Phoenicopterus ruber, or the American Flamingo, is beyond any doubt one of the most spectacular birds of the Western Hemisphere. Once abundant in the southern portion of North America, it is now seen only rarely in southernmost Florida.

Karl E. Karalus

(*Overleaf*) YELLOW-CROWNED NIGHT HERON
Nyctanassa violacea violacea (Linnaeus).
Englewood, Florida, May 20, 1976. A.O.U. Number 203

THE WADING BIRDS OF NORTH AMERICA

Books Written by Allan W. Eckert

THE GREAT AUK
THE SILENT SKY
A TIME OF TERROR
WILD SEASON
THE DREAMING TREE
THE FRONTIERSMAN
BAYOU BACKWATERS
THE KING SNAKE
WILDERNESS EMPIRE
IN SEARCH OF A WHALE
BLUE JACKET
THE CONQUERORS
THE CROSSBREED
INCIDENT AT HAWK'S HILL
THE COURT-MARTIAL OF DANIEL BOONE
THE OWLS OF NORTH AMERICA
THE WADING BIRDS OF NORTH AMERICA
THE WILDERNESS WAR
SAVAGE JOURNEY
SONG OF THE WILD
TECUMSEH! (DRAMA)

Books Illustrated by Karl E. Karalus

WILD SEASON
THE CROSSBREED
HOME LIFE OF NORTH AMERICAN BIRDS
THE OWLS OF NORTH AMERICA
FIELD GUIDE TO THE BIRDS OF THE SUN COAST
THE WADING BIRDS OF NORTH AMERICA
SAVAGE JOURNEY

THE WADING BIRDS OF NORTH AMERICA

(NORTH OF MEXICO)

TEXT BY

Allan W. Eckert

PAINTINGS AND DRAWINGS BY

Karl E. Karalus

DOUBLEDAY & COMPANY, INC., GARDEN CITY, NEW YORK

1981

ISBN: 0-385-01339-6
Library of Congress Catalog Card Number 80-1090

Design by M Franklin-Plympton

PRINTED IN THE UNITED STATES OF AMERICA
FIRST EDITION

AUTHOR'S DEDICATION

For my friend,
Edward J. Farran

ARTIST'S DEDICATION

The color plates in this book are dedicated to three young people who have brought much joy to the artist:

Charlene Anette Karalus
Julie Anne Eckert
Joseph Matthew Eckert

CONTENTS

COLOR PLATES AND SPECIES SKETCHES

(Plates appear after the given page number)

ACKNOWLEDGMENTS

The illustrations for this book could hardly have been possible without the help of so many kind and patient people.

Melvin A. Traylor, Curator of Animals, Field Museum, Chicago, and a friend over the years, for criticism, encouragement, and the loan of many bird skins;

E. Joseph Koestner, Director of the Dayton Museum, Dayton, Ohio, for his encouragement;

Dr. Emmet Blake, Ornithologist, Field Museum, Chicago, Illinois, for criticism and patience;

Ms. Dianne Maurer, Curator of Birds, Field Museum, Chicago, Illinois, whose lunch hours were often spent aiding me in the selection of bird skins for this book, as well as *The Owls of North America;*

Tom O'Conor Sloane, III, Senior Editor, Doubleday & Company, Inc., for patience and understanding through difficult and trying times;

Diana Klemin, Art Director at Doubleday, for extreme patience;

Joseph Eckert, my field assistant, an unselfish young man whose willingness to tackle autopsies, skinning, and many other chores contributed enormously to this book;

The people at the Lemon Bay Conservancy, founded by Allan W. Echert at Englewood, Florida, for saving forever a series of beautiful islands where one may study the wading birds in comparative comfort: Mr. Jerry Chambers, Mr. James Cook, Mrs. Joan D. Eckert, Dr. Emil Swepston, Mr. Howard Mensel and Dr. Richard Campbell—sincere thanks to all;

Last but not least, my thanks to Russell Mason of Englewood, Florida, outdoor sports writer and an excellent field naturalist.

KARL E. KARALUS

Least
Bittern
Reddis
Egre
Young
Night
Heron's
Green
Heron
Green
Heron
Black
Crowned
Ibis
Tricolored
young
Bittern
yellow
crowned
Egret
chick
at nest
snowy
Egret

INTRODUCTION

In the preparation of this book, all known species and subspecies of wading birds of the North American continent north of Mexico have been studied closely. Mostly these are the typical waders—the long-legged and long-necked birds common to marsh and swamp. Yet, to aver that all the wading birds have long legs and long necks would certainly be incorrect, since in some cases the characteristics have become modified or are even absent.

In a book of this scope, it was important to include all known aspects of the life histories of each of the species and subspecies included under the orders Gruiformes and Ciconiiformes occurring on this continent north of Mexico. Since the Ciconiiformes and Gruiformes have many similar characteristics and these become progressively abundant as the classification is narrowed down through suborder, superfamily, family, subfamily, genus, species, and subspecies, tedious repetition in the text was likely to occur. It was necessary to avoid this possibility, yet without undermining the value of the descriptions for each of the subspecies. To do this, the most prominent, familiar, or representative wading bird of each genus and species has been selected for a major description. Other subspecies falling under each major species designation are described only as far as they *differ* from the representative species that is described in detail.

A word about subspecies is advisable here. The terms race, subspecies, and geographic variation are essentially synonymous. Subspecies are rarely constant in coloration, markings, and characteristics in the same sense that there is a constancy to species determination. The geographic variations—races or subspecies—are rarely separable into distinctly bounded geographic areas. Variation of a species on any continent is almost invariably continuous in smooth clines of intergrades and intermediates and therefore not neatly separable. Yet, to establish some sort of order, the subspecific scientific names become a necessity, however lacking they may be in the clarity one would hope to ascribe to them.

This, in itself, was a problem of considerable moment when it came to a determination of which geographical variations should be included in a book

---

Neck and head attitudes of resting herons, bitterns, ibises, etc. Field sketches made in the Everglades and elsewhere in south Florida.

(Overleaf) Field sketches of herons and egrets in flight, made on Manasota Key, Englewood, Florida, April 1974.

(Page xv) Sketches of dead birds washed ashore at Stump Pass, Englewood, Florida, April 20, 1974. (Thumbnail sketches not intended to show detail or scale.)

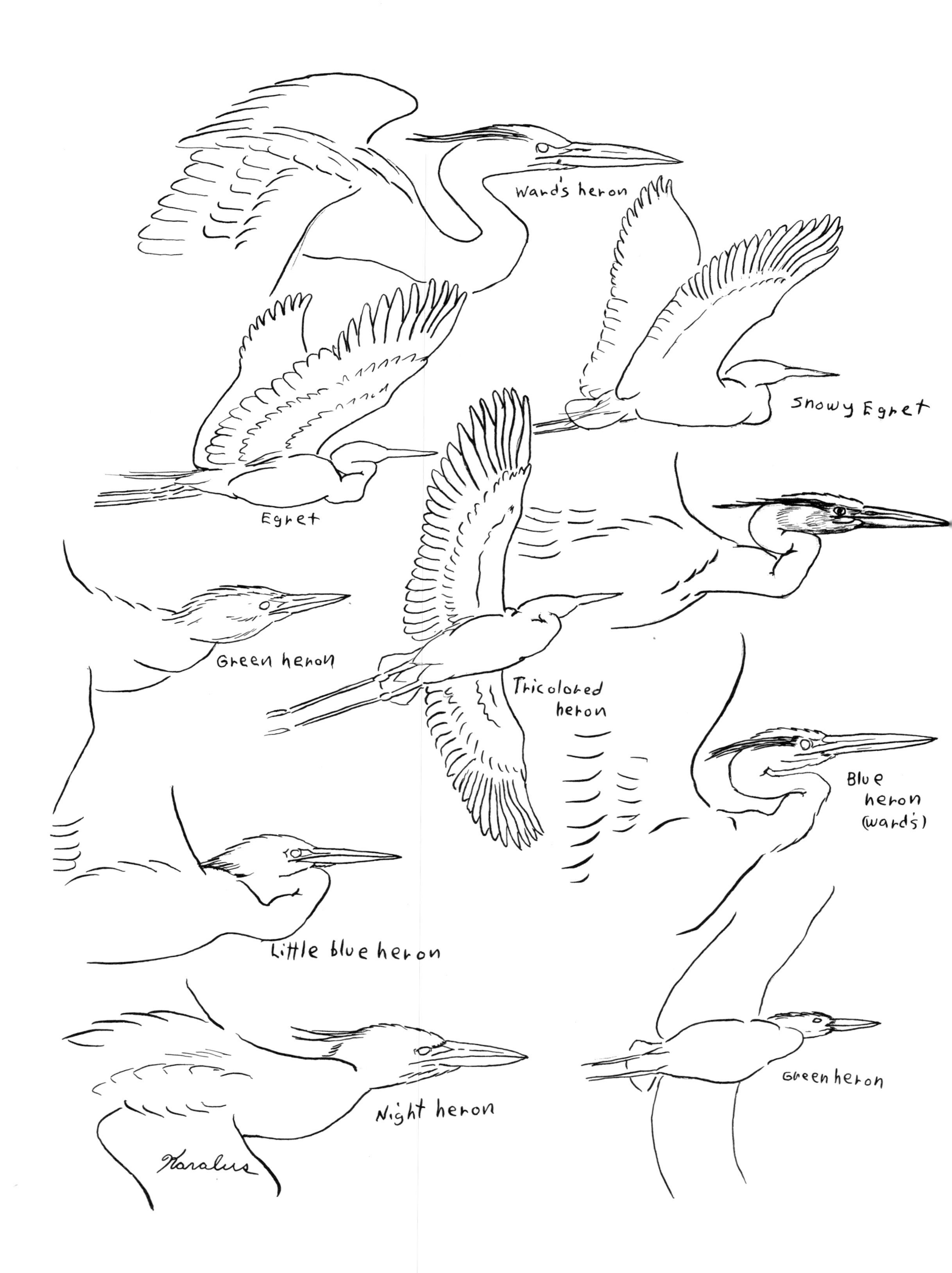
Ward's heron
Snowy Egret
Egret
Green heron
Tricolored heron
Blue heron (ward's)
Little blue heron
Night heron
Green heron
Karalus

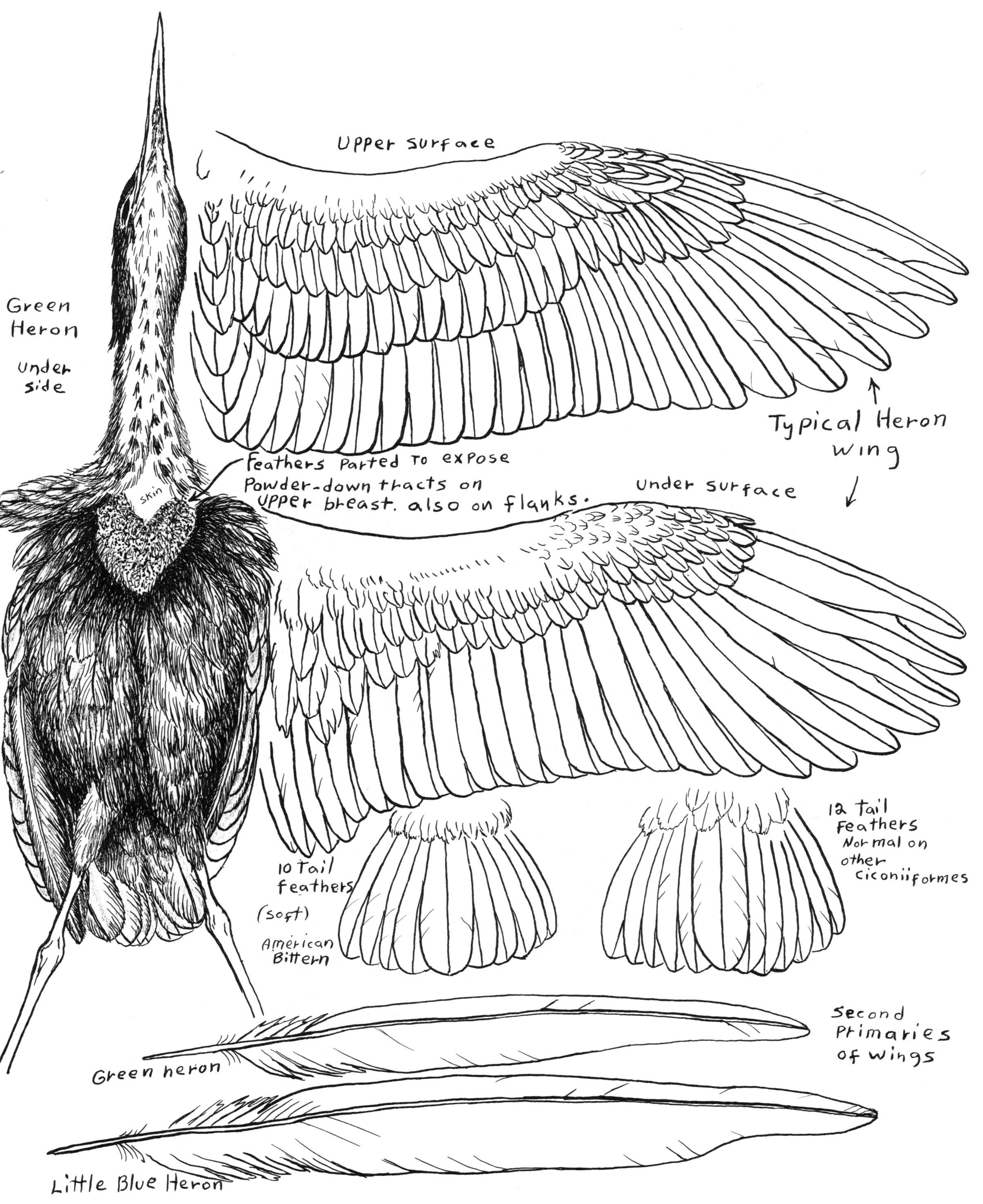
Green Heron
Under side
Upper surface
Feathers parted to expose Powder-down tracts on upper breast. also on flanks.
skin
Under surface
Typical Heron wing
10 Tail feathers
(soft)
American Bittern
12 Tail Feathers
Normal on other ciconiiformes
Second Primaries of wings
Green heron
Little Blue Heron
.E.K.

Karl E. Kara

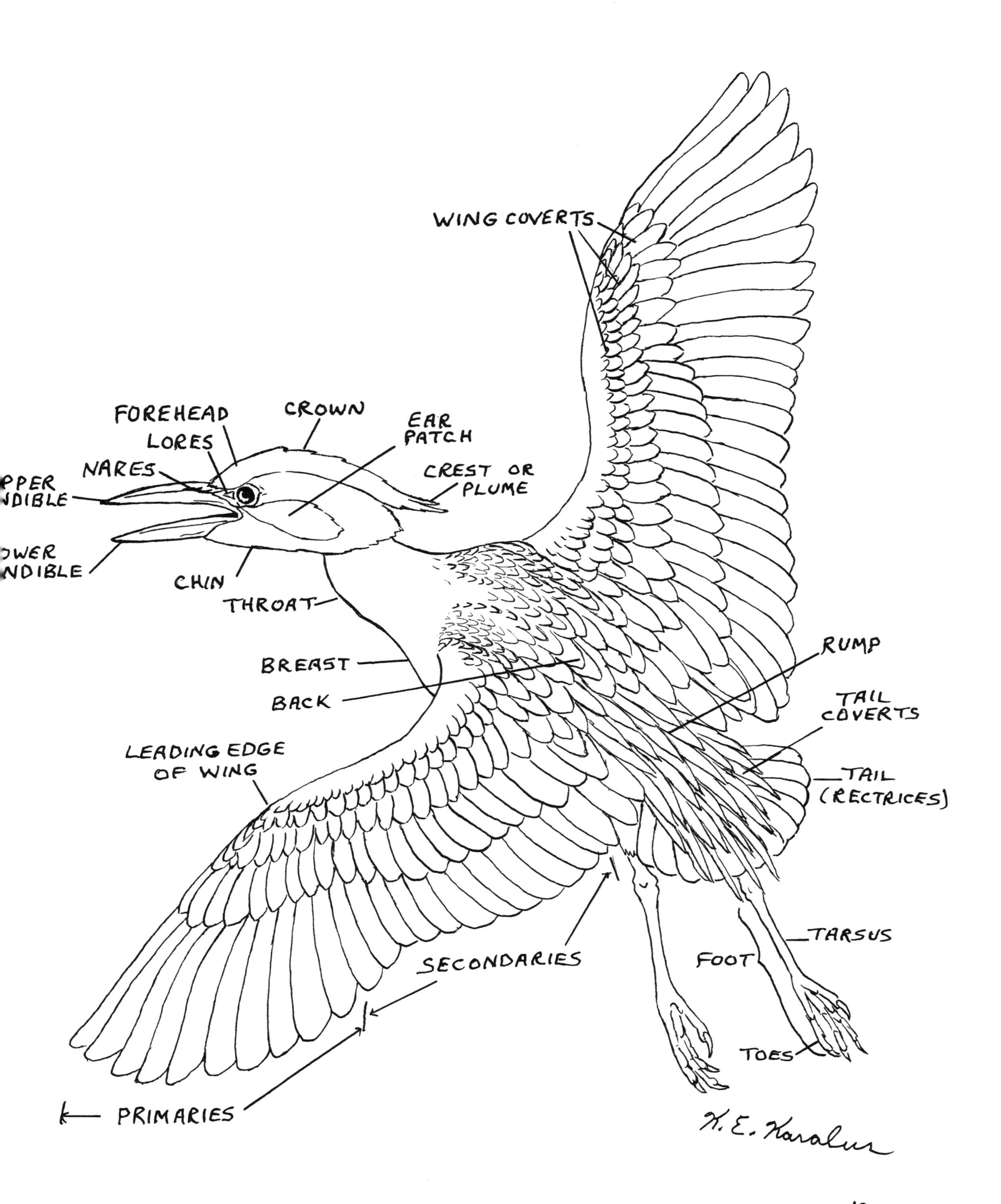
WING COVERTS
FOREHEAD
CROWN
EAR PATCH
LORES
NARES
CREST OR PLUME
CHIN
THROAT
BREAST
BACK
RUMP
TAIL COVERTS
LEADING EDGE OF WING
TAIL (RECTRICES)
TARSUS
FOOT
SECONDARIES
TOES
PRIMARIES

1976

purporting to describe all continental subspecies of any one order of birds. The matter of taxonomy is more often than not a touchy issue. In some cases, wading birds that were accepted as legitimate species or subspecies some years ago may now be part of another species or themselves broken down into more extensive subspecies. Further, new subspecies continue to be named and described and often it becomes difficult to keep pace. The process of subspecification is a living, continuing thing.

In no respect is it the province of this book to attempt to establish new races of wading birds, nor is it proper here to eliminate races whose validity may be questionable. Rather, the authors, after considerable research, after discussion with authorities far more able in these matters than we, and after exhaustive study of specimens from all over North America (including, in many cases, the actual type specimens from which the species or subspecies were described), have included those subspecies (or races) with characteristics which seem truly to set them reasonably well apart from others. Beyond any doubt, questions will be raised by knowledgeable readers as to whether this wading bird or that should have been included or excluded.

(Page xvi) Yellow-Crowned Night Heron, *Nyctanassa violacea violacea* (Linnaeus). This bird was studied for many hours on the property of Mrs. Joan D. Eckert, Lemon Bay, Florida. It would come in early afternoon to hunt wharf and soldier crabs until dusk. Normally shy, the bird allowed very close approach.

(Overleaf) Topography of a Yellow-Crowned Night Heron.

BUTORIDES HERONS

ORDER:	*CICONIIFORMES*
SUBORDER:	*ARDEAE*
FAMILY:	*ARDEIDAE*
SUBFAMILY:	*ARDEINAE*
GENUS:	*BUTORIDES* Blyth
SPECIES:	*STRIATUS* (Linnaeus)
SUBSPECIES:	*virescens* (Linnaeus) Eastern Green Heron
	frazari (Brewster) Frazar's Green Heron
	anthonyi (Mearns) Anthony's Green Heron

COMMON NAME

Eastern Green Heron
(Color Plate I)

SCIENTIFIC NAME

Butorides striatus virescens (Linnaeus). The generic name derives from the Latin *butio,* meaning "a heron," and the Greek *eidos,* signifying "resembling." The specific name is the Latin *striatus,* meaning "streaked." The subspecific name is the Latin *virescens,* meaning "growing green." In essence, then, the scientific name can be loosely translated to mean a bird "bearing a resemblance to a bittern, and streaked, but greener."

OTHER COMMON OR COLLOQUIAL NAMES

CHALK-LINE After the white line of fecal matter often left behind when the bird is flushed.

CHRISTMAS HERON The origin of this name is unclear, but it is possibly based on the bird's predominantly green and reddish coloration, reminiscent of the Christmas colors.

CRAB-CATCHER From a particular item of prey it is fond of catching and eating in coastal waters, especially in southern Florida.

FLY-UP-THE-CREEK From its habit of doing just what the name suggests, when the bird is flushed along a stream.

GREEN BITTERN For its color and relationship to the bittern, especially the Least Bittern.

GREEN HERON For the lustrous coloration of its crest, shoulders, back, and wing coverts.

INDIAN PULLET Allegedly because formerly it was used as a food source, like chicken, by certain woodland tribes of American Indians.

KOP-KOP After the explosive call it makes.

LITTLE GREEN HERON For its size and coloration.

POKE Bag, as a diminutive of Shitepoke (see below), which is another common name.

REED HERON For its marked agility in moving about among the cattail reeds.

SHITEPOKE Literally, "bag of shit," after its habit of defecating voluminously when first flushed.

SKEER Apparently a dual-name form; first, after the fear it displays when flushed; second, after the piercing cry it utters at that time.

SKEO For much the same reason as Skeer, but with more consideration given to the articulation of the call.

SMALL BITTERN After the original description basis.

SHAPE AT REST AND IN FLIGHT

The usual shape at rest is a hunched, drawn-in position on a branch, normally in protective cover, with the head couched on the body and showing little or no sign of the neck, or sometimes with the head drawn so far back that it seems to be growing out of the back. In this latter position it bears little resemblance to the characteristic at-rest pose of a heron. Relatively small and dark, it is not as large as a crow and often it is seen in its hunting posture along the margin of a stream or pond. That posture is with head, neck, and back nearly horizontal and the shanks of the legs so flat to the ground that the bird itself appears to be outstretched on the surface upon which it is standing. At such times it has been described as having a loglike appearance. Now and then, when startled unexpectedly, it will freeze in place to escape detection and its position then will be whatever position it happened to be in when it "froze." Occasionally it will stand with neck outstretched, head held high, beak slightly upward, and crest raised and spread. The tail is so short that it appears to be abnormally cut off. Sometimes the bird will "break" from its frozen position into an in-place nervous movement wherein it raises and lowers its crest and twitches its tail in irregular jerks. This is one of the smallest of the herons on the North American continent.

Although its initial takeoff when disturbed is not smooth it swiftly levels and can dart directly and with great skill through the overhanging branches of trees with relatively rapid wingbeats; strokes which are slightly faster than those of the closely related herons and equally faster and more coordinated than those of the Least Bittern, with which it is sometimes confused when it first rises. As well as the tail being short, the legs are relatively short and extend beyond the tail only a couple of inches. This, too, serves as a recognition factor since the legs and feet extend farther behind in flight than among other heron species. Ordinarily, in flight, the head is couched slightly on the shoulders, but it is not usually drawn in as much or with as great a neck curvature as is apparent with some of the other heron species.

LENGTH AND WINGSPAN

The average length is 18 inches (457mm) and the average wingspan is just under 25 inches (629mm).

BEAK

As in all the heron species, the beak is sharply pointed and, in the dorsal-ventral silhouette laterally, more or less symmetrical. In its coloration, the beak ranges from a pale clear greenish to a distinctly dusky greenish, with the lower mandible paler and more yellowish toward the base than the upper. In younger birds, the beak has a dusky ridge and is generally duller and a paler greenish than in adults.

LEGS, FEET, AND CLAWS

In both adult and young birds, there is a slight webbing between the middle and outer toes. This aids young birds in swimming when they fall out of the nest, and aids adults when they deliberately plunge into the water after prey and return to shore or their hunting perch with it. The middle toe, including the claw, is about the same length as the tarsus, with legs and feet yellow in the adult and a pale and dull greenish gray in the young.

Green Heron, *Butorides striatus.*

serrate section
on inside of bill
Franklin Park Illinois
May 20 1963
♂
studies near
Dayton Ohio
K. E. Karalus
chicks from nest
at Myakka River
Charlotte co
florida
2 days old
12 days old

CRESTS, PLUMAGE, ANNUAL MOLT

The long, soft, occipital crest is always raised when the bird is nervous and, at such times, is uneven and unruly, as if not properly combed. When the bird is hunting, the crest almost always lies flat against crown and nape. The crest feathers are a deep lustrous dark green. Although the crest is normally in its lowered position during flight, on very short flights not only is the neck extended and the head high but the crest is raised and spread. Very little seasonal difference occurs in adult plumage. A postnuptial partial molt occurs in late winter and early spring. Yearling birds tend to undergo their first postnuptial molt, at which time full adult plumage is acquired, occasionally as early as April, but more often in May or June.

VOICE

Butorides striatus virescens makes a variety of sounds, some of them so distinctive to the bird that it has been dubbed with colloquial names which try to emulate the sound. Such names as Kop-Kop, Skeo, and Skeer, are derived from the sounds made by the bird, especially when startled from its perch. The most familiar of the cries is a loud, alarmed, raucous screech of *keow* or *skeow,* repeated as the bird wings away. Such a call is always explosively uttered and very distinctive. Once heard and identified, it is not mistaken for anything else when next encountered. In addition to that alarm call, however, there are a number of soft clucks, clicks, chuckles, squawks, cackles, and grunts made by the bird, especially during courtship and nesting. A particular courtship cry uttered by the male as he struts and displays before the female is a series of soft little sounds like *qua-qua-qua-qua-qua.* Sometimes this sound emerges as little more than a grunting repeated twice with a pause between of irregular duration before the call comes again. It may continue for an hour or more if the bird is undisturbed. A similar but slightly louder sound is sometimes made as the adult bird lands near the nest bearing young.

SEXUAL DIFFERENCES: SIZE, COLORATION, VOICE

The male is slightly larger than the female, with a broader wingspan. There is no extensive difference in coloration between the sexes as adults and no real difference in tonal quality of the voice.

COLORATION AND MARKINGS: ADULT

A deep, lustrous-but-not-quite-iridescent dark green is found on the crown and crest, and on the longer feathers of the shoulders and back. The latter plumage has a bluish-green, rather bronzish cast. The wing coverts are also green, but the edges of these feathers are buffy to tawny in color. The entire head (other than crown and crest) and neck are a deep, rich chestnut, sometimes tending toward a purplish cast. The upper throat is white with brownish-gray streakings. The gular area is dark brownish and the abdomen directly below is streaked with white. The primaries, secondaries, and rectrices are a dusky greenish, except that the leading edges of the wings are white. The beak is generally greenish above and paler greenish below, this color graduating to a chartreuse and then more distinctive yellowish near the base of the lower beak. The legs are yellow, but on occasion certain individuals will show more of a deep yellow ocher coloration on shanks and feet. The irides are a bright golden yellow and the bare skin surrounding the eyes is a pale bluish-green.

COLORATION AND MARKINGS: JUVENILE

There is no crest and no green on the head of the juvenile bird. The head is generally brownish, with the neck and sides of the body a faintly lighter brown streaked with lighter tan. The throat and center of the gular area are dusky-streaked white. The back is a plain, non-lustrous greenish brown. The same occurs on the wing coverts and secondaries, but these feathers are white-tipped and white-edged. The undertail coverts are a dingy white, the legs are dusky green, and the beak is greenish with a grayish-green ridge. The irides are yellow.

GENERAL HABITS AND CHARACTERISTICS

The Eastern Green Heron is commonly a very solitary bird, rarely associating with other birds, even of its own species. Except at times of courtship, nesting, or migration, it is almost always found by itself, generally along the margin of pond or stream.

HABITAT AND ROOSTING

The Eastern Green Heron is rather selective about its habitat, preferring the edges of watercourses or ponds, especially where the water is sluggish and where there is dense growth of brush and trees to the water's edge and extending over the water. Areas of alders, willows, cottonwoods, and other such growth are particularly favored. This heron also shows a marked preference for areas where broken branches or logs extend from shore into the water, as these are favored as hunting perches. Even in coastal areas of salt water or brackish water, *Butorides striatus virescens* seeks out the tangled mangroves or areas of densest cover. In regard to roosting, it normally roosts alone in thick brush or close to the trunk of a dense tree growth near the water. Occasionally two will roost together and, even less often, three, but ordinarily the bird remains solitary.

ENEMIES AND DEFENSES

The harsh alarm note it voices as it flushes may provide some sort of benefit in frightening or disconcerting would-be attackers. Also, the habit of waiting until the last possible moment to flush and then, in the very moment of flushing, defecating heavily may have considerable protective benefit. More than one would-be attacker has been struck full in the face with the bursting expulsion of the feces and been temporarily blinded and very thoroughly discouraged in the process. Becoming absolutely rigid at the sight of danger approaching is definitely another defense mechanism of considerable value. Even though the bird, moving, may be quite visible to an approacher, when it freezes in whatever position it may happen to be in, it is remarkable how difficult the bird is to detect, even though it is known where the bird was last moving. Even the very young Eastern Green Herons and subspecies utilize this process of freezing to avoid detection, doing so at a signal from the parent birds. Sometimes the "frozen" position will be held by young or adult birds alike until the intruder has approached to within a few short feet. Another trait which acts toward defense, though its utilization may be entirely accidental, is regurgitation of the stomach contents toward an intruder who is very close. Again, this is done by both young and adult birds, but whether it is an instinctive action brought about solely by fear or a deliberate attempt at defense against an enemy has not been ascertained positively. *Butorides striatus virescens* discriminates quite well in what constitutes danger and may be found perfectly content in an area where there is much adjacent auto traffic, human movement, and noise, as long as it is not molested. As an adult the bird has relatively few enemies and it is likely that more are killed by youngsters with air guns or small-caliber rifles who just wander along watercourses and "plink" at anything which catches their attention than by any other cause.

FOOD AND FEEDING HABITS

What the Eastern Green Heron eats depends largely upon the environment in which it finds itself, whether marsh or swamp, saltwater or freshwater or brackish. The principal food, wherever it hunts, is fish—a variety of small species making up about 40 per cent of its diet. Insects are next in importance, making up close to 30 per cent of food intake, followed by crustaceans at 24 per cent and a variety of other material—spiders, snails, worms, small mammals—making up the remaining percentage. Surprisingly few reptilians are taken (snakes and lizards) and even more surprisingly, hardly any frogs. A partial listing of some of the prey most favored by the Eastern Green Heron would include a wide selection of minnows, especially including killifish, other fish up to about 6 inches in length, including carp, catfish, sunfish, eels, pickerel, goldfish, white perch, etc. Also favored are water insects and their larvae, dragonflies and damselflies, katydids and crickets, grasshoppers, crayfish and small crabs. Essentially a day-feeder, the Eastern Green Heron prefers to hunt in the morning hours, take a midday siesta, and then resume hunting again in late afternoon until twilight. It frequents the shallows when hunting, sometimes taking a perch on a branch or log just over the water and spearing whatever comes past which might represent food, but more often it stalks stealthily and with great skill and caution along the shorelines, head drawn back and couched between the hunched shoulders, as if on a spring and ready to snap forward and downward with unerring aim when prey appears. Infrequently the bird will actually plunge headlong into the water, usually successfully, after prey and then swim to shore or back to its perch with whatever it has caught, devouring it en route. It will frequently hunt in marshy meadows, especially for insects, but usually stay relatively close to good covering bushes along the edges.

COURTSHIP AND MATING

Butorides striatus virescens will prance and dance in the most outlandish manner at times, sometimes on a gravel or sand bank, sometimes on a mud flat, sometimes in an inch or so of water. Most often it appears to be doing this for its own amusement, but such is not the case. Invariably the dancer is a male and he is performing a courtship ritual for a female who is close by, but probably well hidden from the eyes of an intruder. At such times the male will raise and twitch his crest, spreading it in a ragged fashion and tilting his head in a ludicrous manner as he dances, his tail bobbing up and down rapidly. He gets very caught up in the tempo of his display and sometimes will take several successive hops on one foot, then switch and do the same on the other; then spring forward four or five feet, then backward, then turn in small, dizzying circles. It is a fascinating display, but oddly graceless and appearing rather awkward and ridiculous, especially because he gives the illusion of doing it for his own amusement. Other courtship activities are not well documented, no doubt because of the solo habits of the bird. The actual copulation is reported to occur sporadically, several times daily over a period of from three to six or seven days.

NEST AND NESTING HABITS

The Eastern Green Heron breeds anywhere within its range, but almost always only in pairs, rarely in small groups, and only in exceptional cases in any kind of breeding rookery. Its nest is by far the most frail constructed by any North American heron; a very poorly built platform of sloppily interwoven twigs which is almost flat on top. There is no cup shape to the nest, nor even a saucerlike depression to keep the eggs in the center, yet oddly enough there are virtually no accounts of the eggs having fallen out, even as the result of storms. Nevertheless, the nest is so flimsy that one can almost always see the eggs by standing right below the nest and looking up through the sticks of which the nest is constructed. The actual body of the nest is about 10 inches to a foot in diameter and, though ordinarily built anywhere from 10 to 20 feet high in living trees, it may sometimes be built in the very tops of trees or, contrarily, in low bushes or even on the ground in marsh grasses or thick meadow grasses. The nest is never lined with grasses, leaves, or any other sort of softening or buttressing material. Although the Eastern Green Heron prefers as a nesting site a tree in or very close to the water, such as dense willow or mangrove, it often nests quite far from the water in dry upland woods or even in orchards. Ornithologists of the past have written about relatively large rookeries of breeding Eastern Green Herons, but none of these writings are more recent than thirty or

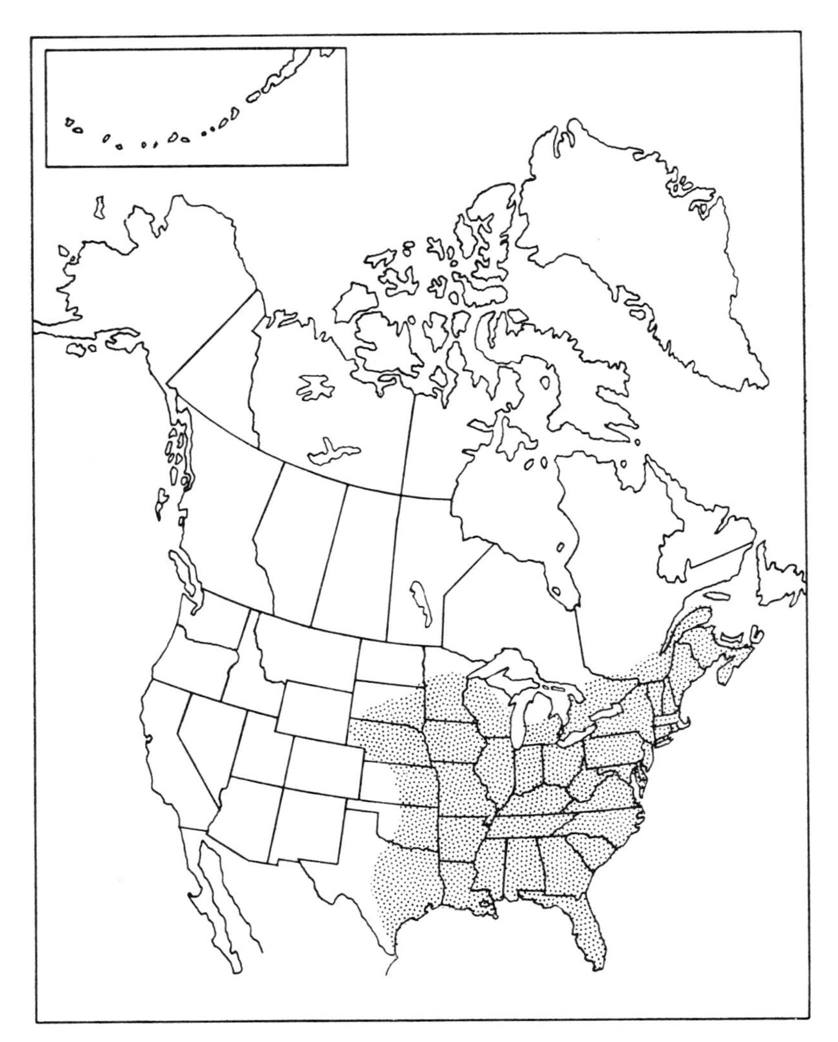

EASTERN GREEN HERON

Butorides striatus virescens (Linnaeus)

forty years ago. No recent accounts speak of any sort of nesting rookery, although occasions are mentioned when, perhaps more or less accidentally, Eastern Green Herons nest near to or in conjunction with other heron species, or sometimes in the same areas with grackles or other birds.

EGGS AND INCUBATION

Three to nine eggs are laid, though the usual number is four or five. They are smooth-shelled, pale greenish or bluish, and in size they average about 1.5 inches by 1.1 inches (38mm x 30mm). The twenty-day incubation is shared equally by the parent birds.

YOUNG

All the eggs hatch at essentially the same time, almost without exception on the same day. They weigh approximately 21.25 grams on hatching (¾ ounce) and their weight increases by about 14 grams (½ ounce) daily until about the tenth day. They are fed by both parent birds, but the morning feeding (usually six or seven separate visits by the parents) generally occurs only between dawn and sunrise. A similar evening feeding begins in the later afternoon, perhaps no more than an hour before sunset, and continues until dusk, again with six or seven separate visitations by the parent birds. Feeding is by regurgitation, but the food material is not predigested by the parent birds. While still downy chicks, before beginning to assume juvenal plumage *(see Coloration and Markings: Juvenile)* the baby birds are clad in a nondescript down which ranges from a medium brown on the crestless crown to a light buff or buffy gray on the underparts. The young are quite ugly in the down period and until juvenile plumage is reasonably well developed.

MIGRATION

The southern movement begins, from the northern portion of its range, from as early as during the first few days of September to as late as mid-to-late October. Winters in north-central Florida (sometimes southern Georgia) southward through the West Indies and South America, with southward migration completed usually no later than November 25. The northern movement begins as early as mid-March and the birds have settled into the northernmost portions of their range before the end of April.

ECONOMIC INFLUENCE

Butorides striatus virescens, except in very isolated cases, has no significant economic impact. Its dietary habits are generally beneficial within the scheme of natural balance, except for occasions when it is of some economic detriment because of preying upon goldfish or minnows in areas where these are raised commercially. Probably is of considerable benefit in controlling injurious insects.

COMMON NAME

Frazar's Green Heron
(Subspecies Sketch 1)

SCIENTIFIC NAME

Butorides striatus frazari (Brewster). This subspecies was first discovered among the coastal mangroves at La Paz, Lower California, in 1887 by M. Abbott Frazar, who provided the type specimen for William Brewster.

OTHER COMMON OR COLLOQUIAL NAMES

BAJA GREEN HERON For primary residence locality.

FRAZAR'S GREEN HERON

Butorides striatus frazari (Brewster)

COLORATION AND MARKINGS: ADULT

It is generally darker and rather duller in coloration than *Butorides striatus virescens,* with the coloration more generally uniform. The neck is somewhat more purplish, the back and sides tend to be slightly more glaucous, and the light-colored throat line is more restricted.

GENERAL HABITS AND CHARACTERISTICS

Since the habits of Frazar's Green Heron are virtually the same as those of the Eastern Green Heron, the principal differences are those of coloration and size, with Frazar's Green Heron averaging slightly larger and darker than the Eastern Green Heron.

HABITAT

More frequently in mangrove areas and less often in upland areas or stream valleys.

---

1. FRAZAR'S GREEN HERON

Butorides striatus frazari (Brewster). Ensenada Baja, California. A.O.U. Number 201a

Karl E. Karalus

COMMON NAME

Anthony's Green Heron
(Subspecies Sketch 2)

SCIENTIFIC NAME

Butorides striatus anthonyi (Mearns). Dr. Edgar A. Mearns collected the first specimens of this subspecies just north of the Mexican border in the valley of the Colorado River in California during 1895. One of the birds he collected was the type specimen, and he named the bird in honor of his friend from San Diego, California, A. W. Anthony.

ANTHONY'S GREEN HERON
Butorides striatus anthonyi (Mearns)

OTHER COMMON OR COLLOQUIAL NAMES

VALLEY GREEN HERON After the Colorado River valley which it inhabits.

DITCH HERON After the irrigation ditches it frequents throughout its range.

DESERT HERON Because it is the desert form of the Green Heron.

COLORATION AND MARKINGS: ADULT

This is a much lighter subspecies; all the markings are paler, with those of the throat, neck, and wings being much less restricted and considerably paler than those of *Butorides striatus virescens.* Some of the markings fade out practically into whiteness in this desert form of the bird.

NEST AND NESTING HABITS

On the average, the nest of Anthony's Green Heron is positioned slightly higher in the nesting trees than is the nest of the Eastern Green Heron, with the average nest height of the former approximately 30 feet high instead of 20.

---

2. ANTHONY'S GREEN HERON

Butorides striatus anthonyi (Mearns). San Diego, California. A.O.U. Number 201c

Karl E. Karalus

BLACK-CROWNED NIGHT HERON

GENUS: *NYCTICORAX* Forster
SPECIES: NYCTICORAX (Linnaeus)
SUBSPECIES: *hoactli* (Gmelin)

COMMON NAME

Black-Crowned Night Heron
(Color Plate II)

SCIENTIFIC NAME

Nycticorax nycticorax hoactli (Gmelin). *Nycticorax* means "Raven of the Night."

OTHER COMMON OR COLLOQUIAL NAMES

QWOK From the call it utters.

NIGHT HERON Due to its almost exclusive tendency to hunt and fly nocturnally; and because the bird is rarely seen at any other time than during the night or the very deep twilight hours of morning and evening.

STRIPED NIGHT HERON Primarily due to the clear stripings on the plumage of birds less than four years of age, birds which have not yet acquired full adult plumage.

SHAPE AT REST AND IN FLIGHT

Except when poised to strike prey, the Black-Crowned Night Heron almost always stands in a generally hunched posture with the head usually well couched on the shoulders. The bird is easily identifiable because of the stockiness of its body, stoutness of beak, and shortness of legs and neck in comparison with most other heron species.

The wings are long and broad, seeming almost abnormally so in flight for the size of the body, which appears to be blunt and short. In flight the head is tucked back in the shoulder plumage and the legs are drawn up tightly against the abdominal plumage, with the lower legs and feet trailing beyond the tail, as is the nature of all herons and egrets.

At takeoff, the wingbeat pattern is strong but fluttery, although very quickly the wingbeats settle to powerful, fairly slow regularity of approximately forty strokes per minute.

LENGTH AND WINGSPAN

Average length of the Black-Crowned Night Heron is 26 inches (667mm) and the average wingspan is almost 46 inches (656mm).

EYES

In adult birds, the irides are bright red. Young birds, however, go through a progression of iris coloration, from gray to yellow, to orange in the subadult, and red in the adult.

CRESTS, PLUMAGE, ANNUAL MOLT

Generally, immature birds are streaky brown and white. Adult birds, from a distance, give the uniform impression of grayish coloration. There are no particular plumes except for the two or three

common at dusk and at
night at Englewood F
Charlotte Co
Stump Pass channel
Englewood Florida
Dec 23 1976
K. E. Karalus

extremely long filamentous feathers which spring from the hind head. These few feathers are normally imbricated into one bundle. The average length of the longest plume in such a bundle is about 7 inches (183mm). There are eight complete plumage changes before full adult plumage is acquired. The annual molt, beginning about early June and completed by late October, is progressive and in no way hampers the bird's flight. The greasy, powdery substance exuded by the powder-down tracts on the breast is used to dress and oil the heron's contour feathers, as is the case with other heron species.

VOICE

A brief and well-spaced series of deep-throated sounds similar to *quck* and *whuk* or *quock* are usually uttered immediately as the bird goes into flight, especially if it has been startled or forced to fly. A few of these same sounds may be uttered, in a somewhat lower and more placid tone, just prior to landing. When angered, especially during territorial squabbles or during incubation altercations *(see Eggs and Incubation)*, the bird may utter a harsh, grating screech.

SEXUAL DIFFERENCES: SIZE, COLORATION, VOICE

The male bird is generally somewhat larger than the female, but coloration is identical. The voice of the male bird tends to be a shade deeper and stronger and farther-carrying than the female's.

MORTALITY

Hatchlings which are left unprotected in the nest can and quite often do fall prey to avian predators, especially crows and sometimes vultures and gulls. However, the highest death rate among young birds occurs when they are blown out of their flimsy nests during severe storms. It is believed that the Black-Crowned Night Heron in its wild state may live to around twenty years of age, and those in captivity may live to around age thirty.

COLORATION AND MARKINGS: ADULT

The shoulders, back, and entire crown of this bird are jet black, while the remainder of the upper parts are a pale ash-gray, including wings and tail. The sides of the head, forehead, and throat are white, except that the throat generally blends into a pale lilac coloration. The remaining underparts are white. The beak is glossy black, the irides are scarlet, and the bare space around the eye is a light, delicate chartreuse. The legs are generally yellow.

COLORATION AND MARKINGS: JUVENILE

In its natal plumage, the bird has head, neck, and dorsal tracts which are a dark mouse gray to a deep neutral

---

Black-Crowned Night Heron, *Nycticorax nycticorax hoactli* (Gmelin).

gray. The outer three quarters of the crown filaments are white and these are especially conspicuous during the first few hours after hatching. The down of the ventral tract ranges from pallid neutral gray on the lower belly to a medium gray on the breast and then to a dark mouse gray on the neck. The down on the crown is always much longer than the body down and forms a distinct crest. The down, when dry, conceals the wings and aptera. When the hatchling is five days of age, the upper down fades to a neutral gray which can best be described as a mouse gray, as opposed to the lighter pale dull gray which the down becomes ventrally. Later, the entire plumage becomes grayish-white and is streaked on the head and breast as well as on the underbody with dark brown. There are also streaks and spottings of rusty-reddish and white on the back. The wing coverts are brown and these feathers have triangular white tips. The primaries are simply a dirty grayish-brown. The beak is a dull yellow and the feet are a pale chartreuse.

GENERAL HABITS AND CHARACTERISTICS

This is a fairly large but decidedly stocky bird, with comparatively short legs for a heron. The neck, too, is much shorter than is commonly noted in other members of this family, and the beak is relatively short and stout. When seen perched from reasonably close up, the immature birds are generally brownish with much darker brown stripings, while the adults are a handsome gray with white underparts, and jet-black crown, back, and shoulders. Black-Crowned Night Herons breed in colonies. They also occasionally gather in small groups of from three to seven individuals to feed or roost. Their migration is always in large flocks.

HABITAT AND ROOSTING

This species particularly likes marshy areas with heavy reed growth and mangrove shorelines, especially those of small islands. It is uncommonly fond of alighting upon pilings, rocks, low docks, and other protuberances which project from the water. The Black-Crowned Night Heron is especially drawn to docks and other structures where artificial lighting at night tends to bring minnows and other small marine life to the surface. Roosting is usually low in dense, leafy trees—especially red mangroves in the coastal areas—fairly close to the water. In freshwater areas, roosting often occurs on floating matted bundles of dead cattails, especially within heavy standing growths of cattails.

HUNTING METHODS, FOOD AND FEEDING HABITS

Unlike many of its longer-legged kin, the Black-Crowned Night Heron prefers *not* to stand in water when hunting. Rather, it likes to take a perch on a

Crustaceans most hunted by Black- and Yellow-Crowned Night Herons in the Lemon Bay, Florida, study area. These sketches were made from specimens collected by Joseph Eckert. They represent both live material and the stomach content of birds.

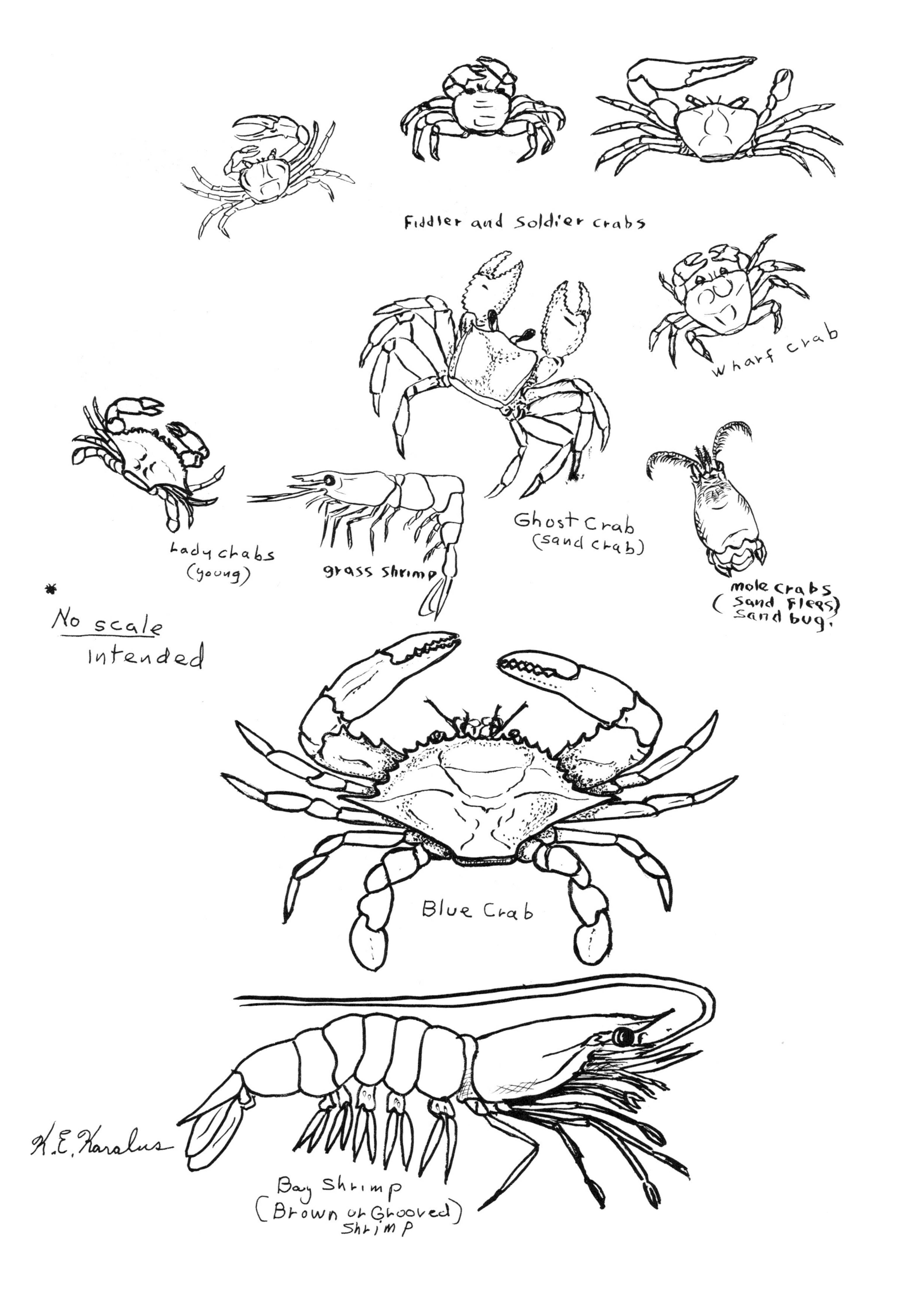
Fiddler and soldier crabs
Wharf crab
Ghost Crab
(sand crab)
Lady crabs
(young)
grass shrimp
mole crabs
(Sand fleas)
Sand bug.
No scale
intended
Blue Crab
K. E. Karalus
Bay Shrimp
(Brown or Grooved)
Shrimp

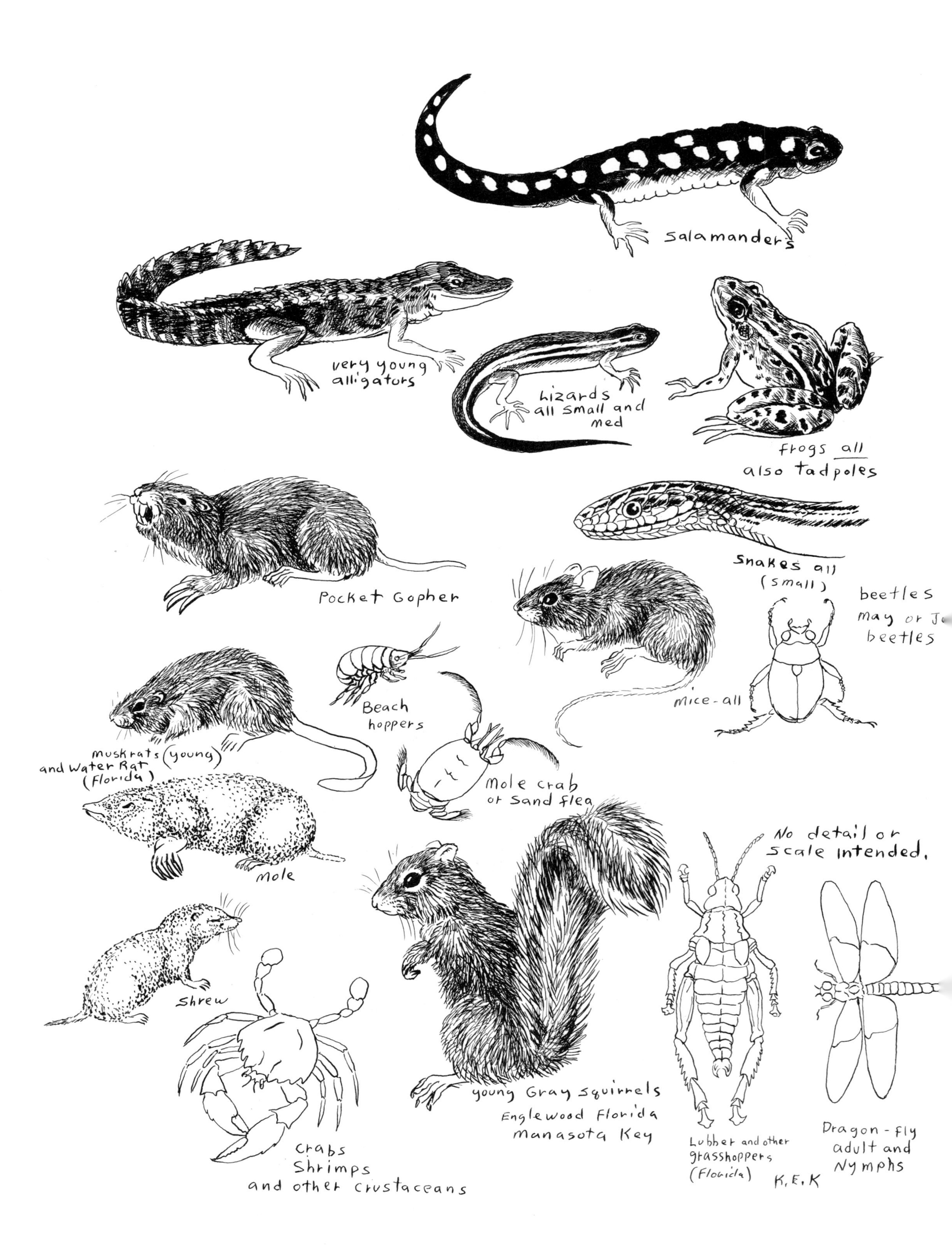
Salamanders
very young alligators
Lizards all small and med
Frogs all
also tadpoles
Snakes all (small)
Pocket Gopher
beetles
may or J
beetles
Beach hoppers
mice-all
muskrats (young) and Water Rat (Florida)
Mole crab or Sand flea
mole
No detail or scale intended.
Shrew
young Gray squirrels
Englewood Florida
Manasota Key
Crabs
Shrimps
and other crustaceans
Lubber and other grasshoppers (Florida)
Dragon-fly adult and Nymphs
K.E.K

branch, mangrove root, piling, post, rock, or light fixture right at the water's edge and lean down to snatch up small unsuspecting prey swimming past on the water surface or just under the surface, or circling aimlessly in the halo of artificial light on the surface. Serrations of the beak aid in holding the often slippery prey.

Small fish of almost any variety up to four or five inches and occasionally even up to nine or ten inches are taken avidly by the Black-Crowned Night Heron. Occasionally it will also feed upon crayfish, shrimp, squid, insects, lizards, and amphibians. The captured prey is held very tightly crosswise in the beak and is usually shaken vigorously until thoroughly stunned and limp, or else dead. The prey is rarely dropped on the ground and speared, as is so often done by the larger herons with their prey. When the prey has been shaken to limpness, the bird then tosses it gently in its beak, juggling it about adroitly until it is positioned in a head-first manner toward the bird's throat. It is then swallowed.

The bird's digestive acids are so powerful that there is very little regurgitation of any ingested material. Almost all bone matter is dissolved in the digestive acids and this results in the feces taking on an unusually white, limy character due to the high content of dissolved bone calcium. More often than not, the nesting and perching areas used regularly by the bird become extremely unsightly because of the defecations which coat everything for yards.

Heron food-prey aside from fish. Lizards are grasped by the head and beaten repeatedly before being swallowed. The young of ground-nesting birds also make up part of the heron's diet.

COURTSHIP AND MATING

Since much of this activity occurs during the nighttime hours, only the most spectacular efforts have been observed and described at any length. The males perform a sort of dance display and it is believed that at times the female will join in the prancing and leaping as the tempo seems to become infectious. On the whole, however, courtship displays are relatively simple and ordinarily rather brief. The male alights near the female and bends quite low, raising his crest and his back, breast, and neck feathers in display, to which the female responds similarly. Then begins a mutual caressing and preening with their beaks for a few minutes, after which they sit side by side, close together without movement. On occasion, it is the female who will fly in and perch close to the male and initiate the ceremony with an urgent squawking. In all cases, the male will grip the head of the female in his beak as he mounts her, at the same time raising his plumes and spreading his wings, as much for display as for maintaining balance as the copulation takes place.

NEST AND NESTING HABITS

The nest is a crude, loosely constructed platform of coarse branches. It is usually quite low in the sturdier branches of low trees. Both male and female are active in the construction of the nest, a job which takes them from two to five days. This species will often nest in association with other species of herons and egrets.

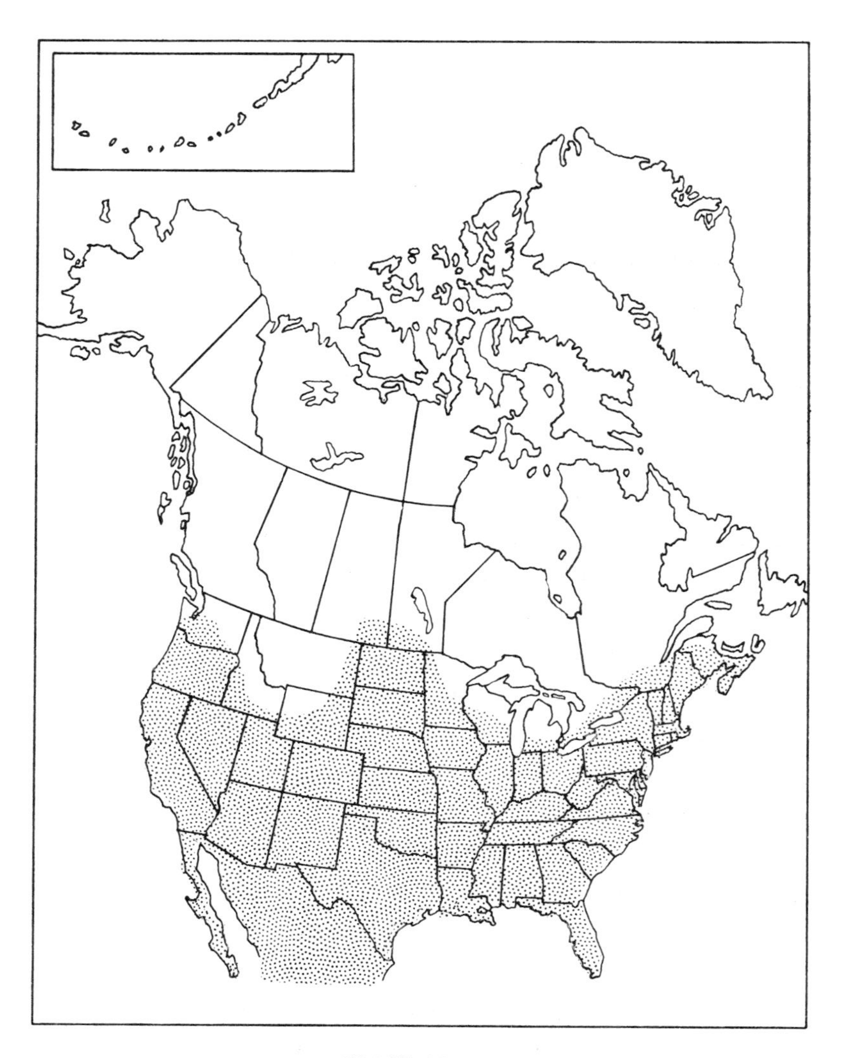

BLACK-CROWNED NIGHT HERON

Nycticorax nycticorax hoactli (Gmelin)

EGGS AND INCUBATION

The Black-Crowned Night Heron usually lays three or four bluish-green eggs, averaging 2.5 x 2 inches, between February and March and between June and July.

Incubation, beginning with the laying of the first egg, is undertaken by both parent birds. The incubation period of each egg is twenty-four to twenty-six days.

YOUNG

Because of the interval of egg-laying, some of the chicks in the nest will often be a full week ahead in their development beyond the last-hatched chick. Quite frequently the egg is pipped fully twenty-four hours before actual emergence occurs. The chick's eyes are open from the very beginning and by the end of twenty-four hours after hatching it can sit erect and be somewhat active. The hatchling utters a faint sound similar to a high-pitched "pip-pip-pip" when hungry or left alone. By the tenth day numerous pinfeathers appear, but vestiges of down remain on the young birds even after they have left the nest. The post-natal molt is not completed until the bird is from five to six weeks of age.

At the beginning of its fourth week, the bird has acquired the smooth, contoured appearance of the adult bird, but the complete growth of juvenile plumage does not occur until about the fiftieth day. There are eight distinct plumage changes before the full adult plumage is acquired.

MIGRATION

Nycticorax nycticorax hoactli migrates in large flocks and almost without exception at night, resting in secluded areas during the daylight hours. The migration in spring to the north generally occurs from mid-February through mid-May. The autumn migration southward generally occurs from mid-July through October. Much of the population does not follow the pattern of a true migration, but merely moves about within the southern portions of its distributional range.

YELLOW-CROWNED NIGHT HERON

GENUS: *NYCTANASSA* Stejneger
SPECIES: *VIOLACEA* (Linnaeus)
SUBSPECIES: *violacea* (Linnaeus)

COMMON NAME

Yellow-Crowned Night Heron
(Color Plate III)

SCIENTIFIC NAME

Nyctanassa violacea violacea (Linnaeus). *Nyctanassa* derives from the Greek for "night fish trap." Species and subspecies name of *violacea,* from the Latin, "violet-colored."

SHAPE AT REST

Although *Nyctanassa violacea violacea* is stocky in build, it is nonetheless more slender and graceful than *Nycticorax nycticorax hoactli* and its legs are slightly longer, its beak slightly stouter. A distinctive white check patch and yellow crown are good field marks.

LENGTH AND WINGSPAN

The species averages, in length, about 24 inches (610mm) and the wingspan is just over 42 inches (1084mm).

CRESTS, PLUMAGE, ANNUAL MOLT

The adult plumage includes a crest extending backward from the pate throughout the year. During the breeding season, however, both sexes produce from two to seven or eight long narrow white feathers, upward of 8 to 9 inches in length, that usually rest along the contour of the bird's back. Adult birds undergo a complete molt from August to October and a partial molt in late January and early February. Young birds get their first complete adult plumage at the age of thirty months when they undergo a complete postnuptial molt during July and August.

COLORATION AND MARKINGS: ADULT

Generally the bird appears to be a medium grayish to violet-gray throughout its body at first look. The general blue-gray of the underparts is lighter than that of the back, where the feathers have dark centers and are strongly margined with lighter gray. The beak is black and the lores a pale greenish to greenish-gray. Crown and crest, including plumes, are creamy white to tawny yellow, with occasionally several jet-black plumes in the crest during the breeding season. The cheek patch extending backward from beneath the eye is whitish. The irides are bright orange-red in the adult, yellow in the juvenile. The upper body is dark violet-gray with long narrow streaks of black; lighter violet below. The wings also have black streakings and the primaries and rectrices are uniformly dark slate-gray. Legs and feet are yellow and black. Except for the cheek patch and crown-crest, the head and throat are black.

♀
comb
fiddler
crab
uca. sp
Yellow-crowned Night
Herons show a
strong preference for
crustacea in Florida
fiddler's a favorite food
Karl E. Karalus

GENERAL HABITS AND CHARACTERISTICS

The Yellow-Crowned Night Heron, despite its name, is not essentially a nocturnal bird. Though it will often feed during the nighttime hours, it is as frequently found feeding during the daylight hours. The single exception, as adults, is when a pair is nesting in solitary manner, at which time they can sometimes be approached quite closely. When nesting in colonies, they take alarm easily and slip away from the nest before an intruder can come very close. While usually found only with its own kind, on rare occasions it will sometimes be found in mixed colonies made up of Ward's Herons, Little Blue Herons, Louisiana Herons, and Black-Crowned Night Herons.

HABITAT AND ROOSTING

Most often *Nyctanassa violacea violacea* roosts alone or in company with only one or two others of its own species, usually in a dense tree close to the water. However, during nesting and migrational periods, colony roosting is not uncommon. The bird has a wide variety of habitat preference, ranging from rocky coasts or high cliffs or desert conditions to bayou swamp, cattail marsh, banks of rivers and creeks, and even forests in conjunction with slow-moving or stagnant water, such as with large cypress swamps and forests of Spanish moss-bedecked tupelos, water oaks, gum trees, and magnolias.

FOOD AND FEEDING HABITS

The principal items of food for the Yellow-Crowned Night Heron are crawfish and crabs, although at times it will also eat such small coastal-area life as small fishes, small snakes and other reptiles, snails, baby birds that have tumbled from their nests, eels, young leeches, and aquatic insects. Oddly, very few frogs are eaten and there is no recorded instance of toads having been eaten. Although it is not unusual for this species to feed at night, it does so much less often than the Black-Crowned Night Heron. It is essentially diurnal, feeding most heavily during the early morning and late evening hours.

NEST AND NESTING HABITS

Among the herons, *Nyctanassa violacea violacea* builds one of the most substantial of nests, constructed of relatively well-interwoven sticks. It is generally 18 to 22 inches in diameter and as much as 16 inches in depth, with a shallow depression in the center which is sometimes sparsely lined. The most common nesting site seems to be in a dense willow or black mangrove about 15 to 30 feet high. Most often the nesting occurs in conjunction with from ten to twenty pairs of its own species.

Yellow-Crowned Night Heron, *Nyctanassa violacea violacea* ♀ (Linnaeus). Field sketches made at Manasota Key, Englewood, Florida, April 1975.

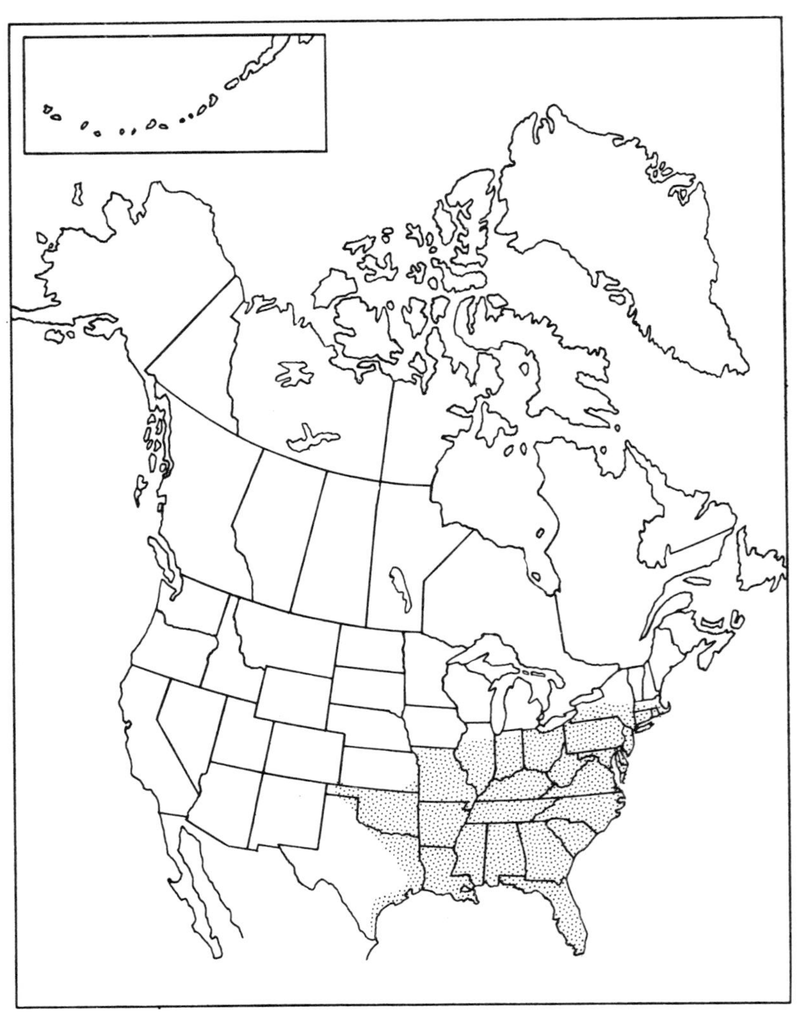

YELLOW-CROWNED NIGHT HERON

Nyctanassa violacea violacea (Linnaeus)

EGGS AND INCUBATION

The four or five smooth-shelled eggs are a pale greenish-blue and, in size, average 2 inches x 1.4 inches (51mm x 37mm). Incubation appears to be identical to that of the Black-Crowned Night Heron and parental care is also the same. Eggs are laid from March through May. Incubation requires twenty-four to twenty-six days.

YOUNG

Characteristics and development essentially the same as for the Black-Crowned Night Heron, the principal difference being that the young of the Yellow-Crowned Night Heron are a lighter slate color, with less brownish generally.

ARDEA HERONS

GENUS: *ARDEA* Linnaeus
SPECIES: *HERODIAS*
SUBSPECIES: *herodias* (Linnaeus)
Great Blue Heron

fannini Chapman
Northwestern Coast Heron

wardi Ridgway
Ward's Heron

treganzai Court
Treganza's Heron

hyperonca Oberholser
California Heron

occidentalis Audubon
Great White Heron

COMMON NAME

Great Blue Heron
(Color Plate IV)

SCIENTIFIC NAME

Ardea herodias herodias (Linnaeus). From the Latin *ardea,* meaning heron, and the Greek *erodios,* also meaning heron.

OTHER COMMON OR COLLOQUIAL NAMES

Practically all of its local names have to do with its size and color, sometimes coupled with (erroneously) the term "crane," which it is not. Often the bird is locally called simply a "crane," but this is in error. The other common or colloquial names include:

BIG BLUE HERON
BLUE CRANE
COMMON BLUE CRANE
CRANE

SHAPE AT REST AND IN FLIGHT

When standing, the Great Blue Heron is about four feet high to the top of its raised head, a distinctive attitude of this bird. The legs are long, the neck thin and long, the tail relatively short, and the beak, which is thick at the base, symmetrically tapers to a very sharp point. Occasionally the neck will be folded and the head couched on the shoulders. Often the bird will stand on one foot only, the other drawn up and all but hidden in the underside plumage. With the encroachment of another Great Blue Heron on its territory, the bird will stretch its neck upward fully, point its beak toward the sky, and advance slowly and menacingly toward the intruder, and chase it away.

In flight it is an uncommonly large bird, with long, broad, round-tipped wings. Except when first taking off and landing, the neck is folded back and the head is couched upon the folded neck. This, incidentally, quickly differentiates it from cranes and flamingos, which fly with heads and necks outstretched. The Great Blue Heron also trails its long legs far behind in flight.

The flight begins as the bird leans forward with neck outstretched. Then (sometimes with an assisting step or two) the great wings beat powerfully and it is launched. For a moment the neck remains outstretched and the legs dangle; but then the legs go back straight and stiff, trailing behind and acting as a rudder to assist the very short tail. At this point the head is couched on the folded neck. The early vigorous wingbeats settle down to slow, powerful strokes. Landing is slightly more graceful than the takeoff, as head and neck are again outstretched and long legs come forward, reaching for purchase as the broad wings brake the bird which drops lightly to the ground or onto its selected perch.

LENGTH AND WINGSPAN

This species averages about 47 inches in length (1206mm) and has an impressive wingspan of around 70 inches (1789mm).

BEAK

The sharp beak is about 5 inches long and yellowish, often turning considerably more orange during the breeding season.

LEGS, FEET, AND CLAWS

Legs and feet are blackish in coloration, except that the soles of the feet are yellowish. The outer toe is longer than the inner. The hind toe is not elevated, but is on the same level with the others; all toes are long and slender, with small webbing connecting the base of the outer and middle toes. The long claw on the middle toe has comblike serrations on the underside (pectinations) which are used as an aid in preening.

CRESTS, PLUMAGE, ANNUAL MOLT

The body plumage, generally, is loose and long. In the breeding season, the bird's back is without any lengthened and loosened plumes. The lower foreneck has considerably lengthened feathers and in the breeding season the crest, which is more or less present all year, becomes much more pronounced and develops two very long, slender, filamentous occipital plumes. The lores are bare.

VOICE

The voice is a hoarse *gronnk* or *graack,* or occasionally a low, heavy, and coarse grunting *quuck.* It has been reported, though not verified, that when extremely angry, the Great Blue Heron will sometimes issue a very harsh shrieking sound not unlike the sound of a heavy desk being pulled across a wooden floor.

SEXUAL DIFFERENCES: SIZE, COLORATION, VOICE

In coloration and voice, the sexes are virtually identical. The male is slightly larger than the female.

COLORATION AND MARKINGS: ADULT

The sharply pointed beak is generally yellowish, especially on the lower mandible, with the upper mandible having a dusky greenish ridge. The lores are a faintly dusky bluish-green and the irides are a bright, clear chrome yellow. The brow and crown are pure white, but with the sides of the crown and the plume feathers black. The neck is a light gray with streaks of white, black, and rust on the sides of the neck toward the front. Cheeks and chin are white. The back and scapulars are a general slate-blue-gray. The tail is deeper slate-gray, as are the primaries, which shade into black. The longish plumes of the lower neck and breast are a light gray with, on the abdomen, streaks of rust interspersed on the white background. Undertail coverts are pure white and the legs and feet are a dusky gray, with the soles of the feet yellowish.

COLORATION AND MARKINGS: JUVENILE

Much like the adults except for a generally browner coloration. Most of the crown is black and there are no lengthened feathers, either crest or plume, on the head. There is a strong rufous edging to the feathers of back and scapulars, while the lesser wing coverts are a rufous brown. The underside is an ashy gray-white, with the legs dingy grayish-black.

GENERAL HABITS AND CHARACTERISTICS

The Great Blue Heron is the largest member of the heron family in the northern United States and Canada. It is also the most widely distributed, most commonly sighted, and therefore best-known of the North American herons. It is normally seen while flying with slow, graceful strokes of its great broad wings at relatively low (treetop) altitude, or while standing in dignified sentinel-like motionlessness in the shallows of stream, marsh, or bog. Yet, though it frequents watery areas, it is equally at home in meadows and highlands and is often seen in such areas walking about with stately grace, occasionally snatching some sort of prey—insects, young birds or small mammals, reptiles or amphibians. Most often solitary in its habits, *Ardea herodias herodias* shows a marked disdain for other wading bird species and even for other individuals of its own species, except during breeding and migratory seasons. Although it appears to be a tremendously large bird, equaling the turkey in general size, its weight is far less than that of the turkey, averaging only 6 to 8 pounds. Certainly it has to be considered as one of the most stately and recognizable of American birds.

HABITAT AND ROOSTING

A wide variation of habitat is enjoyed by the Great Blue Heron but almost always on a solitary basis. It might be seen in newly plowed farm fields, in meadows, in marshes, swamps, bogs, and along the edges of lakes, streams, and ponds. Roosting is sometimes done on the ground and frequently the bird will sleep (often standing on one leg) while in knee-deep water. Most roosting is done, however, in relatively dense cover: heavy mangrove growth, deep willow margins, low swamp oak, and similar growth near watery areas. The roosting bird normally perches in a hunched position on a sturdy branch close to the trunk for long-period roosting. However, for short-term resting or observation, *Ardea herodias herodias* will very frequently land in the very uppermost branches of a tree and stand silhouetted against the sky.

ENEMIES AND DEFENSES

Once it has acquired its full growth, the Great Blue Heron has few natural enemies. Its powerful beak is a formidable weapon. Unfortunately, because of its great size and distinctiveness, the Great Blue Heron is often destroyed by thoughtless or uncaring people with guns who are just looking about for something to shoot.

FOOD AND FEEDING HABITS

Ardea herodias herodias is most often seen standing motionless waiting for prey in shallow waters. In the shallows it may move about in a very stealthy manner, walking slowly and carefully, so that no sound is heard and scarcely a ripple made. Very frequently in the marshes this is the principal means used by this species for capturing frogs and small turtles, which it devours greedily. In upland meadows and plowed fields it hunts field mice, shrews, moles, garter snakes, leopard frogs, and the young of ground-nesting birds. The principal prey, however, is fish of almost any variety. It captures fish by thrusting the powerful beak spearlike into the fish's side or back; then, partially opening the beak, it prevents the impaled fish from wriggling free until the fish can be carried to dry ground and stabbed again repeatedly until dead. The fish is then juggled until positioned headfirst and is swallowed with a series of convulsive gulpings. Often the size of the fish swallowed is remarkable. The authors have watched Great Blue (and Ward's) Herons in Florida coastal waters catch and quite successfully swallow ladyfish nearly two feet in length and just over two pounds, mullet upward of two pounds, and other such fish. Instinctive care seems to be taken, however, with species such as catfish which have spines that might prevent regurgitation. Smaller prey—whether fish, amphibian, or reptile—caught while the bird is wading, is not usually taken to shore. If not killed with the first thrust, the prey will be repeatedly tossed into the air, caught, and mouthed until dead (sometimes beaten against the water surface or against floating debris) and then juggled in the mouth until it is headfirst down the throat and swallowed. Practically without exception, immediately after swallowing the prey, whether in the water or out of it, the Great Blue Heron will dip its beak into the water and shake it back and forth several times, apparently to clean off any slime or other foreign matter which may be clinging to it, before resuming the hunt. Digestion is rapid and the digestive juices are of such acidity that bone matter swallowed is almost completely dissolved. Occasionally a compact pellet of undigested or partially digested feathers and fur is regurgitated.

COURTSHIP AND MATING

Shortly after the spring migration north has been completed, the Great Blue Herons will sometimes assemble in large numbers to engage in mock fights. Soon the paired birds begin leaving for nesting areas.

Great Blue Herons usually copulate with the female standing on the ground. Even if she is on a low limb, invariably she will come to the ground itself before permitting the male to mount her for the brief copulatory activities.

Breeding displays of Great Blue Heron. Sketches made at Buttonwood Rookery, Lemon Bay, Englewood, Florida.

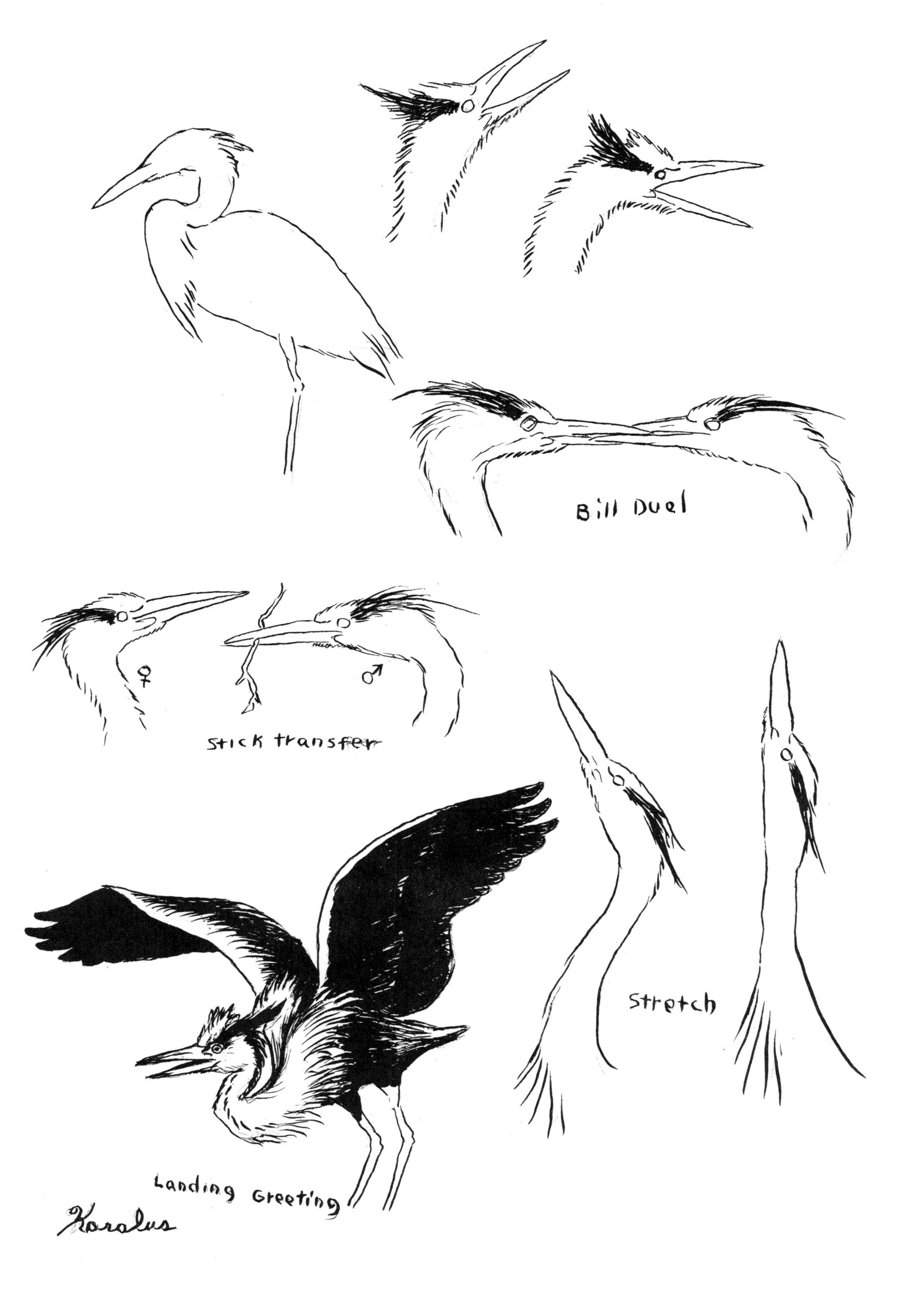
Bill Duel
♀
♂
stick transfer
Stretch
Landing Greeting
Karalus

NEST AND NESTING HABITS

The Great Blue Herons usually tend to nest in small colonies of perhaps ten to thirty pairs, although sometimes the groups are larger. The nests are usually at the very uppermost branches of a tree, although the tree might be as low as 10 feet tall or as high as 100. Now and then numerous nests will be placed in a single tree. *Ardea herodias herodias* will sometimes nest in association with other wading birds, such as Little Blue Herons, Louisiana Herons, White Ibises, and even such swamp birds as Anhingas. Where colony-nesting successfully occurs, the Great Blue Herons are inclined to come back year after year to renest in the same area. In such colonies, the old nests are almost always enlarged and reused. Twigs from old nests may be used in the construction of new nests.

Choice of tree species does not seem to be a terribly important consideration, although a certain preference is shown for larger mangroves, high pointed conifers, and cypresses with expansive umbrellas. Sometimes the herons will nest in the top of very low bushes. Some ground-nestings have been reliably reported. Where the habitat is conducive to it, nesting will occur in crevices or on ledges of cliffs. Of prime importance in nest site selection is isolation—far more so than height of nesting tree. *Ardea herodias herodias* demands isolated remoteness in its choice of nesting sites.

The nest is a large affair, usually from 30 to 40 inches across but sometimes as much as 4 feet in diameter and rarely smaller than 20 inches. The nest and the ground beneath it become, as the nesting season progresses, increasingly whitened by the excrement of the adult Great Blue Herons and their young.

EGGS AND INCUBATION

The three or four pastel blue or green eggs are usually smooth-shelled, though sometimes there is a slight granulation. They are fairly large, averaging 2.5 inches x 1.7 inches (65mm x 45mm). The incubation, shared equally by both parent birds, lasts for twenty-eight days.

YOUNG

Great Blue Herons in the nest, from the time of hatching until fully feathered, are among the ugliest birds in the world. In addition to being ugly, they are ungainly and awkward. They tend to keep crouched down and out of sight while the parent birds are away, but as soon as a parent returns, they stand and start a great hubbub of squawking and vying for position in the nest. Though they're fed in order, the largest and most aggressive youngster usually winds up getting the most food. At first the food is predigested (or partially digested) fish. The baby bird grips the parent's beak crosswise in its own and the parent thereupon, with crest and plumes erect, pumps until regurgitation occurs, the result of which is avidly swallowed by the young. Later, as the young grow more able to fend for themselves, the parents cease regurgitation of predigested food, and instead regurgitate small whole fish into the bottom of the nest. These are then picked up by the youngsters and swallowed.

The young birds remain in the nest, under ordinary circumstances, until fully fledged and as large as the adults. However, they frighten easily and in such case will leave the nest and walk out on the slender surrounding branches and remain perched there.

Full adult plumage is not assumed by the young bird until the first post-nuptial molt in its second year. After that there is little seasonal change except that the adult may be slightly more handsome in the spring breeding season than at other times of the year.

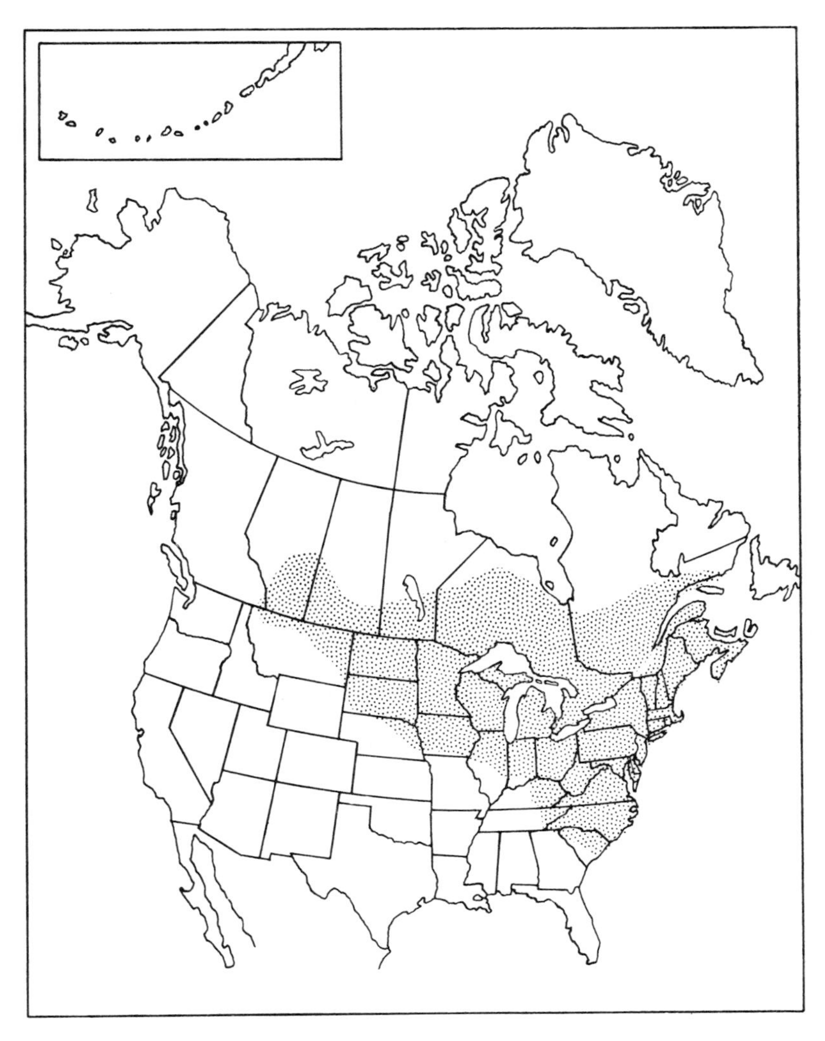

GREAT BLUE HERON

Ardea herodias herodias (Linnaeus)

MIGRATION

Ardea herodias herodias is definitely migratory in the northernmost portion of its range. Sometimes the bird migrates by itself or in flocks of from five to thirty birds. Many of the Great Blue Herons have winter ranges which overlap with the Ward's Heron or other subspecies to the south or west. The southward migration in autumn usually begins early in October. Northward migration in spring occurs in March or early April. Following the breeding and nesting season, young birds wander in all directions.

ECONOMIC INFLUENCE

The Great Blue Heron has earned the enmity of man in some areas where goldfish, turtles, frogs, or trout are raised commercially. Once one of these herons learns how simple it is to obtain food at a trout hatchery, for example, it may have to be trapped or shot. However, only individual troublesome birds justify this practice, which can only be done by permit.

COMMON NAME

Northwestern Coast Heron
(Subspecies Sketch 3)

SCIENTIFIC NAME

Ardea herodias fannini Chapman.

BASIC SUBSPECIFIC DIFFERENCES

The Northwestern Coast Heron is the same size as, but considerably darker than, the Great Blue Heron. It is limited in distribution to the Pacific coastal area of the Northwest.

NORTHWESTERN COAST HERON
Ardea herodias fannini Chapman

3. NORTHWESTERN COAST HERON
Ardea herodias fannini Chapman. Campbell River, Vancouver Island, British Columbia, Canada.
A.O.U. Number 194a

Karl E. Karalus

COMMON NAME

Ward's Heron
(Subspecies Sketch 4)

SCIENTIFIC NAME

Ardea herodias wardi Ridgway. At first suspected of being an intergraded hybrid of *Ardea herodias herodias* (Great Blue) and *Ardea herodias occidentalis* (Great White), but this distinction was ultimately given to a variety previously known as Wuerdemann's Heron.

SHAPE AT REST AND IN FLIGHT

Generally larger than *Ardea herodias herodias,* but identical in basic contour.

LENGTH AND WINGSPAN

Ward's Heron has an average length of about 51 inches (1315mm) and a wingspan over 6.5 feet (2033mm).

COLORATION AND MARKINGS

The middle of the forehead is white, the sides of the crown and occiput are black, and the feathers are lengthened. The throat and sides of the head are white, while the neck is light drab streaked with black in front. The back, wings, and tail are a dark smoky gray, with the primaries dark plum color. Underparts are mixed black and white and leg plumage is tawny. Unlike the Great Blue Heron, in which only the upper portion of the upper mandible is greenish, the entire beak of Ward's Heron is this color.

The variety formerly called *Ardea herodias wuerdemanni* (Wuerdemann's Heron), actually a hybrid of the Great White Heron and the Great Blue Heron (and found almost entirely in the Florida Keys), has white head and occipital crest feathers and a fuscous forehead. The underparts, also, are grayish-white.

GENERAL HABITS AND CHARACTERISTICS

Ward's Herons will often construct their large nesting colonies in close proximity to (sometimes even surrounded by) such other species as the

I EASTERN GREEN HERON

Butorides striatus virescens (Linnaeus). Franklin Park, Illinois, May 11, 1953. A.O.U. Number 201

II BLACK-CROWNED NIGHT HERON

Nycticorax nycticorax hoactli (Gmelin). Near Dayton Museum of Natural History, Dayton, Ohio. A.O.U. Number 202

III YELLOW-CROWNED NIGHT HERON

Nyctanassa violacea violacea (Linnaeus). Adult (left) and immature (right). Bay Oaks Circle, Manasota Key, Englewood, Florida. A.O.U. Number 203

IV GREAT BLUE HERON

Ardea herodias herodias (Linnaeus). Lemon Bay, Sarasota County, Florida, January 19, 1974. A.O.U. Number 194

arl E. Karalus

Karl E. Karalus
1973

E. Karalus

Karl E. Karalus

Crown raised
in anger or display
K. E. Karalus
Little Blue Heron
Florida caerulea
Serrate section on bill of Green heron
Green Heron
Butorides striatus
Ward's Heron
Ardea herodias wardi
Southern variety of Great blue heron

WARD'S HERON

Ardea herodias wardi Ridgway

Great White Heron, Great Egret, Snowy Egret, Reddish Egret, Louisiana Heron, and Black-Crowned Night Heron. Sometimes Boat-Tailed Grackles will be close by and even build their own nests in the bottom sticks of the Ward's Heron nests.

HABITAT AND ROOSTING

The habitat most used, both for roosting and nesting, is densely tangled areas of mangrove and other trees on floating islands or hammocks amid surrounding heavy marsh growth. Ward's Heron usually roosts and nests in an area of around 150 to 200 feet in diameter in the thickest portions.

NEST AND NESTING HABITS

Ardea herodias wardi begins nesting activities as early as late November and continues right on through April. The nests themselves are usually quite large; built of interwoven sticks and measuring around 3 to 4 feet in diameter and 15 to 18 inches thick. Such nests are reused year after year if the nesting area remains undisturbed, with certain improvements made in the nest each new season. There may be as many as ten nests in a single tree, although occasionally the birds will nest on the ground amid clusters of prickly-pear cactus growth. If nesting among the oaks, water elms, or cypresses, Ward's Heron generally likes the nest to be about 40 to 50 feet from the ground.

EGGS AND INCUBATION

The eggs are a bit larger than those of the Great Blue Heron, measuring on the average 2.5 inches x 1.8 inches (65mm x 46mm).

(Overleaf) Head and beak/bill studies from life; Stump Pass, Lemon Bay, Englewood, Florida; April 25, 1977. (Not to scale.)

4. WARD'S HERON

Ardea herodias wardi Ridgway. Englewood Beach, Florida. A.O.U. Number 194b

Karl E. Karalus

COMMON NAME

Treganza's Heron
(Subspecies Sketch 5)

SCIENTIFIC NAME

Ardea herodias treganzai Court.

BASIC SUBSPECIFIC DIFFERENCES

While slightly larger than the Great Blue Heron *(Ardea herodias herodias)*, at an average height of 42 inches, it is somewhat smaller than Ward's Heron *(Ardea herodias wardi)*.

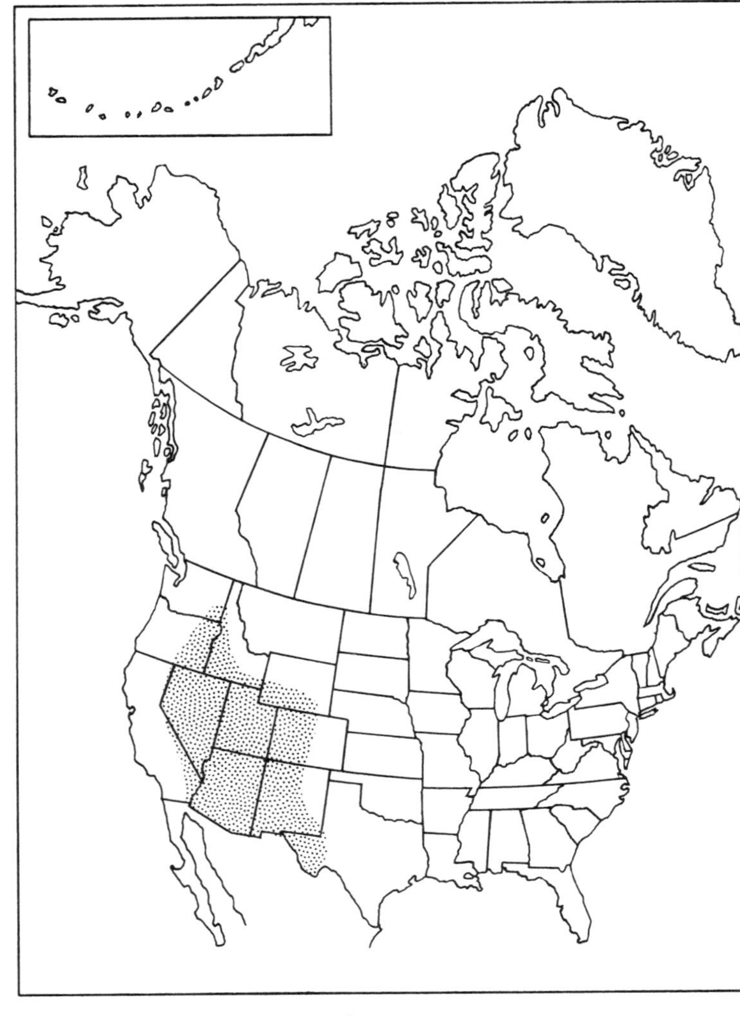

TREGANZA'S HERON

Ardea herodias treganzai Court

5. TREGANZA'S HERON

Ardea herodias treganzai Court. Green River, Wyoming. A.O.U. Number 194c

Karl E. Karalus

COMMON NAME

California Heron
(Subspecies Sketch 6)

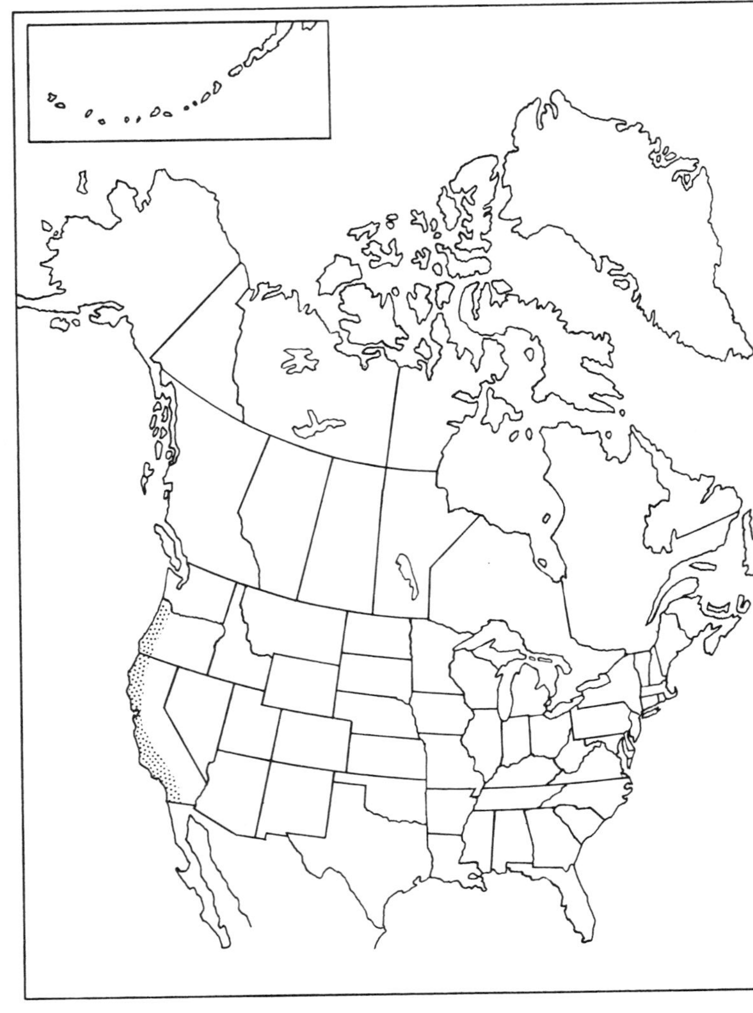

CALIFORNIA HERON

Ardea herodias hyperonca Oberholser

SCIENTIFIC NAME

Ardea herodias hyperonca Oberholser. *Hyperonca* means "of greatest bulk."

BASIC SUBSPECIFIC DIFFERENCES

Identical in shape to the Great Blue Heron, but much larger than *Ardea herodias herodias,* and much darker than *Ardea herodias treganzai.*

LENGTH AND WINGSPAN

The average length of the California Heron is about 50 inches (1287mm) and the average wingspan is almost 6 feet (1832mm).

NESTING HABITS

The California Heron, which shows a somewhat more marked proclivity for colonial nesting than others of the subspecies, prefers a heavy tangle of brushy growth, from the midst of which rises one or more large trees. Here, at a height of about 40 to 80 feet, and sometimes with as many as twenty or more nests in the same tree, is where this subspecies is most inclined to nest. Having water close by is desirable, but evidently not a prerequisite.

---

6. CALIFORNIA HERON

Ardea herodias hyperonca Oberholser. Bakersfield, California. A.O.U. Number 194d

Karl E. Karalus

COMMON NAME

Great White Heron
(Color Plate V)

SCIENTIFIC NAME

Ardea herodias occidentalis Audubon. The Latin name simply signifies that this is a heron of the Western world.

SHAPE AT REST AND IN FLIGHT

When at rest, this bird almost invariably sits on a mangrove branch outstretched over the water at a height of 6 to 20 feet, its head drawn down and couched on the shoulders, and often standing on one leg. As a matter of fact, frequently one leg is a little larger than the other as a result of its being used more. When the bird is fishing it is usually standing erect in water nearly reaching its underside, patiently waiting for a fish to swim close enough to impale. At such times its head may be raised to its greatest height for better visibility downward into the water, or poised at an angle on a neck bent into an S-curve like a tight spring ready to be released, as the bird observes prey coming close. Its basic shape in flight is very similar to that of the Great Blue Heron.

LENGTH AND WINGSPAN

The average length of the Great White Heron is 52.7 inches (1350mm) and the wingspan averages 81.8 inches (2097mm).

BEAK

The beak is yellow on both mandibles, usually becoming slightly greenish toward the tip. This is especially noticeable on the lower mandible.

LEGS AND FEET

The legs are yellowish, shading to greenish on the front. The feet are also yellowish with a faint greenish cast. The general yellow coloration of the legs is the best way to separate the Great White Heron from the Great Egret, since the legs of the latter are black.

CRESTS, PLUMAGE, ANNUAL MOLT

The plumage of the Great White Heron is much like that of Ward's Heron, but white.

EYES AND VISION

The irides of the Great White Heron are a clear chrome yellow (with the lores a pale bluish-green). The bird's vision is excellent.

COLORATION AND MARKINGS: ADULT

The adults are always pure white in plumage, with the only coloration occurring in the irides (chrome yellow), the lores (bluish-green), the legs and feet (yellowish, tending toward greenish on the "shin" portions and on the upper surface of the toes), and the beak, which is yellow on both mandibles but usually slightly greenish toward the tip, especially on the lower mandible.

COLORATION AND MARKINGS: JUVENILE

Like the adults, pure white, but often with the beak a little more greenish at the base than in the adult bird. The sequence of plumage and molts is the same as that in the Great Blue Heron, with fully adult plumage not being acquired until at least two years of age.

HABITAT AND ROOSTING

This is the only heron species of the continent which is entirely coastal maritime in its choice of habitat. The rare occasions when the Great White Heron has been observed farther inland have almost without exception followed hurricanes or other severe storms. The preferred habitat is strictly of the low mangrove coastal area type, where extensive

GREAT WHITE HERON

Ardea herodias occidentalis Audubon

shallows afford good fishing and small but dense and tangled mangrove islands afford good nesting sites. Roosting almost always occurs in the denser areas of mangroves, relatively close to open water.

COURTSHIP AND MATING

Courting activities which have been recorded are similar to those of *Ardea herodias wardi.*

LITTLE BLUE HERON

GENUS: *FLORIDA* Baird
SPECIES: *CAERULEA* (Linnaeus)
SUBSPECIES: *caerulea* (Linnaeus)

COMMON NAME

Little Blue Heron
(Color Plate VI)

SCIENTIFIC NAME

Florida caerulea caerulea (Linnaeus). The Latin name signifies a sky-blue heron of Florida.

OTHER COMMON OR COLLOQUIAL NAMES

BLUE EGRET For general coloration and for type of bird.

BLUE HERON For general coloration and type of bird, but might lead to confusion with Great Blue Heron, which is also often called simply "Blue Heron."

CALICO BIRD For the spotted coloration displayed by adult-sized immature birds.

CALICO HERON

LITTLE WHITE HERON Common for the adult-sized juvenile which may even be raising its own young, yet still wears the juvenile plumage of pure white with bluish primary tips. This name was used very commonly some years ago when it was incorrectly believed that the white bird was a color phase of the adult bird and that the Little Blue Heron was dichromatic.

PIED HERON After the coloration and mottled plumage of the young bird as it changes from white to the blue of the true adult.

SPOTTED CRANE For the same reason, but with erroneous designation of the type of bird.

SPOTTED HERON Again, for the type of bird and its mottled, intermediate plumage.

SHAPE AT REST AND IN FLIGHT

This is a slender, streamlined heron which seems to be taller than it actually is because of its very slenderness and the fact that it rarely crouches and hunches when standing or perching, as other herons do. The neck is long and the head usually held high, with generally alert attitude and crest plumes not readily apparent. The beak is long and slender and very pointed and often the neck will be bent as if broken. At first glance from a little distance, the bird appears to be dark.

As do most herons, it flies with the head drawn in upon the shoulders and the long legs trailing behind, but with the body silhouette being somewhat less bulky than most other heron species.

Sometimes, when circling on a high wind, and almost always when coming in for a landing, *Florida caerulea caerulea* will set its wings and glide for a considerable distance. At times it will do this in unison with upward of a score of other birds of the same species, especially if it has been frightened from its perch. At such times it will frequently make a wide circle on relatively fast wingbeats and then come back, gliding the last dozen yards or more and landing lightly and gracefully with delicate strokes instead of with excessive wingbeating. Indeed, lightness and grace are characteristic of the flight of the Little Blue Heron.

LENGTH AND WINGSPAN

The average length of the Little Blue Heron is just slightly over 2 feet (620mm) and its wingspan averages 40.25 inches (1032mm).

BEAK

The beak is one of the features by which the white, immature but adult-sized Little Blue Heron can be told apart from the similar-sized and shaped Snowy Egret. The beak of the Little Blue Heron has a black tip and shades into a dark blue and then lighter bluish toward the base, while that of the Snowy Egret is essentially black or shading to grayish-black. Also the beak of the Snowy Egret is not quite as thick at the base as that of the Little Blue Heron, even though the latter's beak is relatively slender and very acute. On the upper mandible there is a gentle curve from base to tip (convex) and the lower mandible is straight or with only a very slight concave curvature.

LEGS AND FEET

Again, as with the beak, legs and feet are a good means of distinguishing the immature Little Blue Heron from the Snowy Egret. The latter has black legs and bright yellow feet, while the immature Little Blue Heron has legs and feet which range from a medium greenish-yellow to a dark greenish.

CRESTS, PLUMAGE, ANNUAL MOLT

Adult Little Blue Herons have a few short plume-like feathers in the back, but not really any outstanding aigrette feathers as do many of the related species. Beginning in February, the adult birds undergo a partial molt just prior to nuptials. Afterwards there is a complete molt beginning at the end of June and continuing until the wings themselves are finally molting in August. In its breeding plumage, *Florida caerulea caerulea* is a dark but extremely handsome bird with a beautiful plum-colored plumage frosted with a faint blush of powder from the powder-down tracts which imparts a delicate, temporal quality to the bird's general appearance.

VOICE

The Little Blue Heron is usually a silent bird. However, there are times when it becomes downright garrulous, as during the nest-building period, when it seems to murmur constantly as it works, and during the early days of the hatching of its eggs, as it comes to the nest to feed its young through regurgitation. It often utters a loud, harsh, croaking cry when frightened.

COLORATION AND MARKINGS: ADULT

Plumage of the head and neck range from a dark purplish-maroon to a purplish-red which is especially intense in the nuptial plumage (it is at this time that the slate-blue lengthened plumes on the back are more apparent). The lores and eyelids are blue and the rest of the bird's body and wings are dark plum color to slatey blue, but dusted with a delicate frosting of powder down of pale blue coloration. The Little Blue Heron is not dichromatic and does not have a white color phase, as was once believed. In winter plumage the head and neck are more evenly purple-colored with some white occurring on the throat and below the lower mandible. The irides are bright yellow.

COLORATION AND MARKINGS: JUVENILE

The juvenile is snowy white with a tinge of blue tipping the primaries. The legs are green and the beak is bluish but tipped with black. Some of the young reach breeding age while still pure white, and this is what initially gave rise to the belief that dichromatism occurred in the species. However, it has now been proven that a white or pied bird is merely a young one changing color to the full adult plumage. When the change in plumage does occur (a change which takes place gradually over the entire year) the white birds get blotched, speckled, patched, and spotted with blue—a phenomenon unique among the herons.

GENERAL HABITS AND CHARACTERISTICS

Probably the most immediately evident characteristic of *Florida caerulea caerulea* is its shy nature. It is not particularly reclusive, since it does take considerable pleasure in the company of its own kind as well as other heron species, but it tends to like isolated places to which it can retire and feed, roost, and nest undisturbed. When it travels to such areas, it generally travels in loose, rather disorganized flocks, with rarely more than fifteen or twenty birds in any one flying group, although these groups often converge at the final resting or feeding place. The Little Blue Heron shows a marked affinity for the company of the Louisiana Heron, and together they frequent isolated small ponds with densely tangled willow and myrtle banks, or else broad grassy open areas surrounding them. During daylight hours, when the birds are principally active, they like being in relatively small groups or even alone, but as evening comes on, they begin to collect in larger groups and then, in the twilight, take wing and fly to the roosting area, which may be several miles distant. As they reach it, they generally make an inspection pass first, then wheel about and glide in for their landing. These areas are shared not only with the Louisiana Heron, but sometimes with the Black-Crowned Night Heron and the Little Green Heron.

HABITAT AND ROOSTING

Little Blue Herons generally roost among considerable numbers of birds, primarily of its own species, but sometimes, as noted above, with other herons. The roosting colonies are sometimes as small as twenty to fifty pairs of birds, but colonies as large as two thousand pairs have been recorded. The usual number seems to be anywhere from a hundred to three or four hundred birds. This roosting is done usually relatively low in clumps of bushes or dense trees on the margins of swamps and ponds, or on islands, generally well isolated and safe from molestation by man. Almost without exception these rookeries are far inland from the coast, even though the birds may have spent the day at the coastal flats feeding. In all cases, a freshwater habitat is preferred over a saltwater habitat, although now and then large colonies will frequent the dense mangrove swamps of the salt or brackish coastal areas. In the southern states the bird is especially fond of marshes and small pond habitats which are well grown with pickerelweed *(Pontederia cordata)* and dense barrier screens 8 to 20 feet high, closely stemmed bushes called ti-ti (or sometimes ty-ty). These *Cliftonia monophylla* borders become almost impenetrable to any enemy and certainly cannot be crossed without considerable disturbance being made. In addition to the swamps and marshes described above, Little Blue Herons like dense, tangled tree growths of willow, myrtle, black gum, sweet gum, pine, bay, water oak, and live oak, all growing from or on the margin of water that is mere inches to 2 or 3 feet in depth. These are the same sort of areas where nesting occurs and they are farther inland than the breeding areas of any of the other herons that breed in vast rookeries. After roosting for the night, the birds begin to fly away from the roost at the first light of early morning in small detached groups, heading for distant feeding grounds.

FOOD AND FEEDING HABITS

Most often the Little Blue Heron feeds alone or in small groups during early morning and late evening, wading carefully about in the shallows and striking swiftly and usually unerringly with its sharp beak. Rarely if ever a night feeder, this heron usually feeds most determinedly in the early morning and early evening hours. If the small fish it is hunting in the shallows are specially abundant, it will often move about with great alacrity, stabbing here and there with its beak and rarely missing. Sometimes, like the Cattle Egret, it will alight near grazing cattle and follow them to pluck up the insects which are disturbed by the bovine movements. Most often, though, the food is small fish—ordinarily various species of minnows and killifish, along with occasional bluegills, sunfish, catfish, and other species, plus a fair amount of crawfish and a lesser number of grasshoppers, locusts, mole crickets, aquatic beetles, frogs, salamanders, small snakes and lizards, cutworms, and very young turtles.

COURTSHIP AND MATING

The courtship of *Florida caerulea caerulea* is almost identical to that of *Hydranassa tricolor ruficollis* (the Louisiana Heron). The display begins with the male flying in to perch on the highest point of a low bush or small tree near

---

V GREAT WHITE HERON

Ardea herodias occidentalis Audubon. Big Pine Key, Monroe County, Florida. A.O.U. Number 192

VI LITTLE BLUE HERON

Florida caerulea caerulea (Linnaeus). Adult male (right) and immature (left). Stump Pass, Charlotte County, Florida. A.O.U. Number 200

Karl E. Karalus

Karl E. Karalus

Karl E Karalus

Karl E. Karalus

which a female bird is perched. There he begins his display by bowing low to her numerous times and moving farther and farther out on the branches until there is hardly a perch left for his feet. There he swings and sways precariously—yet with perfect balance—with every breeze which touches him. His neck moves in graceful serpentine curves and he rarely takes his eye from the female of his choice. Every now and then he will freeze in an especially attractive attitude and stay that way for five or ten seconds before once again beginning the dancing which moves him ever closer to the female. At last, when they are finally so close that their shoulders are actually rubbing, they lean against one another and rub heads and necks together and then copulation occurs. Following the mating, the paired birds fly off together and generally begin construction of their nest on the same day.

NEST AND NESTING HABITS

The nest is usually in a bush or tree, sometimes as low as 2 feet above the water but more commonly at a height of 3 to 8 feet. On rare occasions it may be placed as high as 40 feet.

The extremely flimsy nests are actually no more than relatively flat unlined platforms of loosely interwoven twigs, perhaps 12 to 28 inches in diameter with a slight depression in the center. Sometimes some smaller, finer twigs are used for the top layer and for the depression. The nests have no lining other than that. Nest-building usually begins in mid-March and ends by mid-June, but on occasion it will take place much later—rarely as late as mid-August. Often numerous Little Blue Herons will nest in the same bush or tree.

EGGS AND INCUBATION

There are usually four or five (sometimes six) smooth, delicate bluish-green eggs. The average egg size is 1.7 inches x 1.3 inches (44mm x 34mm).

Incubation, shared by both parents equally, begins with the first egg laid. It is not uncommon to find nests in which there is not only still a viable egg, but young ranging in age from one day to one week.

YOUNG

Because of the staggered hatching, very often the smallest herons in the nest are eventually shoved out by the older nestlings. The baby birds appear in a first down that is pure white, and it is the body plumage which appears first, also pure white. The entire back is ordinarily well feathered before the baby bird is even half grown and considerably before the flight feathers break through their sheaths. The primaries and rectrices are not complete until the bird is

---

VII LOUISIANA (OR TRI-COLORED) HERON

Hydranassa tricolor ruficollis (Gosse). South Manasota Key, Charlotte County, Florida (Nature Conservancy land), May 15, 1973. A.O.U. Number 199

VIII CATTLE EGRET

Bubulcus ibis ibis Linnaeus. Cape Haze, Charlotte County, Florida, May 15, 1973. A.O.U. Number 201.1

LITTLE BLUE HERON

Florida caerulea caerulea (Linnaeus)

fully grown. The white plumage (with dark-tipped primaries) remains all during the first summer, fall, and winter. By the following February, some of the blue body plumage begins appearing. By this time the bird is old enough to breed itself and so some breeding takes place with young adults in interim plumage, ranging from pure white (pied) to almost all blue. Full adult plumage is apparent with the first post-nuptial molt when the young bird is just over a year old.

MIGRATION

The movement northward which occurs from midsummer onward into autumn is not a true migration, but rather the wandering of the young adult birds out of the nest. Because these young are essentially in pure white plumage, they are very frequently mistaken for Snowy Egrets and reported as such. The northern population does undergo a true southward migration in late fall, withdrawing from the northern tier of its breeding range and not returning until late February to early May.

ECONOMIC INFLUENCE

The Little Blue Heron is considered to be quite beneficial because of its habit of devouring large numbers of injurious insects (grasshoppers and locusts, along with cutworms of various kinds) and, in the areas where rice is grown (primarily Louisiana and southern Arkansas), eating great numbers of crayfish which dig holes into the embankments, weakening them and causing considerable damage. Because of these habits, *Florida caerulea caerulea* is probably the most beneficial of all the North American herons.

LOUISIANA (or TRI-COLORED) HERON

GENUS: *HYDRANASSA* Baird
SPECIES: *TRICOLOR* (Muller)
SUBSPECIES: *ruficollis* (Gosse)

COMMON NAME

Louisiana Heron (or, almost as frequently, Tricolor Heron, or Tri-Colored Heron) (Color Plate VII)

SCIENTIFIC NAME

Hydranassa tricolor ruficollis (Gosse). The name stems from the Greek and Latin and means "rufous-necked, three-colored water queen"—*hydr* meaning water, *anassa,* a queen, *tricolor,* three-colored, *rufi,* rufous, and *collis,* neck.

OTHER COMMON OR COLLOQUIAL NAMES

AMERICAN DEMIEGRET A misappelation meaning that the bird is half egret and half heron.

DEMOISELLE Because of its grace and elegance.

LADY-OF-THE-WATERS Due to the delicate, dainty, and feminine mannerisms of the bird when it is in and near the water.

LOUISIANA EGRET Same as in Louisiana Heron, but misapplied to egret.

SHAPE AT REST AND IN FLIGHT

The Louisiana Heron is generally alert, bright, and quick, moving with dainty and delicate movements. It is a medium-sized heron, as compared to the Little Blue Heron and the Great Blue Heron. The bird is slender, with a smooth, clean silhouette.

Its shape in flight is similar to that of other herons. The firm, regular wingstrokes are slightly faster than those of the Great Blue Heron, but slower than those of the Little Blue Heron. The graceful flight usually terminates with the wings gently cupping the air and the outstretched feet neatly gripping the perch without fumbling or stepping about to retain balance. At times the birds engage in some rather outstanding aerial maneuverings. They approach the feeding grounds, for example, with the usual steady wingbeat, while flying at an altitude of perhaps 200 feet or more. Directly over the feeding ground they will fold their wings and drop or tailspin downward and then spread their wings and swing from side to side as they come in for the landing. This same action, often in much greater numbers, is performed over the roosting grounds in the evening, once a preliminary pass has been made over the area where the roosting is to be done. The actual flights to and from these areas in morning and evening are usually made in non-formation flocks or sometimes in rather ragged, fluctuating long lines, often at considerable height. On the whole, this heron is the most graceful of its entire family.

LENGTH AND WINGSPAN

The average length of the Louisiana Heron is just over 25.5 inches (656mm) and its wingspan averages 37.4 inches (958mm).

BEAK

The beak is very slender and, toward the middle, becomes contracted, so that the outline of both upper and lower beaks is slightly concave. It tapers on both mandibles to a very sharp point. During breeding season the beak is black at the end, shading into blue toward the base, then lilac at the base and to the lores. During non-breeding season, the beak is black and yellow.

LEGS

The legs are a dingy yellowish-green behind and a dusky grayish in front, giving a general aspect of grayishness from a slight distance.

EYES

The irides are a very bright and clear true red. During breeding season the lores are a pale lilac, but this becomes pale yellowish at other times.

CRESTS, PLUMAGE, ANNUAL MOLT

The adult birds undergo a complete postnuptial molt beginning in late August, and lasting into early October. A partial molt, not including the flight feathers, occurs prenuptially in February and March. The nuptial plumage itself results in the growth of long white head plumes which are not evident at other times of the year. However, the other well-developed purplish head plumes are visible the year around, as are the purplish and dusky cinnamon back plumes. At all times except winter there is an exceptionally fine fringe-like train of feathers extending beyond the tail.

VOICE

A variety of croaks and squawkings are issued at various times by the adults, sometimes low and chuckling in character, sometimes harsh. The young birds in the nests make an almost constant whining sound, low in tonal quality and inaudible very far from the nesting tree. However, they also make a very loud peeping cry, especially when hungry. This cry, which intensifies when an adult appears, can be heard for a considerable distance.

SEXUAL DIFFERENCES: SIZE, COLORATION, VOICE

Males and females are essentially similar in coloration and voice.

MORTALITY AND LONGEVITY

Hydranassa tricolor ruficollis is by far the most widespread and abundant heron species in the South, which may be due, in part, to the fact that the bird has been unmolested by plume or meat hunters.

Louisiana Heron, *Hydranassa tricolor ruficollis* (Gosse).

South Beach
manasota Key
Charlotte co
april
7.1975
Florida
K. E. Karalus
♂
♀
at nest
Peterson Island
Lemon Bay
Florida

Also, because it builds a more substantial nest than other heron species, there is less likelihood of storms destroying the nests and their contents.

COLORATION AND MARKINGS: ADULT

On a very general basis, the bird is a dark grayish-blue in color with a white underside and white rump. This highly contrasting white underside (which is unique to the Louisiana Heron) is a key identification marking, and is apparent at all stages of the plumage and in all seasons. The adult's legs are a dingy yellowish-green in the rear and dusky grayish in front and on the tops of the toes.

COLORATION AND MARKINGS: JUVENILE

Juveniles lack a crest and elongated plumes; the neck and back plumage is a dusky cinnamon in color, while the upper neck sides, nape, and head range from a deep chestnut to a bright reddish-bay in color. The center of the throat, the entire belly, and the underwings (exclusive of the primaries) are all white. The underwing primaries are purplish-blue, tipped with a deep chestnut. On the back, the primaries and rectrices are a pale mauve to lavender. The legs are one color—a dingy dust-green. Just after the nuptials, when the young bird is about sixteen months old, a molt occurs in which the last of the juvenile plumage is lost and the bird emerges with complete adult plumage for the first time.

GENERAL HABITS AND CHARACTERISTICS

Hydranassa tricolor ruficollis is among the least shy of all the North American wading birds and sometimes can be approached and observed from very close range as it moves daintily about in its normal activities. As if conscious of its inherent elegance, this pretty heron may spend hours in the process of preening its plumage and thoroughly working the grease-powder from its powder-down tracts into the feathers, providing them with not only a degree of water repellency but also with an attractive dusty, almost silvery sheen.

HABITAT AND ROOSTING

The rookeries—both breeding and roosting—are ordinarily located in wooded swamps or on densely treed and bushy islands or hammocks. The Louisiana Heron especially prefers as a habitat areas of tidal marsh, mangrove fringes in the coastal areas, small freshwater pond margins, the edges of lakes, creeks, and rivers, especially where these are well grown with brushy cover, marshy meadows, and along flooded ditches. Once in a while it will associate with the Cattle Egrets and Little Blue Herons as they follow meandering cattle through pasturage areas, in order to feed on the insects disturbed by the movements of the cattle.

FOOD AND FEEDING HABITS

The Louisiana Heron prefers to move about slowly in the shallows, looking for prey, and, when it enters an area where prey is abundant, to dance about with rapid and agile steps, wings partially or fully outspread, spearing or snatching minnows or whatever other prey it has found. It is believed that this delicate prancing-about serves to muddy the water, causing the fish to get confused and to rise closer to the water surface, where the bird can more easily snap them up. When the Louisiana Heron strikes, it rarely misses. It has even been observed skillfully snatching flying insects out of the air. When feeding it prefers wading in water not over 6 inches in depth and preferably 3 or 4 inches deep. Like the Great Blue Heron, it will eat almost any fish, insect, crustacean, reptile, or amphibian it can catch, kill, and swallow.

COURTSHIP AND MATING

Although the actual courtship dance is virtually identical to the dance of the Little Blue Heron, one part of it appears to be unique to *Hydranassa tricolor ruficollis.* This occurs when the male, toward the end of his display, allows his wings to droop until the tips of the primaries are dragging at which point he raises his head with the beak pointed skyward and the neck outstretched to its greatest limits, and gives voice to a peculiar low moaning sound. This sound is so muted that an observer only a dozen or so yards away would have to strain his ears to hear it, but it seems to excite the female.

NEST AND NESTING HABITS

The Louisiana Herons usually nest in rookeries of considerable size. Accounts from years ago indicate that nesting colonies very often consisted of four to five thousand pairs of birds. Except that the nest is slightly more sturdily built, it is almost indistinguishable from that of the Snowy Egret. In Florida most of the nesting is done in mangrove tangles and dense willow clumps, and elsewhere the densest possible growth adjacent to water is what the Louisiana Heron likes most. Yet, in some areas where tree growth is scant and even bushes are few, it is not uncommon for this heron to nest on the ground or amid clusters of prickly-pear cactus. In the areas of willows and mangroves, the Louisiana Herons often nest in close proximity to other heron species, and in the ground nestings, they often share the area with nesting black skimmers, terns, and gulls. In the West, where tall cane borders marshy areas, strips of cane are often used for major braces in nest construction, while finer strips of the same material are used to line the nests. In their nest-building, the Louisiana Herons have a system that is seldom altered. The male seeks out the proper sticks and returns with them to the nesting site. There he gives them to the female, who does the actual nest construction. With each such stick presented to the female, the male raises his crest feathers, aigrettes, and neck plumage, struts with wings widespread, and utters a special long crooning cry. The female responds with a similar display and cry and then takes the stick from him. Almost at once he leaves to find another, while the female occupies herself with weaving the new stick into the nest, positioning and

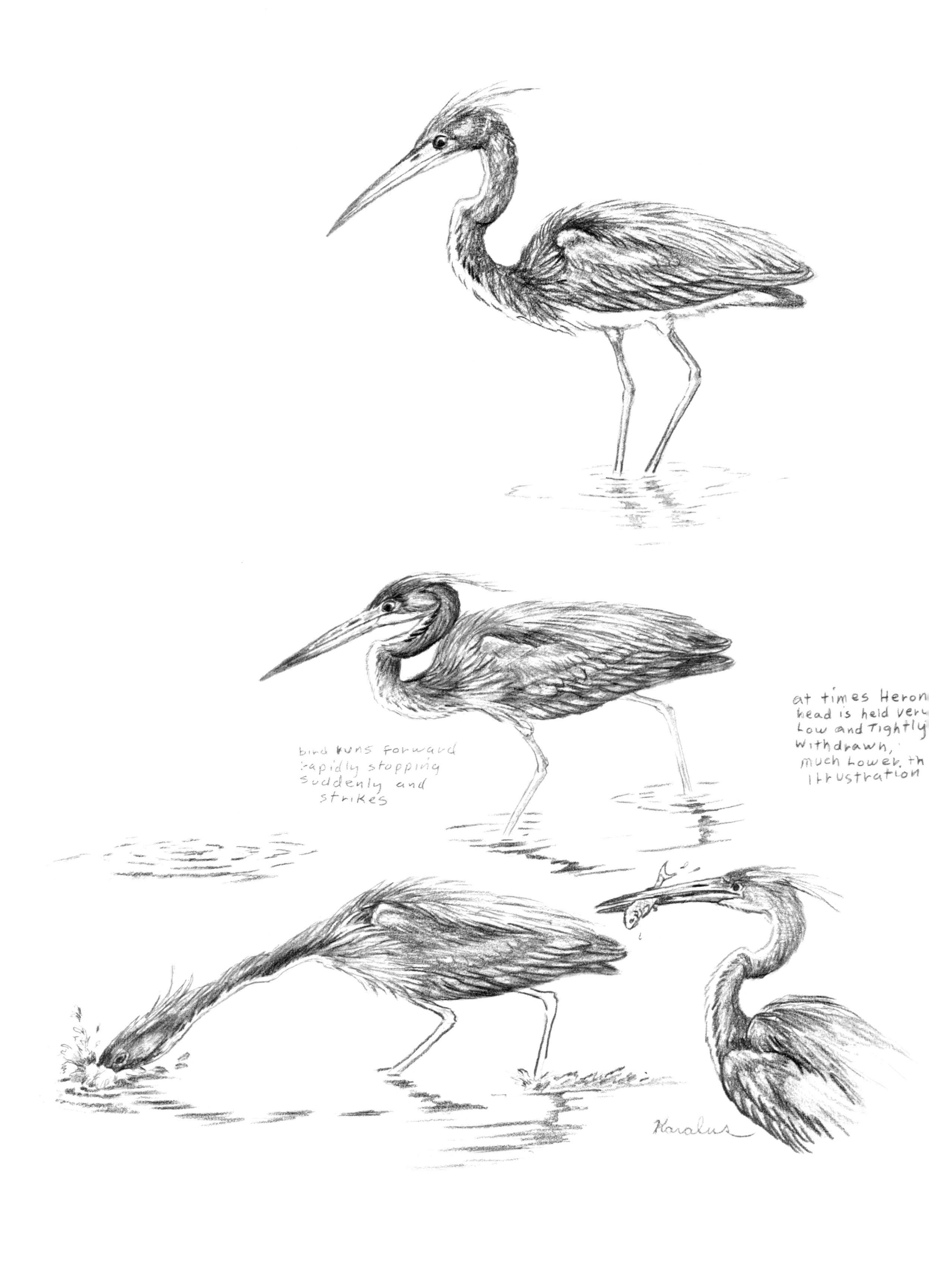
bird runs forward
rapidly stopping
suddenly and
strikes
at times Heron
head is held very
Low and Tightly
withdrawn,
much Lower th
illustration
Karalus

repositioning it until he returns with another.

EGGS AND INCUBATION

The eggs are almost indistinguishable from those of the Snowy Egret. Both parents incubate in relatively equal segments during the daytime, usually changing position four times during the course of a day; but it is the female who does the incubating throughout the night, while the male roosts on a branch close by. Whenever one bird relieves another of the incubation duties, a ceremony of some importance is enacted. The approaching bird presents the sitting bird with a brief display of outstretched wings and a short crooning note as it hops from one branch to another while nearing the nest. The relieved bird relinquishes its position, but before leaving the area for any length of time, it presents the bird on the nest with anywhere from one to three twigs, which are then woven into the nest by the newly incubating bird. The incubation of an individual egg takes twenty-one days, but hatching is not simultaneous, due to staggered laying, and may occur over a period of four or five days, perhaps even a week.

YOUNG

Young Louisiana Herons stay in the nest, under normal conditions, until they are fully two thirds the size of the adult birds. Only then will they begin to climb about in the surrounding tangle of branches. They soon become quite adept at this, using feet, beak, and wings to do so. Falls often occur but rarely result in tragedy (such as a young bird hanging itself from a crotch or being gobbled up by an alligator). Most often when a fall occurs, the bird swims back to the tree and manages to climb back up, gradually working its way back to the nest, plaintively peeping all the while.

The downy baby birds have coloration unlike that of any other downy-young herons. The crown is covered with inch-long fawn-colored hairlike plumes, and the back is dense with a soft down of brown. Oddly, the white down of the underparts is rather more coarse. The beak, feet, and unfeathered skin all range from a dusky green to a dingy chartreuse in coloration.

The initial appearance of the juvenile plumage occurs on the back, then successively on head, neck, underparts, and tail. The last feathers to grow to full length are the flight feathers, and this doesn't occur until the bird has grown to full adult size.

MIGRATION

Throughout its range, the Louisiana Heron is relatively permanent and abundant except for those populations in the coastal areas of Texas and Louisiana which abandon their usual habitat during the winter months. There are casual records from California, Arizona, southern Nevada, southern New Mexico, western Texas, southern Arkansas, southern Missouri, western Kentucky, southern Il-

---

Feeding habits of the Louisiana Heron. Field sketches made at Manasota Key, Englewood, Florida, April 1974.

LOUISIANA (OR TRI-COLORED) HERON
Hydranassa tricolor ruficollis (Gosse)

linois, southern Indiana, and even as far north as New Jersey and New York.

ECONOMIC INFLUENCE

Hydranassa tricolor ruficollis is considered to be an ecologically valuable bird because of the large number of injurious insects and invertebrates it consumes, especially weevils and grasshoppers, which it devours in great quantities. It is also considered agriculturally valuable in rice-growing areas since it eats large numbers of crawfish, whose burrowing does considerable damage to rice dikes.

CATTLE EGRET

GENUS: *BUBULCUS* Bonaparte
SPECIES: *IBIS* Linnaeus
SUBSPECIES: *ibis* Linnaeus

COMMON NAME

Cattle Egret
(Color Plate VIII)

SCIENTIFIC NAME

Bubulcus ibis ibis Linnaeus. *Bubulcus* is Latin for herdsman; *ibis* is Greek for wading bird.

OTHER COMMON OR COLLOQUIAL NAMES

BUFF-BACKED HERON

SHAPE AT REST AND IN FLIGHT

A short, stocky bird, easily identifiable because of the bright yellow beak, which distinguishes it from the black-beaked Snowy Egret. Even though stocky, it tends to stand very erect and its beak is much stouter than the beak of any other heron or egret with which it might be confused. Somewhat more erratic than that of other herons or egrets within its range, the flight pattern of the Cattle Egret tends to suggest a bouncing sort of movement through the air rather than the smooth level flight so characteristic of others of this family.

LENGTH AND WINGSPAN

Average length for the Cattle Egret is 20 inches (514mm) and the average wingspan is 27.4 inches (702mm).

BEAK

One of the most accurate and immediate means of identifying the Cattle Egret is its beak. In general physical appearance, only two other North American birds bear resemblance to the adult Cattle Egret; one is the mature Snowy Egret and the other is the immature Little Blue Heron. In the Snowy Egret and Little Blue Heron, however, the beak is very dark, whereas in the Cattle Egret it is yellow or greenish-yellow. Furthermore, the beaks of the other two birds are much more slender, longer, and more pointed than that of *Bubulcus ibis ibis.* During the breeding season the beak of the Cattle Egret may become a more vivid yellow, yellow-orange, or even reddish, but it is never dark (blackish or bluish) as in the case of the Snowy Egret or Little Blue Heron.

LEGS

The legs may range in coloration from a dull, dingy yellowish or greenish-yellow to a darker orange. In winter, however, the legs are always a dark greenish-brown or blackish.

EYES

The irides range from pure yellow to yellow-orange.

CRESTS, PLUMAGE, ANNUAL MOLT

During the breeding season, elongated feathers appear on the back, lower nape, and crown; these range from distinctly pinkish in color to a rich cinnamon-buffy. The distinctive feathers are another excellent differentiating factor between this bird and the Snowy Egret and Little Blue Heron.

VOICE

Although it is a gregarious bird in its normal daily activities, the Cattle Egret does not often vocalize beyond a few short *quck* sounds when alarmed. The hungry young in the nest will peep or make a faint squealing sound as the parent bird approaches, but otherwise are mostly silent.

COLORATION AND MARKINGS: ADULT

Pure white plumage except in breeding season, when the feathers of the crown, lower rear of the neck, and upper back become buffy, cinnamon-buffy, or pinkish. Legs are greenish-yellow to dull reddish at this time, but dark olive-brown to blackish at other times.

COLORATION AND MARKINGS: JUVENILE

Same as in the adult bird, except that there are no elongated buffy or pinkish feathers in crown, neck, or back. The beak is yellow and the legs are dark brown to greenish-brown or greenish-black.

GENERAL HABITS AND CHARACTERISTICS

Probably the most characteristic trait of the Cattle Egret is that which gave it its name—its proclivity to associate with cattle. Often groups of three or four to twenty or more of the birds will follow close at the feet of grazing cattle, alert and ready to snatch up any grasshoppers or other insects, lizards, small snakes, and other such creatures which the casual movements of the cattle may disturb into motion. Sometimes the birds will land on the backs of the cattle, which are not bothered in the least by their presence. Not infrequently, the Cattle Egrets are joined in this activity by Snowy Egrets, Louisiana Herons, and Little Blue Herons, and occasionally even by Great Egrets. *Bubulcus ibis ibis* frequently engages in a very peculiar physical motion that is foreign to other birds of the family. During the midst of its feeding, it will pause and raise its head high, at which time a waving motion will begin in the head and neck and

---

IX REDDISH EGRET

Dichromanassa rufescens rufescens (Gmelin). Light and dark phases. Tampa Bay, Florida. A.O.U. Number 198

X GREAT EGRET

Casmerodius albus egretta (Gmelin). Bay Oaks Circle, Manasota Key, Charlotte County, Florida, April 20, 1975. A.O.U. Number 196

Karl E Karalus

Karl E. Karalus

then, like a wave in a ribbon, move down the entire length of the bird's body. Usually two or three such waves will traverse down the bird's body before it lowers its head and resumes its normal feeding activities.

HABITAT AND ROOSTING

The bird generally prefers to remain in pasture lands, associating with cattle in the manner mentioned above. Roosting is generally done in tangled areas of low trees or high bush growth and in groups of anywhere from twenty to one hundred birds. In recent years, as their numbers have increased and the range of the bird has become extended in North America, Cattle Egrets have become familiar sights in the ditches, on the shoulders, and on the median strips of modern highways and expressways. *Bubulcus ibis ibis* is also fond of foraging for food in marshy meadows, but it does not wade as much as other birds of its family.

FOOD AND FEEDING HABITS

Insects make up by far the greater bulk of the Cattle Egret's diet. Snails, slugs, worms, frogs, salamanders, small snakes, and lizards are also eaten, though in lesser volume. Feeding is done throughout the daylight hours, but most heavily in early morning and late afternoon.

XI SNOWY EGRET

Egretta thula thula (Molina). Palm Island, Stump Pass, Charlotte County, Florida. A.O.U. Number 197

XII AMERICAN BITTERN

Botaurus lentiginosus (Rackett). Englewood, Florida, November 19, 1974. A.O.U. Number 190

NEST AND NESTING HABITS

As nesting sites, low dense bushes are favored, well out of ordinary traffic areas which might bring danger. The basic foundation of the nest is a poorly built structure of twigs, to which is added a lining of smaller twigs (usually green) and both grasses and leaves which the bird plucks for the purpose. The nesting colonies ordinarily include around thirty or forty pairs of birds.

EGGS AND INCUBATION

Usually five smooth-shelled, pale blue eggs are laid. Their average size is 1.4 inches x 1.1 inches (35mm x 29mm). Incubation is performed almost equally by both parent birds during the daylight hours, but more so by the female than by the male at night, at which time he roosts nearby.

DISTRIBUTION

Each year the range of *Bubulcus ibis ibis* becomes more extended. This bird represents perhaps the classic example of a bird distributing itself throughout the world. Found on all major continents, the Cattle Egret is widely established throughout the Old World, Asia Minor, southern Asia, and Africa. It is

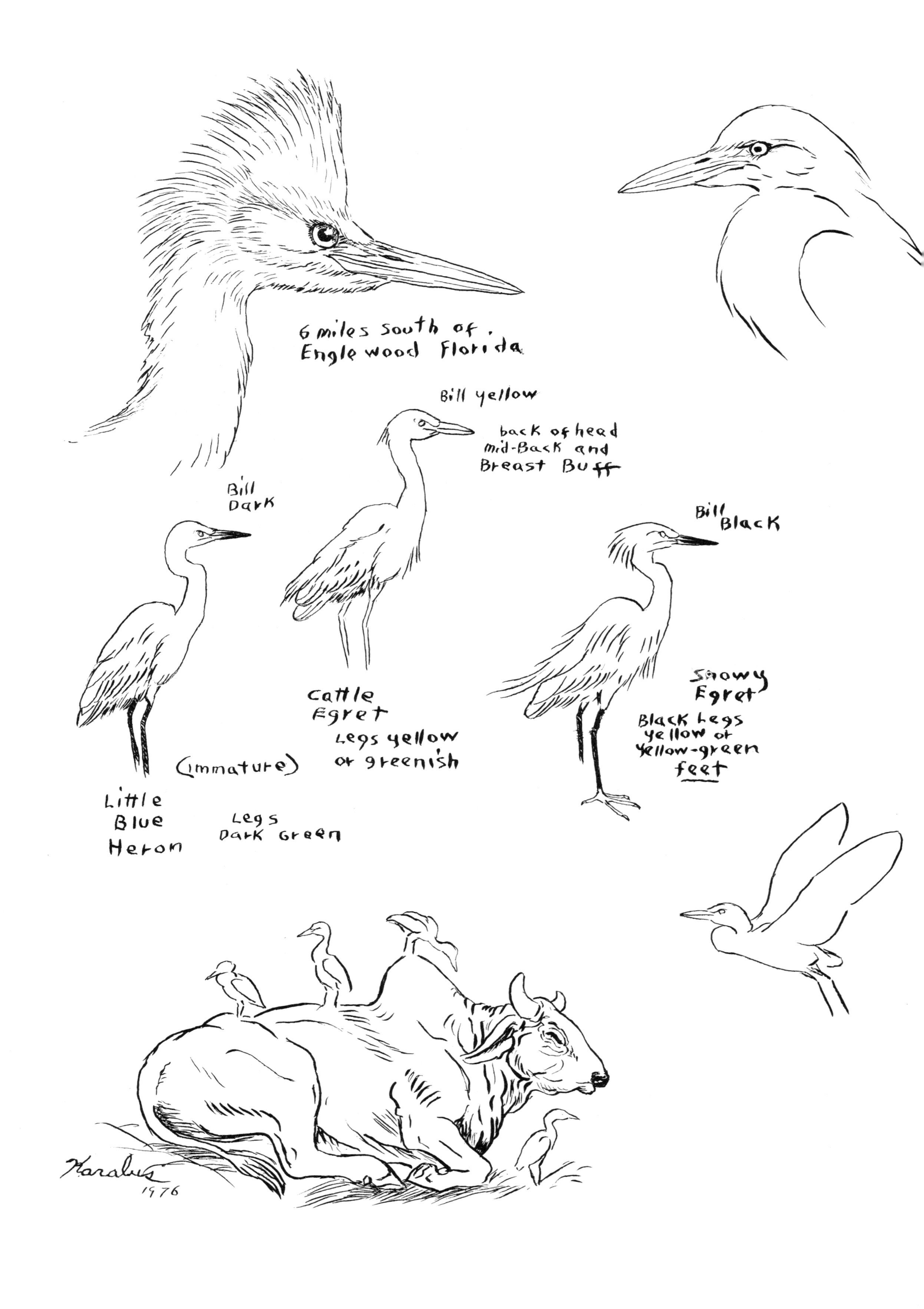
6 miles south of
Englewood Florida
Bill yellow
back of head
mid-Back and
Breast Buff
Bill
Dark
Bill
Black
Cattle
Egret
Legs yellow
or greenish
Snowy
Egret
Black Legs
yellow or
yellow-green
feet
(immature)
Little
Blue
Heron
Legs
Dark Green
Karalus
1976

believed to have come to the Western Hemisphere first in migration from Africa to Brazil sometime after 1850. By about 1877 it had spread to Surinam and by 1911 to Guyana. Movement through the Caribbean area via Central America and Mexico, and from island to island in the West Indies, was slow but relatively steady, with at least two major setbacks due to devastating hurricanes. However, by the late 1930s and early 1940s it had reached the Florida Keys and then the mainland of Florida. The extension of the bird's range was not particularly noted in ornithological literature until 1952, when, on April 23, a specimen was taken at Wayland, Massachusetts. By 1957 the species was breeding well throughout much of the southeast and spreading westward and northward quite rapidly. It has been nesting in southern Canada since 1962. Because it is continually in motion, it is difficult to state a definite range demarcation.

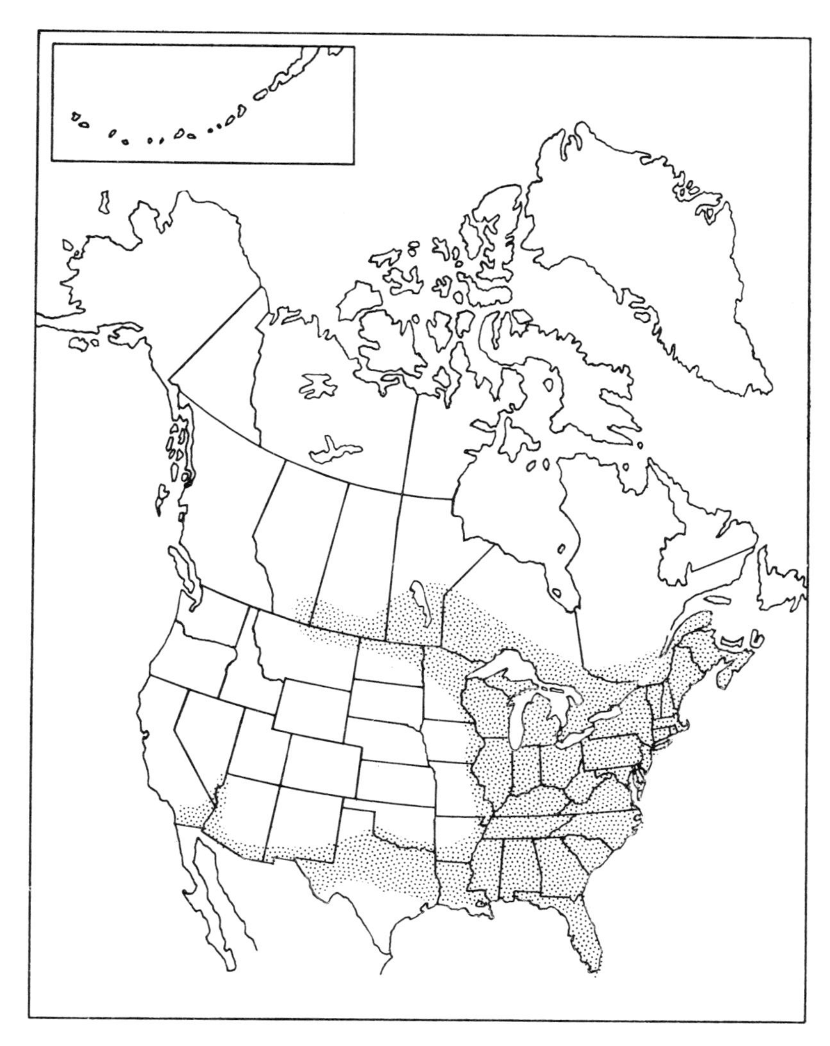

CATTLE EGRET

Bubulcus ibis ibis Linnaeus

MIGRATION

There is a definite withdrawing of *Bubulcus ibis ibis* from the northern portions of its range in autumn, at which time the southern population seems almost to explode. With each spring's northward (and westward) migration, it seems that the bird extends its range. It has now even been reported casually from southern Alaska.

ECONOMIC INFLUENCE

Because of its propensity for devouring insects in large numbers, the Cattle Egret is considered to be a very beneficial bird agriculturally.

Field sketches of various egrets and one immature Little Blue Heron, made at North Port, Florida, September 1975.

DICHROMANASSA EGRETS

GENUS:	*DICHROMANASSA* Ridgway
SPECIES:	*RUFESCENS* (Gmelin)
SUBSPECIES:	*rufescens* (Gmelin) Reddish Egret
	dickeyi van Rossem Dickey's Egret

COMMON NAME

Reddish Egret
(Color Plate IX)

SCIENTIFIC NAME

Dichromanassa rufescens rufescens (Gmelin). Scientific name from the Greek *dis* (twice) and *chroma* (color), referring to the two color phases (reddish and white), and from the Latin *rufus* (reddish).

SHAPE AT REST AND IN FLIGHT

Dichromanassa rufescens rufescens in its colored phase bears a resemblance to the Little Blue Heron, except that it is larger and bulkier, has a slightly heavier beak, and its coloration is generally a bit lighter throughout. In its white phase it bears a resemblance to the Great Egret, except that it is shorter and not so trim and slender. A very distinctive characteristic of the bird is an unusually long tarsus for its size. Its movements on the ground have a peculiar grace.

The Reddish Egret looks most like the Little Blue Heron in shape while flying, except that its body is stouter and its wings broader. The flight pattern is more regular than that of other small or medium-sized herons, and the Reddish Egret generally flies a little higher. Occasionally, it will hesitate in its stroke and glide for two to five seconds before stroking again. The wingstrokes are not as long and slow as those of the Great Egret or Great Blue Heron, and the flight is strong and fast as well as gracefully light.

LENGTH AND WINGSPAN

Reddish Egrets average above 29 inches in length (751mm) and have an average wingspan of 47.3 inches (1213mm).

BEAK

The terminal one third to one half of the beak is black, while the basal one half to two thirds is, in summer adults, a pale fleshy coloration. This particolored beak is a good field identification of the bird in its summer plumage. In winter, however, the beak is dusky.

LEGS, FEET, AND CLAWS

The tibia is bare and, in the white phase, the toes are dark olivaceous instead of yellow, a factor that helps to distinguish the white-phase Reddish Egret from the Snowy Egret. In the colored phase, the legs and feet are blue with blackish scales on the tarsus. The middle toe and claw are lengthy.

EYES

The irides of the Reddish Egret are milk-white, and both the lores and eyelids are a pale flesh coloration.

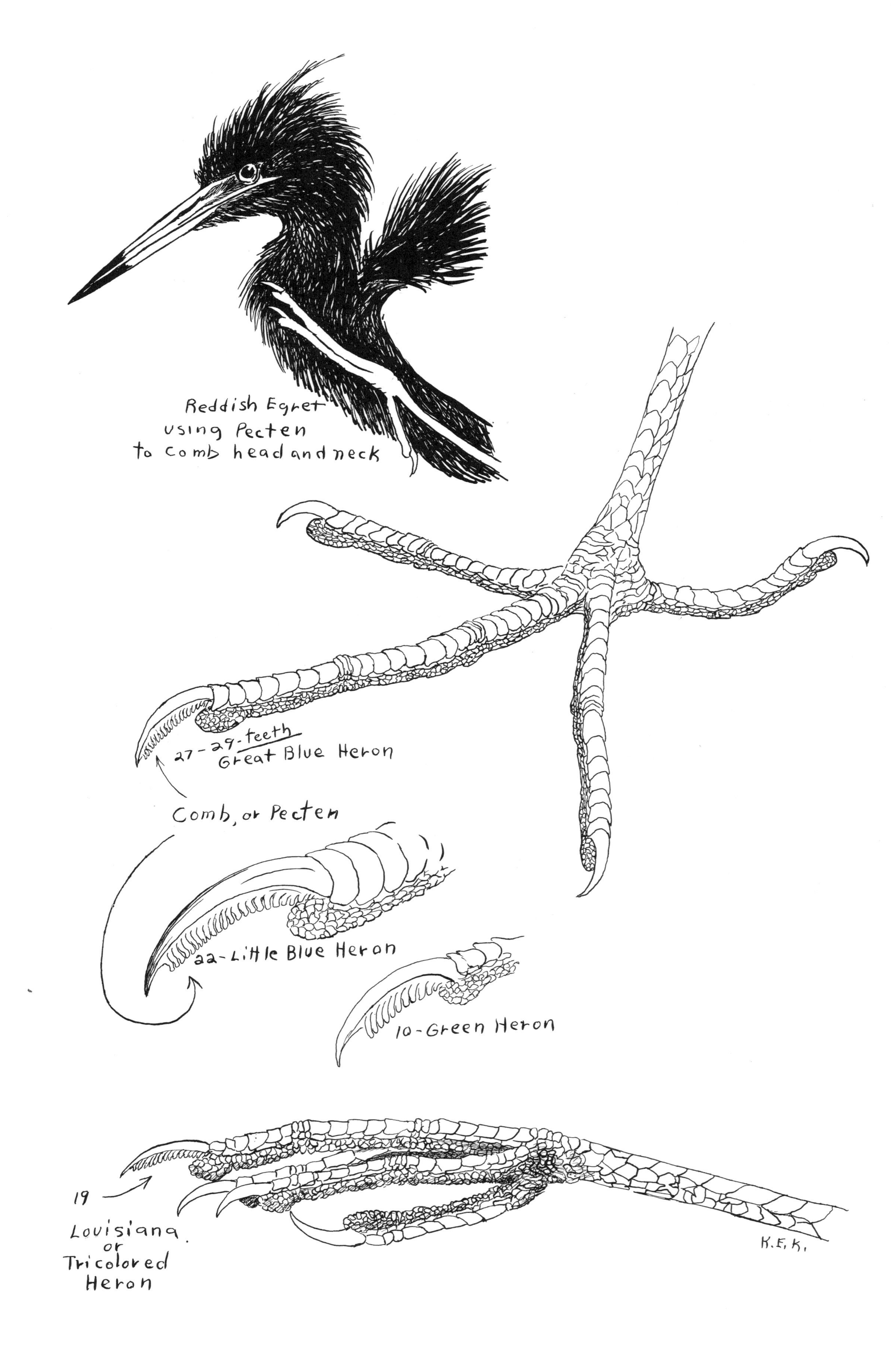
Reddish Egret
using Pecten
to comb head and neck
27-29-teeth
Great Blue Heron
Comb, or Pecten
22-Little Blue Heron
10-Green Heron
19
Louisiana
or
Tricolored
Heron
K.E.K.

CRESTS, PLUMAGE, ANNUAL MOLT

Adult birds undergo a complete molt beginning in early to middle August, and lasting through mid-October. Also, in January and February, there is partial pre-nuptial molt which involves primarily the display plumes. These plumes of the head, neck, and breast are long and distinctive, with a peculiarly attractive pinkish brown to sometimes cinnamon coloration. These quills, when erected by the bird for display, stand out in a bristling array around the shoulders and on neck and back, appearing almost menacing, as if they are quills like a porcupine's. In wintertime, these quills and those of the back, which are a bluish-gray in coloration, are much shorter and less distinctive.

VOICE

In at least one of its vocalizations, the Reddish Egret utters a far more musical note than do any of its heron or egret relations. This is a clear, bugling cry which is often given as it feeds on the tidal flats and, less often, as it settles into the rookery for the night. It also makes the more guttural croakings characteristic of most of the family. One other distinctive note, however, is a sort of booming, hollow sound with a rough, rasping quality which is uttered during the courtship displays.

SEXUAL DIFFERENCES: SIZE, COLORATION, VOICE

There are no obvious differences between the sexes.

COLORATION AND MARKINGS: ADULT

In its white phase, which is the less common, the Reddish Egret most closely resembles the Great Egret, but is shorter and stouter. The plumage is entirely white. The bird is dichromatic, with two well-defined color phases. In the more common colored phase, the bird resembles the Little Blue Heron but with the neck reddish-tan rather than dark purplish-blue. The rest of the body is, along with the wings, a neutral gray to a slight bluish-gray, but paler in this coloration on the underside. The ends of the train feathers are sometimes yellowish.

COLORATION AND MARKINGS: JUVENILE

In the colored phase the young bird is a plain ashy gray, touched here and there with shades of reddish, from cinnamon-brown to rusty and fawn-colored. The beak is uniformly dusky. The white-phase bird is entirely white. The legs and the tops of the feet are a dark greenish-black and the soles of the feet are a dingy yellow.

The pecten, or comb, a peculiar structure found on the middle toenail of herons, bitterns, and egrets, is used to clean and dress plumage, sometimes in conjunction with the powder-down tracts on the upper breast.

GENERAL HABITS AND CHARACTERISTICS

Dichromanassa rufescens rufescens is almost entirely diurnal in its habits, with its peak feeding activities in early morning and evening. At daybreak the birds fly from their rookeries or nesting colonies to the feeding areas, but they return before the sun is very high and spend much of the day dozing or playing at repelling intruders from their nests. Often they spend hours preening. When actively feeding, they are much more lively in their movements than any other heron, darting here and there with partially or fully outstretched wings—a distinctive trait which is called umbrella feeding—and sometimes punctuating these movements with peculiar little hopping flights of a dozen feet or less. Sometimes, however, they are content to stand in the tidal shallows and wait for food to come near enough to spear, or else move slowly about seeking their prey on the mud flats or sandbanks, remaining there until the incoming tide forces them to vacate.

HABITAT AND ROOSTING

Sandy shoals, muddy banks, tidal flats, coastal marshes, narrow winding bays intermingled with mangrove islands—all these are indicative of the type of habitat most favorable for the Reddish Egret. Only on rare occasions does the bird stray very far from the immediate coastal areas, and it even prefers feeding in saltwater areas rather than brackish or freshwater locations. Most roosting is done in low trees on islands in rather isolated areas.

FOOD AND FEEDING HABITS

With the approach of evening, the Reddish Egrets fly to their favorite feeding areas on the tidal flats and either snatch small crustaceans and fish from the shallows where the birds stand waiting, or else prowl about with steady stalking pace, hunting such prey. Often the prancing, darting, hopping sort of pursuit of prey is engaged in, with seemingly good results. The majority of the bird's diet consists of fish, but also a fair amount of crabs, grass shrimp, and snails are eaten. On those occasions when the bird does feed in less saline marshes and on the fringes of ponds or in moist meadows, frogs and tadpoles become important in the diet. Small snakes and lizards will be eaten as well.

COURTSHIP AND MATING

As courtship begins, the males begin chasing one another with hoarse cries and considerable aerial acrobatics as the females watch, usually from the ground. The chasing flights involve swift turns, long curves, and harrowing zigzags low to the water and past obstructions. When the chasing male, whose crest has been raised in anger all during the chase, manages to oust the male he has been chasing, he then returns to where the female has been standing. Time and again, with all his display plumage as erect and bristling as he can force it to be, he parades back and forth in front of her in what seems to be a menacing manner, but in a way which evidently appeals to her greatly. Soon she stands close to him and for a while they rub necks together. Then, usually on the spot where this occurs, copulation takes place. Part of the male's display includes marching back and forth before her with his beak pointed skyward and his neck gracefully curved, all the while a deep, hollow coarse sound rumbling from his throat and his plumes trembling with the effort. No distinction is made among the birds regarding color phase; white and white, colored and colored, and white and colored pair up indiscriminately.

REDDISH EGRET

Dichromanassa rufescesn rufescens (Gmelin)

NEST AND NESTING HABITS

Although the Reddish Egrets nest in colonies largely made up of their own species, they are not opposed to nesting in close proximity to or even among such other species as Great Blue Herons, Louisiana Herons, or Little Blue Herons; boat-tailed grackles also nest in conjunction with them. *Dichromanassa rufescens rufescens* is particularly adept at balancing on the thin and springy outermost branches of low bushes and trees, and it is here that the nests quite often are built. The nest is somewhat better made than the ordinary heron nest. The basic structure is still one of interwoven sticks, but the interweaving is a little better accomplished and the nest is not simply a flat platform, as is so often the case with other species in the family Ardeidae. Measuring from 20 to 26 inches in diameter, the nest is ordinarily about 10 inches high and has an inner hollow about 1 foot in diameter and 3 or 4 inches deep. This hollow is well lined and smoothed with grasses, straws, and fine twigs. Not infrequently, the nest will be built on the ground.

EGGS AND INCUBATION

Three or four pale bluish-green smooth-shelled eggs are laid which average 2 inches by 1.5 inches (52mm x 38mm). Both parent birds incubate on an essentially equal basis. Incubation lasts for twenty-four days.

YOUNG

In their white phase, young Reddish Egrets are pure white, but in the colored phase the downy young have atop their heads inch-long hairlike plumes, a drab cinnamon in coloration, while the rest of the long and soft down is a mousy gray. The unfeathered throat, the beak, and the feet are all a dark olive-green. No fleshy coloration develops on the beak until the second year, when the bird reaches full adulthood.

MIGRATION

There is no real migration among the Reddish Egrets and not as much general movement of young birds northward after they leave the nest as occurs with other heron and egret species.

COMMON NAME

Dickey's Egret
(Subspecies Sketch 7)

SCIENTIFIC NAME

Dichromanassa rufescens dickeyi van Rossem.

PRINCIPAL SUBSPECIFIC DIFFERENCES

Dickey's Egret is included in this work because it moves casually into the United States from Mexico on a more or less annual basis, appearing with some regularity in southern California, especially in the coastal areas of San Diego County, and on occasion in the Colorado River valley as much as 50 miles north of the Mexican border. It has been known to wander as far as the Texas coast and north along the California coast to Los Angeles. Slightly larger than the Reddish Egret, it is also a bit lighter in general coloration. All the toes are markedly short for a member of the family Ardeidae.

The elongated plumes on the head and neck are quite well defined and form into tufts at the throat and occiput. Dickey's Egret, like the Reddish Egret, does not have the white throat line of most herons.

More ground-nesting is done by Dickey's Egret than by the Reddish Egret, but the eggs are almost identical in size and coloration.

DICKEY'S EGRET

Dichromanassa rufescens dickeyi van Rossem

(Overleaf) 7. DICKEY'S EGRET

Dichromanassa rufescens dickeyi van Rossem. Isla Magdalena, Baja California, April 1963. A.O.U. Number 198a

head and neck of
This bird was much
darker compared
to Reddish Egret's
from Texas or florida
K. E. Karalus

GREAT EGRET

GENUS: *CASMERODIUS* Gloger
SPECIES: *ALBUS* Linnaeus
SUBSPECIES: *egretta* (Gmelin)

XIII EASTERN LEAST BITTERN

Ixobrychus exilis exilis (Gmelin). Rotunda, Charlotte County, Florida, September 15, 1975. (On left, color phase known as Cory's Bittern. Ithaca, New York.) A.O.U. Number 191

XIV WESTERN LEAST BITTERN

Ixobrychus exilis hesperis Dickey & van Rossem. Point Reyes, California, 1915. A.O.U. Number 191a

Karl E. Karalus

Karl E. Karalus

Karl E Karalus

Karl E. Karalus

COMMON NAME

Great Egret (formerly American Egret)
(Color Plate X)

SCIENTIFIC NAME

Casmerodius albus egretta (Gmelin). *Egretta,* from the French *aigrette,* a type of heron; also a plume. *Casmerodius* is Greek for gaping heron.

OTHER COMMON OR COLLOQUIAL NAMES

This bird has quite a variety of local or regional names, although all are very similar. It is sometimes referred to as an egret, sometimes as a heron, and sometimes as a crane. For a great many years it was commonly called the American Egret.

BIG PLUME BIRD After its spectacular breeding plumage.

COMMON EGRET After the European egret to which it is so closely allied.

GREAT WHITE EGRET Because of its size.

GREAT WHITE HERON Erroneously, since this is the common name of *Ardea herodias occidentalis.*

LA GRANDE AIGRETTE French Canadian name.

LONG WHITE A very common name at one time, applied especially by the plume hunters in Florida.

WHITE CRANE Another case of misidentification, since the bird is not a crane at all.

WHITE EGRET Because of its pure white plumage.

WHITE HERON A misnomer for the species.

SHAPE AT REST AND IN FLIGHT

A sleek, slender, well-shaped bird of grace and elegance and with uncommonly expressive posturings of the head and neck. Much larger than the Snowy Egret, it is very nearly the size of the Great Blue Heron, though not as bulky in body shape. During the breeding season a train of long graceful plumes extends far beyond the tail. The beak is relatively heavy for its size.

The basic shape in flight of the Great Egret is much like that of others of the heron family, with the neck folded back, the head between the shoulders, and the legs stretched far behind, acting as a rudder. When it takes to flight, the Great Egret springs very lightly into the air with legs and neck extended; even with neck drawn back and couched, this is still, in flight, the slenderest of the her-

---

XV WOOD STORK

Mycteria americana Linnaeus. Placida, Charlotte County, Florida. A.O.U. Number 188

XVI GLOSSY IBIS (left)

Plegadis falcinellus falcinellus (Linnaeus). Naples, Florida. A.O.U. Number 186

WHITE-FACED IBIS (right)

Plegadis chihi Vieillot. Brownsville, Texas. A.O.U. Number 187

ons for its size. It also has an uncommonly buoyant flight silhouette, almost as if it were holding itself down with its wings in flight, instead of lifting itself up.

LENGTH AND WINGSPAN

Excluding the plumes, which extend approximately a foot beyond the tail, the Great Egret has an average length of 37.3 inches (968mm) and a wingspan exceeding 4.5 feet (1489mm).

BEAK

Most individuals have some degree of black on the very tip of the yellow-orange beak.

LEGS AND FEET

The legs and feet are black, which is a key identification factor.

CRESTS, PLUMAGE, ANNUAL MOLT

Casmerodius albus egretta has no crest, but its plumes are among the most beautiful to be found on any North American bird. These pure white plume feathers, as long as 680mm (approximately 26.5 inches), spring from the back and extend far beyond the tail almost in the manner of a bridal veil train. Though the shafts of these feathers are stiff and resilient, the barbs are soft and lack barbules. As many as fifty of the plumes have been found in the back of an individual bird, but the usual number is about thirty-five. These plumes are acquired during the pre-nuptial molt of adults, usually beginning in January, and are usually shed, in worn condition, toward the end of June. A complete post-nuptial molt begins in July or early August; this molt either produces no plumes at all or else back plumes which are relatively short and not as spectacular as those of the breeding plumage. While the plumes in the males generally extend about a foot beyond the tail feathers, those of the female birds average a couple of inches shorter.

VOICE

The most familiar vocalization made by the Great Egret is a sort of coarse rattling croak, unpleasant squawkings, and raspy sounds, with the most raucous of all coming when the bird is alarmed. About the softest utterance is a soft gurgling sound made during courtship, ordinarily only by the male. Young birds demanding food issue a grating, almost constant *kak-kak-kak-kak-kak,* and adults approaching the nest often give utterance to a similar but deeper sound of *quck-quck-quck-quck,* which may go on for a quarter hour or more.

MORTALITY AND LONGEVITY

As in most heron species, the infants suffer a relatively high mortality rate through tumbling from the nest into the water below and either drowning or being taken by predators before they are able to regain the security of the nest.

In former times, the greatest threat to the Great Egret came in the guise of the plume hunter, who destroyed great numbers of birds during the breeding season, with resultant destruction of whatever eggs or young were in the nests at the time.

COLORATION AND MARKINGS: JUVENILE

Pure white, like adults, but without plumes. Legs and feet tend to have a more greenish cast.

GENERAL HABITS AND CHARACTERISTICS

Great Egrets are primarily diurnal, rarely crepuscular, and almost never nocturnal in their habits. If harassed, they become very wary, but can become reasonably tame and easy to approach if left alone. When the breeding season is completed, young and old alike ordinarily scatter in all directions and become more solitary in their daytime habits, though still roosting at night in large groups.

HABITAT AND ROOSTING

The most favored habitat is marshy or mangrove fringe. Sometimes the birds will be on open sand beaches, but far more often feeding occurs in the tidal flats among mangroves, or else in the midst of extensive marshes, usually along the fringes of more open water areas, such as channels or canals. Other areas holding an attraction for *Casmerodius albus egretta* are the margins of lakes, ponds, streams, ditches, rice fields, and bayous. Just prior to dark the birds gather in large numbers in the roosting areas—usually dense mangrove islands—and here they perch throughout the night in trees, only to scatter again after dawn.

ENEMIES AND DEFENSES

The worst natural enemies of the Great Egret are crows, and boat-tailed grackles (the latter often playing havoc with the eggs when they are left unguarded, even briefly). By far, however, the greatest enemy of the Great Egret has been the plume hunter. At one point the species was teetering on the brink of extinction thanks to the vogue for plumed hats. Just before the turn of the century the plumes were worth, ounce for ounce, twice as much as gold. And it took the plumes of four birds to make one ounce. In 1886 New York dealers were paying 90 cents for the plumes of one bird, but the demand became so great and the prices went so high that in eleven years the feathers from one bird brought $10! At a single London auction in 1902, over a ton and a half of Great Egret plumes were sold. The actual weight was 48,240 ounces (3,015 pounds), which, with the feathers of four birds equaling 1 ounce, totals very nearly a fifth of a million birds. Add to this the fact that as a result of this slaughter of adults, probably around 600,000 eggs and young perished. And this was only one auction among a multitude of them! Fortunately, public outcry against such devastation resulted in the passage of tough legislation against plume-hunting. The Great Egret population, at an extremely low ebb by about 1905, has largely recovered and the species is no longer endangered. Due to man's own expansion, however, and the loss of great tracts of natural habitat, it is doubtful that *Casmerodius albus egretta* will ever again regain its former abundance.

FOOD AND FEEDING HABITS

Sometimes in small groups, occasionally in large flocks, and most often in threesomes, pairs, or singly, the Great Egret feeds mainly in the shallows of marshes and coastal mangrove tidal flats. There it stands quietly in the shallows waiting for prey to come past or, nearly as frequently, wades slowly on the flats or in the marshy shallows, its neck drawn back like a coiled spring and its head poised, beak ready to thrust forward and impale or snatch whatever prey may be encountered. Food does not consist entirely of animal matter, although it does play a large part. A certain amount of vegetation, primarily in the form of seeds or small fruits and some green matter, is eaten. Mostly, though, food matter consists of fish, frogs, and crayfish, in about that order of importance. Also frequently eaten are large grasshoppers, dragonflies, moths, and other insects, especially of aquatic variety, along with lizards and small snakes, snails, small birds (rarely eggs), mice and moles, fiddler crabs, and such particularly favored fish as shad, suckers, and sunfish, along with minnows of any species.

COURTSHIP AND MATING

All during the display period prior to actual pairing and copulation, the males show great antipathy for one another and battles of varying degrees of intensity are not uncommon. The male makes a great show of raising his plumes in a flashy manner, strutting, preening, and parading about before the female and crooning to her in a gurgling sort of way until she finally accepts him as mate. This display goes on for six days, each such display being followed by copulation. A lesser form of the display continues, by both sexes, at the nest throughout the remainder of the breeding season, and is especially noticeable at those times when the male and female are relieving one another of incubation or brooding duties.

NEST AND NESTING HABITS

As with all of the herons, the nest is a simple structure of coarse sticks woven together to form a platform with a slightly depressed interior to help prevent the eggs from rolling off during bad weather. The nest is just slightly more substantial than that of the Snowy Egret or Louisiana or Little Blue Heron and it is sometimes lined with Spanish moss or a few mangrove leaves. Great Egrets are especially fond of building their nest in a tree, usually at a height of from 8 to 40 feet and most often about 20 feet high, where two substantial branches converge. Nesting is done in colonies of anywhere from a dozen pairs to fifty or more pairs, sometimes in company with brown pelicans and cormorants as well as other egret and heron species.

In the Gulf coastal areas, isolated mangrove islands are favored nesting sites. Away from the coastal areas, Great Egrets nest on densely overgrown hammocks of willow and bay, along with stands of cypress. Often they will build nests at the very tops of low bushes, but rarely in the tops of trees. The preference is for a nest site directly above water.

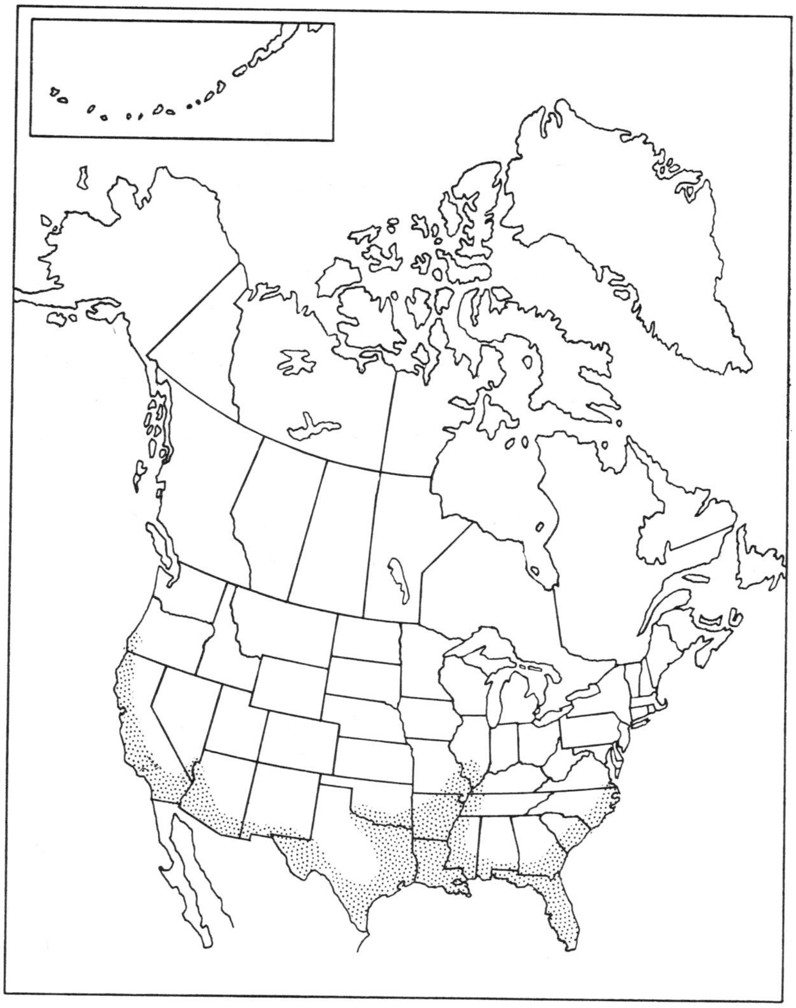

EGGS AND INCUBATION

Ordinarily three or four pale bluish-green eggs are laid. The eggs are usually fusiform (somewhat pointed at both ends) and the shell is smooth. The average size is 2.2 inches by 1.6 inches (57mm x 41mm).

Incubation is undertaken by both sexes, but probably slightly more by the female than by the male. In most cases it is the female who incubates throughout the nighttime hours.

GREAT EGRET

Casmerodius albus egretta (Gmelin)

YOUNG

If the nest is high in a tree, the young are inclined to remain within it until they can fly; if, however, it is low, they will generally leave earlier and crawl about with increasing skill through the low branches, sometimes falling but usually recovering. In most instances, two or three of the young are fed in a single feeding by the parent bird and in some manner not determined, the arriving second parent seems to know very well which of the birds was fed last and thus which should be fed next. Almost always the plumes of the parent bird, regardless of which parent, are raised as feeding is under way. The actual feeding, as with other heron species, is by regurgitation until the baby bird is old enough and capable enough to pick up food dropped into the bottom of the nest.

Juvenile plumage appears in succession on the back, wings, breast, crown, and tail, and finally the wings. The last down to disappear is that of the neck and underside. The growth of plumes in the juvenile plumage is extremely limited or absent. Full adult plumage is not acquired until the first postnuptial molt, occurring when the young bird is about fourteen months of age.

NORTH AMERICAN DISTRIBUTION

Since the Great Egret was eliminated by plume hunters in much of the range it formerly occupied, it appears only casually in areas where once it was extremely abundant. The present breeding range has been expanding gradually, however, and is not quite so limited to the Gulf coastal areas as it was during the first half of this century.

MIGRATION

The Great Egret withdraws from the more northerly portions of its range fairly early in autumn, with most of the birds vacating before mid-October and settling in for the winter in the Gulf coastal areas and southward into the Caribbean and Mexico, Central America, and South America.

ECONOMIC INFLUENCE

Although, at one time, fortunes were made in the millinery trade with the plumes of the Great Egret, the bird is no longer considered economically important, as plume-hunting is now prohibited. Agriculturally the bird is of some benefit because of its habit of eating grasshoppers and other pests.

EGRETTA EGRETS

GENUS: *EGRETTA* Sharpe
SPECIES: *THULA* (Molina)
SUBSPECIES: *thula* (Molina)
Snowy Egret
brewsteri (Thayer & Bangs)
Brewster's Egret

COMMON NAME

Snowy Egret
(Color Plate XI)

SCIENTIFIC NAME

Egretta thula thula (Molina). *Thula,* Greek, means most northern.

OTHER COMMON OR COLLOQUIAL NAMES

BONNET MARTYR This was a nickname affixed to the bird by ornithologists and bird-lovers at the time when plume hunters were making great inroads into the egret populations, and the name still is used in some localities.

COMMON EGRET An often used, though confusing terminology, since the Great Egret is also sometimes referred to by this name.

L'AIGRETTE NEIGEUSE French Canadian name meaning Snowy Egret.

LESSER EGRET As opposed to the "greater egret" (Great Egret).

LITTLE EGRET Descriptive of size and type.

LITTLE PLUME BIRD To differentiate it from the Great Egret, which was the big plume bird, though not referred to by that name.

LITTLE SNOWY Common term used by plume hunters.

LITTLE WHITE EGRET As opposed to "Great White Egret," meaning the Great Egret or, sometimes, the Great White Heron.

LITTLE WHITE HERON Same as the preceding.

SHORT WHITE The most common term for the bird used by the plume hunters, who thereby distinguished it from the "Long White," or the Great Egret. The term referred not only to the actual size of the bird, but to the relative sizes of the plumes.

SNOWY HERON A common appellation simply using the family term instead of the more specific term.

SHAPE AT REST AND IN FLIGHT

A dainty and exquisite little egret, considered by many to be the most charming of all marsh birds and waders, *Egretta thula thula* is quite short and slender, though relatively not as slender as the Great Egret. Also, its beak is quite thin and dainty, as compared to the much heavier beak of *Casmerodius albus egretta.* When sitting hunched with head nestled between the shoulders and one leg drawn up, the Snowy Egret can look especially small.

Relatively speaking, the wings of the Snowy Egret are not as broad as those of the Great Egret and, while the Snowy Egret approximates the Cattle Egret in size, it is not as bulky a bird.

The wingstrokes of the Snowy Egret are somewhat faster than those of the Great Egret, but the flight is essentially as direct and purposeful, though perhaps not quite as light. It is much more inclined to fly close to the water surface—within 3 or 4 feet—than is the larger Great Egret. At times, though, the

Snowy Egret will travel rapidly at a height of about 200 feet until it reaches its destination and then it will abruptly pull its wings almost closed and fairly tumble groundward, braking itself only just in time to keep from crashing into ground or trees.

LENGTH AND WINGSPAN

The average length of the Snowy Egret is just short of 2 feet (597mm) and the average wingspan is just about 38 inches (972mm).

BEAK

The beak of the Snowy Egret is one of its most distinguishing characteristics. The all-black coloration of the beak immediately separates the Snowy Egret from the similarly sized and colored Cattle Egret (which has a yellow-orange beak) and the immature, all-white Little Blue Heron, which has a beak partially black and partially blue.

LEGS, FEET, AND CLAWS

The legs and toes of *Egretta thula thula* clearly identify the species at a glance. The legs of the adult, as well as the tarsus, are black, but the toes are a brilliant yellow. The coloration change is so sharp and so apparent that at first glance it looks exactly as if a bird with black legs and feet had stepped into bright yellow paint which completely stained the toes. This color demarcation is not quite so distinct in the immature Snowy Egrets, whose legs are more greenish than black. The claws are black.

CRESTS, PLUMAGE, ANNUAL MOLT

The Snowy Egret, like the Great Egret, was destroyed in such vast numbers by plume hunters at the turn of the century that the species came very close to being made extinct. Although the plumes of the Great Egret are considerably longer than those of the Snowy Egret (but just as lacy and delicate in appearance), those of the smaller bird were in much greater demand because of the way they recurved toward their ends, with a lovely, graceful swirl. This made them especially appealing in the millinery trade and so literally millions of the birds were destroyed for the recurved plumes from about 1856 through 1905. About fifty of the long, filamentous scapular plumes appear on the bird's back when the Snowy Egret undergoes a partial pre-nuptial molt in mid-January through late February. These feathers, somewhat bedraggled after months of displaying, fighting, and preening, are finally shed with the complete molt which occurs from June to September. In the millinery trade, the recurved feathers of the back were known as "cross-aigrettes" and during the peak of the plume-hunting days, one bird's plumes might sell for as much as $20. Concurrent with the appearance of the recurved scapular plumes are similar but shorter and uncurved plumes on the lower neck. When these and the longer recurved plumes are shed in June, they are replaced by shorter, straighter winter plumes. Unlike the Great Egret, which has no crest feathers, the Snowy Egret has a well developed occipital crest extending over the crown and composed of long, loosely webbed feathers which it erects in a beautiful display during the breeding season as a compliment to the recurved scapular plumes. In its full courtship plumage of lacy white, filamentous, and recurved feathers, the Snowy Egret is indeed one of the most strikingly beautiful birds in the world.

VOICE

The voice of the Snowy Egret is, like the voices of most of the birds of the heron family, ordinarily guttural and coarse. Although this species tends to be somewhat more silent than other species, it can become very vocal during the breeding season.

COLORATION AND MARKINGS: ADULT AND JUVENILE

In both sexes and in both immature birds and adults, the plumage is always a pure, spotless, snowy white. Irides are chrome yellow in adults and slightly lighter yellow in immature birds. The lores are pale yellow.

HABITAT AND ROOSTING

Open sandy beaches are a favorite feeding and resting place of the Snowy Egret, which shares such habitat on occasion with Little Blue Herons. Often the delicate little Snowy Egrets will be seen running or stepping about in the upper portion of the surf, picking up minute fishes and tiny sand fleas. However, even more than on the Gulf beaches, the Snowy Egret is at home in tangled swamps, marshes, and bayous, and along the edges of more open ponds and streams. Probably the most favored roosting area is on the outer edges of a dense stand of mangroves which face the open water of some quiet and secluded bay. Here they roost from dusk to dawn (and sometimes in company with white ibises) in such numbers that the deep green foliage is practically white with them. The Snowy Egret seems to get along better with the white ibis than do any other of the herons, although why this should be so is not known.

FOOD AND FEEDING HABITS

Though occasionally the Snowy Egret will stand silently waiting for food to swim past in the shallows, more often the bird darts about on the flats picking up minnows, shrimp, small crabs, and other food as it moves. In addition to the fry of fish, it also feeds heavily on tiny crustaceans and insects of a wide variety, including especially aquatic forms, such as dragonfly nymphs. In recent years the birds have taken to alighting on golf courses and feeding in early morning on the cutworms that have come to the surface during the night. Lizards and small snakes, along with frogs and tadpoles, make up a small portion of the diet, and some snails are also eaten.

COURTSHIP AND MATING

Male Snowy Egrets tend to become very belligerent and quarrelsome during the breeding season and fights are not uncommon, although these are usually limited to a certain amount of sparring with the beak and batting at one another with their wings until one decides to give up before his beautiful plumage is spoiled. As for the plumage, it is fully displayed to its utmost beauty at every opportunity. Both males and females have plumes, but the males more than the females become highly active in showing off their finery. Passing back and forth before the chosen female, the male extends every plume feather to its utmost, so that he takes on the appearance of a gorgeous animated fan with recurved feather tips and a delicate laciness that is extremely attractive. The crest is raised to its highest vertical position, the breast feathers shoved forward and downward until they nearly touch the ground, the plumes of lower neck are spread wide, and the back plumes are fully extended and erectile. At the same time, the wings are partially opened with their tips sometimes nearly dragging on the ground. It is a lovely sight, evidently every bit as appealing to the female as it is to a human observer. Such displaying is at its peak during courtship, but goes on to a lesser degree all throughout nest-building, incubation, brooding, and later nesting activities.

NEST AND NESTING HABITS

Almost without exception, both male and female birds, when approaching the nest, erect and display their showy plumage, caress one another, and croon softly. Both birds engage in the nest-building, the result of which is much like that made by any other heron. It is usually a flimsy and rather flat platform of intertwined sticks, coarser on the bottom and somewhat finer on the top, and occasionally lined with much finer twigs. Most often the nests are in dense bushes of trees near or directly over the water and from 8 to 20 feet in height. In western portions of their range, nesting is more often closer to the ground—usually under 6 feet high and sometimes on the ground itself. The nest is rarely over 1 foot in diameter and has a faint depression in the top which may be 3 or 4 inches in diameter. The bird almost always nests in colonies of from twenty to one hundred birds of its own species, and sometimes nests in company with such other species as Great Egrets, Louisiana Herons, and Little Blue Herons. Its nest and eggs are virtually indistinguishable from those of the Louisiana Heron and Little Blue Heron. Probably the favorite nesting trees are mangroves and willows, at a height of about 12 feet. Nesting generally begins in late March and continues through June.

EGGS AND INCUBATION

Most often four eggs are laid, which may range in coloration from pale bluish to a pale bluish-green. Almost perfectly oval, these eggs are smooth-shelled but not glossy, and the average size is 1.7

inches x 1.3 inches (43mm x 32mm). Eggs are laid forty-eight hours apart. Incubation begins with the first egg laid and lasts for a term of eighteen days. The sexes share the incubation almost equally.

YOUNG

Since incubation begins with the first egg laid in a nest with four eggs, the first bird hatched may be over a week old before the last egg hatches. The downy young, except for being smaller, are almost identical to the young of Great Egrets, with the naked portions of the skin a pale green and both beak and feet a pale yellow or yellowish-green. The legs shade to duskier greenish on the upper surface. Young birds are fairly helpless until they are about a week old. At twenty to twenty-five days, when they're half-grown, the young birds begin leaving the nest in the daytime to perch on nearby branches, returning to the nest at night. At about six weeks of age they leave the nest for good. Young birds finally become indistinguishable from adults when they are about eighteen months old.

SNOWY EGRET

Egretta thula thula (Molina)

ECONOMIC INFLUENCE

Because of its insect-eating habits and its propensity for seeking out injurious cutworms, the Snowy Egret is held to be a rather beneficial bird.

COMMON NAME

Brewster's Egret
(Subspecies Sketch 8)

SCIENTIFIC NAME

Egretta thula brewsteri (Thayer & Bangs).

BASIC SUBSPECIFIC DIFFERENCES

Brewster's Egret, a western variety of the Snowy Egret, is generally larger than the Snowy Egret, has a larger beak and heavier legs.

BREWSTER'S EGRET

Egretta thula brewsteri (Thayer & Bangs)

8. BREWSTER'S EGRET

Egretta thula brewsteri (Thayer & Bangs). Saint George, Utah. A.O.U. Number 197a

XVII WHITE IBIS

Eudocimus albus (Linnaeus). Myakka River, Charlotte County, Florida. A.O.U. Number 184

XVIII SCARLET IBIS

Eudocimus ruber (Linnaeus). Caroni Swamp, Trinidad, West Indies. A.O.U. Number 185

Karl E. Karalus

E. Karalus

Karl E. Karalus

XIX ROSEATE SPOONBILL

Ajaia ajaja (Linnaeus). Buttonwood Rookery, Englewood, Florida. A.O.U. Number 183

XX AMERICAN FLAMINGO

Phoenicopterus ruber Linnaeus. Andros Island, the Bahamas. A.O.U. Number 182

AMERICAN BITTERN

SUBFAMILY: *BOTAURINAE*
GENUS: *BOTAURUS* Stephens
SPECIES: *LENTIGINOSUS* (Rackett)

COMMON NAME

American Bittern
(Color Plate XII)

SCIENTIFIC NAME

Botaurus lentiginosus (Rackett). From *botaurus,* Latin, meaning a bittern, and *lentiginosus,* Latin, meaning spotted, in reference to the markings on the plumage.

OTHER COMMON OR COLLOQUIAL NAMES

BOG BULL After the booming sound of its voice in the swamp or marsh.

BUTTER BUMP Because the sound of its voice, according to some, can be likened to the thump of a butter churn.

INDIAN HEN After the henlike appearance and size of the bird, and possibly after the fact that it is known to have been a common bill of fare for Seminole Indians in the Everglades as well as other Indian tribes elsewhere in the nation.

SHIT-QUICK Vulgar term extensively used, especially in the South, and descriptive of the habit of the bird to defecate voluminously immediately upon taking off.

STAKE DRIVER For the sound of the bird's voice which at a distance (though not up close) resembles the sound of a stake being driven with a mallet or an ax into the earth or mud.

SUN GAZER After the habit of the bird to assume a protective pose in which its beak is pointed directly skyward.

THUNDER PUMP After the sound of the bird's voice, which, at times, resembles the sound made by a wooden water pump.

SHAPE AT REST AND IN FLIGHT

When alarmed, the American Bittern "freezes" into a posture which causes it to become well camouflaged in its surroundings, its beak pointed skyward and the pattern of its plumage blending almost perfectly with a cattail background. On either side of the neck there is a distinctive black stripe.

Botaurus lentiginosus has considerably smaller wings than similarly sized herons, and the tips of the wings are dark. As the bird first takes off, its legs dangle loosely below, the head is extended on the long, crooked neck, and the wings flap rather sloppily, the whole aspect being rather awkward. However, as it gets well under way, the legs are drawn up and back to extend beyond the short tail and act as a rudder, the neck is drawn in, the head couched snugly between the shoulders, and the wingbeats become more regular.

Ordinarily the flight is quite low, just over the reed tops, and of relatively short duration. The American Bittern alights again on the floor of the marsh or swamp, rarely if ever in a tree, as does the immature Black-Crowned Night Heron, which it most resembles. The American Bittern's takeoff is punctuated with harsh croaks but then, once the flight is well under way, the wingbeats become steady, firm, and powerful, as well as somewhat faster than those of herons of comparable size. The bird is then a strong and good flier.

LENGTH AND WINGSPAN

The average length of the American Bittern is 30.7 inches (787mm) and the wingspan averages about 41.5 inches (1063mm).

LEGS, FEET, AND CLAWS

The legs are a dull yellowish-green, darker and greener behind than in front. The claws are brown, with very little curvature.

EYES

The irides are a brilliant clear yellow, made all the more startlingly bright by the dark brown loral striptin.

CRESTS, PLUMAGE, ANNUAL MOLT

Adults undergo one complete postnuptial molt annually, from about mid-July to September. They are somewhat hampered in their flight by this. There are, as with other heron species, two powder-down tracts on the breast. The neck feathers are quite long and loose. There are well-hidden nuptial plumes on the sides of the breast and neck which become conspicuous only when they are raised during courtship display, by both sexes. At such times these white plumes are raised high above the shoulders.

VOICE

Probably the most common vocalization by the American Bittern is a deep, hollow sound similar to *pump-er-lunk,* voiced mostly in early morning and late evening during spring and summer, and at almost any time of day or night during the breeding season.

COLORATION AND MARKINGS: ADULT

The plumage is an interesting blend of spottings and streakings against a background buffy-brown coloration so like its surroundings that simply by compressing and extending its body, raising itself high, and standing still, the bird can become practically invisible at a distance of only a few feet from the observer. More than one observer has been amazed by the uncanny ability of the bird to blend with its background in an area where such blending seems well nigh impossible. The underparts of the wings of the adult bird are varying tones of yellowish-brown mingled with buffy and pale gray ashy coloration, and with numerous small-sized and irregular bars, spots, freckles, and streaks. The underside of the bird generally is a buffy yellowish-white to pinkish-buff with light brown streakings. There is a highly distinctive black stripe on each side of the

---

American Bittern, *Botaurus lentiginosus* (Rackett).

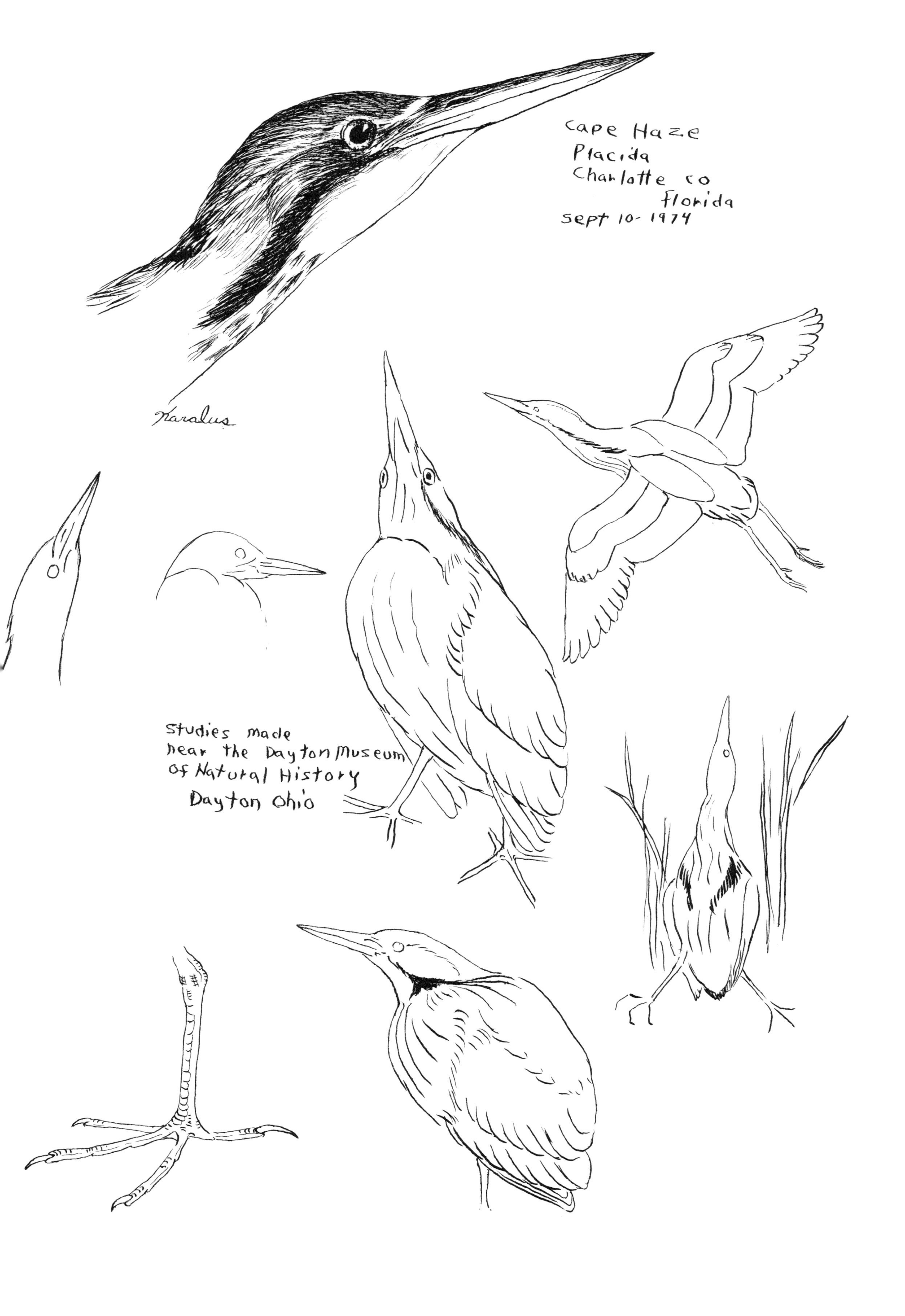
Cape Haze
Placida
Charlotte co
Florida
Sept 10- 1974
Karalus
Studies made
near the Dayton Museum
of Natural History
Dayton Ohio

neck and a rather yellowish to buffy streak over each eye. The throat is a sort of off-white with a dark stripe down the center. Dull brown covers the crown and the primaries are a greenish-black tipped with a warm brown. The tail is a similar brown.

COLORATION AND MARKINGS: JUVENILE

Young birds have no black stripes on the sides of the neck and are somewhat more lightly striped and spotted. Aside from this, they are little different in general coloration and markings from the adults.

GENERAL HABITS AND CHARACTERISTICS

Botaurus lentiginosus is a highly secretive bird, far preferring reclusiveness to gregariousness. Except during the courtship and nesting periods, it is almost always solitary. Very often it will stand well hidden beneath canopied vegetation of the marsh and quietly wait for food of some kind to pass it. When it does move, it moves with great deliberation and stealthy noiselessness.

HABITAT AND ROOSTING

Grassy meadows, extensive marshes, brakes, bogs, canal banks, rush- or reed-choked margins of lakes, ponds, and waterways—all these form excellent habitat for the American Bittern, but most especially favored are the extensive cattail marshlands. The bird sometimes visits salt marshes and the vegetative areas bordering tidal marshes. Swamplands, willow and alder thickets, and lake shallows densely grown with bulrushes are also well-favored areas. Occasionally the birds will be found in drier upland meadows, stalking about looking for grasshoppers. Almost always the roosting is done in solitude on a pile of cattails, either dried or growing, which the bird has trampled into a heap. If the private roost remains undisturbed, the bird may return to it night after night for weeks, perhaps even for months.

FOOD AND FEEDING HABITS

Frogs, crayfish, and small fish make up by far the greatest bulk of the American Bittern's normal diet, but there are a variety of other items this bird will eat, including snails, small snakes, lizards, tadpoles, grasshoppers, dragonflies, eels, mollusks, and even some vegetable food. Almost any sort of small animal life will be eaten, even animals as large as meadow mice. Smaller prey is usually grasped in the beak, tossed lightly in the air, recaught, and swallowed in a smooth, quick movement. Larger prey is generally speared with an accurate thrust of the powerful beak and if this is not enough to kill it, it is held in the beak and beaten against the water surface or against a floating stick or other piece of debris until dead, then torn apart and eaten.

NEST AND NESTING HABITS

The American Bittern, unlike the other North American heron species, does not nest in colonies or even in small groups, but in separate pairs. The nesting is always on the ground level, or just above the water level in a nest constructed of reeds and either suspended just over the water or built up to be several inches above the surface. In the latter case it is built by the birds bending down dead dry reed stalks—or sometimes live ones—and forming them into a suspended platform in which some sticks may also be woven. The nests formed on the surface are also of reed material, usually either those that have been bent over or else material collected from close by where it has been floating in the water. At any rate, such a nest, loosely constructed, is built up to form an almost flat 7-inch platform a few inches above water level. At times the nest will be as much as a foot in diameter. There is practically no depression whatever in it for the eggs, but somehow the eggs manage to stay on the platform, even in severe weather. Rarely will the nest—either the suspended one or the one on the water surface—be constructed in an area where the water depth is over 18 inches. Now and then an American Bittern will nest in wet meadows or even in deeper grasses of dry fields.

Almost without exception, the American Bittern constructs out of trampled-down reeds or grasses two paths leading away from the nest. The bird lands at the end of one and walks to the nest through it, but exits from the nest using the other path, not going into flight until it has emerged from the opposite end. If the bird feels danger is close by, it may land at the end of the pathway it has built, but take anywhere from ten to twenty minutes just to walk the forty feet to the nest. In other areas of the marsh, where it is not following premade paths, the American Bittern will often walk a foot or so above the water by grasping clumps of reeds in the feet and moving along in a very agile manner and with surprising swiftness. Quite frequently a canopy of growing reeds will be bent over the nest by the American Bittern, hiding it from view. However well it hides its nest and endeavors to keep its location secret, by the time the nesting season is well under way, the whole nest area is pretty well befouled by fecal waste from the parent birds, and in time from the young ones as well.

EGGS AND INCUBATION

Usually four or five eggs are laid. They are brownish-olive drab with a gray undertone, which matches exactly the coloration of dry cattail stalks, and which therefore helps in concealment of the eggs. The shell is smooth and has a slight gloss. The average egg size is 1.9 inches x 1.5 inches (49mm x 37mm).

Incubation begins with the second or third egg laid, and is primarily the responsibility of the female. Each egg requires twenty-four days of incubation. As the incubation (and later the brooding) proceeds, new cattail growth tends to cover the nest and make it even less visible than at the outset.

YOUNG

Newly hatched nestlings are well covered with a long fluffy down of light buff coloration on back, rump, and head. On the underside the down is lighter in color and not as thick. The eyes are

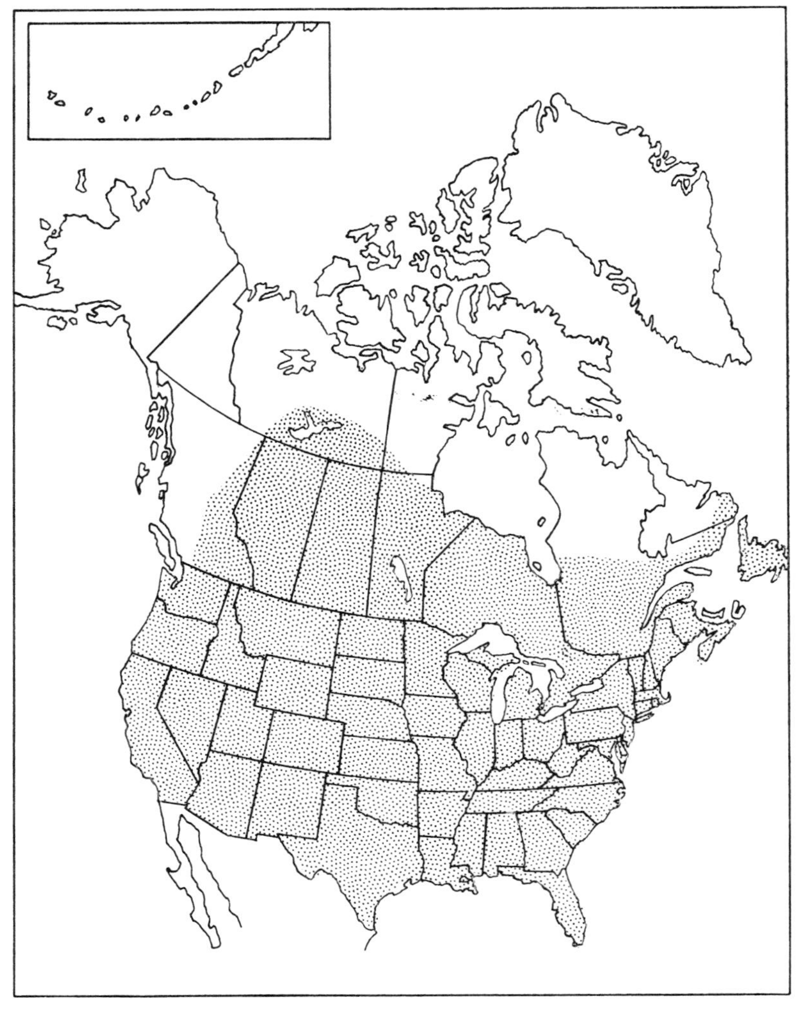

AMERICAN BITTERN

Botaurus lentiginosus (Rackett)

yellow, the feet are flesh-colored with a greenish cast, and the entire beak is flesh-colored. By the time the nestlings are seven to ten days of age, they are already one half adult size and juvenile plumage has begun appearing. They begin leaving the nest at fourteen days.

Feeding of the nestlings is much the same as among the other heron species, through regurgitation by the adults. When the parent bird comes to the nest, the young become extremely excited and leap about until one grips her beak crosswise at the base and shakes and jerks her about. This causes the muscles of her throat to begin working in convulsive spasms. She drops her head and neck flat on the nest for a moment and then regurgitation occurs. All the young in the nest are fed at the same feeding and each, upon being fed, lies flat in the nest and rests.

MIGRATION

The American Bittern is migratory, but the migrational flights are normally solitary, without the company of others of the same or other species. On the whole, it is more inclined to stay farther north in winter than any of the other herons of this continent. It has, for example, been found in winter as far north as Massachusetts in subzero weather. However, the population generally withdraws considerably farther south in winter, especially into the Gulf coastal regions, and most particularly to Florida. Florida's population of American Bitterns during summer, however, is very slight. The Everglades in Florida become heavily populated with American Bitterns during the winter months.

ECONOMIC INFLUENCE

The American Bittern is, on the whole, considered to be a beneficial bird, largely because of the large numbers of injurious insects and crayfish which make up its diet.

IXOBRYCHUS BITTERNS

GENUS: *IXOBRYCHUS* Billberg
SPECIES: *EXILIS* (Gmelin)
SUBSPECIES: *exilis* (Gmelin)
Eastern Least Bittern

hesperis Dickey & van Rossem
Western Least Bittern

COMMON NAME

Eastern Least Bittern
(Color Plate XIII)

SCIENTIFIC NAME

Ixobrychus exilis exilis (Gmelin). *Ixobrychus* is from the Greek, meaning deep bird lime; *exilis* is Latin for slender.

OTHER COMMON OR COLLOQUIAL NAMES

CORY'S BITTERN After the form which was temporarily accepted as a subspecies and, later, a color phase.

LEAST HERON Former common name prior to separation of Eastern and Western forms of the Least Bittern.

SHAPE AT REST AND IN FLIGHT

This is the smallest North American member of the heron family, and its small size immediately separates it from other heron species. In basic form it is very similar to the American Bittern, but in size it is no larger than the Wilson's snipe or the eastern meadowlark. When it is seen at rest, it is often in an uncommonly distorted pose, its body compressed into an extremely narrow form.

Ixobrychus exilis exilis has short wings and a short tail. On brief flights, which are normally all it takes except during migrations, the long slender neck is extended, the feet are dangling, the wings are fluttering rapidly, and prominent buffy patches are visible on the wings. On long migrational flights the Least Bittern assumes more of the true heron flight posture, with neck drawn back, head tucked down between the shoulders, and legs drawn up and extended beyond the tail.

LENGTH AND WINGSPAN

The Least Bittern has an average length of just under one foot (11.33 inches—291mm) and its wingspan averages less than a foot and a half (17.4 inches—446mm).

BEAK

The slender beak is mostly pale yellow in coloration, with a dusky ridge ranging from brownish to blackish.

LEGS AND FEET

The toes are yellow and the legs are a dull greenish.

EYES

The irides are a very bright yellow and very distinct against the pale green coloration of the lores.

Rail-like in fligh
Englewood florida
sept 20 - 1975
Karalus

CRESTS, PLUMAGE, ANNUAL MOLT

A complete annual molt takes place post-nuptially, beginning in late June or early July and extending into late August or early September. While there is a vague crest on the crown, there are no truly outstanding plumes, although the feathers of the lower neck are long and loose.

VOICE

Far more silent than *Botaurus lentiginosus,* the Eastern Least Bittern is seldom heard or, if heard, the voice is seldom recognized by the listener. Yet, the bird has a fairly wide range of sounds. When intruded upon, it will sometimes hiss, and then utter a low *uk-uk-uk* sound. In the spring the male gives a soft cooing sound, of from five to eight notes, repeated for many minutes. This call will often draw a responsive clucking from the female, which the male evidently uses to locate her. When disturbed into flight, the bird utters a loud, harsh *qua* sound and, if really upset, flies off with a loud and rather startling *ca-ca-ca-ca.*

SEXUAL DIFFERENCES: SIZE, COLORATION, VOICE

The sexes are dissimilar in size, coloration, and voice. The most apparent sexual difference is in coloration. The tail, back, and crown of the male bird are a glossy greenish-black, whereas these areas in the female are a dark chestnut in color; in addition, she has two white streaks along the shoulders. In young birds, the sexual difference in the plumage becomes apparent in the first spring, when the bird is approaching one year of age.

COLORATION AND MARKINGS: JUVENILE

Juvenile coloration is similar to that of the adult female, but with the black feathers tipped with buff, and the crown and back plumage a lighter brown. Prominent dusky shaft streakings give a very distinct striped appearance to the upper breast and lower neck.

GENERAL HABITS AND CHARACTERISTICS

Because it is so secretive and so retiring in its general habits, the Eastern Least Bittern is sometimes thought to be rare or even absent in areas where, in actuality, it is quite common. It is essentially a rather timid bird which endeavors to remain inconspicuous. It is rarely seen walking around on the ground or amid the reeds, but when it is seen in the shallows or walking on mud, matted vegetation in the water, or on dry land, its movements are quick and graceful, with the head characteristically shooting forward in a very distinctive manner at each step. This bird can compress its body laterally so much that it can pass through extremely narrow places.

Least Bittern, *Ixobrychus exilis.*

HABITAT AND ROOSTING

Cattail marshes, reedy swamps, along with margins of sluggish streams and ponds that are well grown with reeds, bulrushes, and heavy grasses, all these are habitat areas highly favored by the Eastern Least Bittern. Roosting is solitary. Freshwater marshy areas seem to be preferred, but the bird is no stranger to tidal flats and saltwater marshes, and it is sometimes seen moving about delicately through the most densely tangled coastal mangrove roots.

ENEMIES AND DEFENSES

The principal natural enemies include birds of prey, crows, reptiles, and predatory mammals common to marshy habitat. Crows and snakes are especially detrimental to the eggs, and even the marsh wren has been observed deliberately destroying the unguarded eggs, though not eating them. Fledgling Least Bitterns evade danger or elude pursuit by climbing with great skill and speed among the reeds and hiding in the densest portions of reedy cover. The adult birds also escape danger by walking. Where the water is too deep for wading and the reeds grow closely together, the Eastern Least Bittern climbs swiftly through them about 2 or 3 feet above the water surface, as skillful in grasping the reeds with its feet and moving among them as a squirrel is in moving about in the trees. But, while able to slip away unnoticed in most cases, far more often the Eastern Least Bittern prefers to avoid danger by "freezing" in place and allowing its quite remarkable natural camouflage to hide it from any enemy.

FOOD AND FEEDING HABITS

Insects, tiny fish, and small crustaceans make up the bulk of the Eastern Least Bittern's diet. Very young sunfish and perch, bluegills, topminnows, mud minnows, killifish, gambusias, and others are high on the preferential list, as are freshwater crayfish and such aquatic insects as dragonfly nymphs, giant water bugs, and marsh-dwelling caterpillars. Also eaten in fair amounts are frogs and tadpoles, shrews, mice, lizards, snails, very small snakes, leeches, and slugs. Almost the entire bulk of food is found by the bird within the marshy, reedy habitat in which it dwells. Only rarely will it leave this habitat to possibly catch grasshoppers in more open areas along the fringes of meadows and grassy fields.

NEST AND NESTING HABITS

Most commonly the Eastern Least Bittern's nest is located in cattails and is itself made of cattails pushed and bent

---

XXI FLORIDA CRANE (left)

Grus canadensis pratensis Meyer. Englewood, Florida, July 10, 1974. A.O.U. Number 206a

SANDHILL CRANE

Grus canadensis canadensis (Linnaeus). Green Lake, Wisconsin, October 15, 1963. A.O.U. Number 205

LITTLE BROWN CRANE (right)

Grus canadensis tabida (Peters). Bassett, Nebraska, October 20, 1964. A.O.U. Number 206

XXII WHOOPING CRANE

Grus americana (Linnaeus). Aransas National Wildlife Refuge, Texas. A.O.U. Number 204

Karl E. Karalus

Karl E. Karalus

arl E. Karalus

Karl E. Karalus

down to form a loosely matted and yet fairly compact platform supported by the surrounding vegetation and from several inches to several feet above the water. The water itself is rarely over 2 feet deep where the nest is built. The same sort of nest construction is done in the Florida Everglades with saw grasses. The flat surface of the nest ordinarily measures about 5 inches x 7 inches. The Eastern Least Bittern is by no means gregarious and does not nest in colonies.

EGGS AND INCUBATION

Normally there are four or five pale bluish-white smooth-shelled eggs which average 1.2 inches x .9 inch (31mm x 24mm). Though both sexes alternate in covering the nest, incubation, which takes sixteen to eighteen days, is primarily the responsibility of the female.

YOUNG

The head and back of the young are fully covered with long, soft, buff-colored down. On the underside, this down is scantier and lighter in coloration. The young are fed by the typical heron family method of regurgitation. If young birds are discovered, they will not hesitate to thrust their beaks with considerable viciousness at the intruder if he comes close enough.

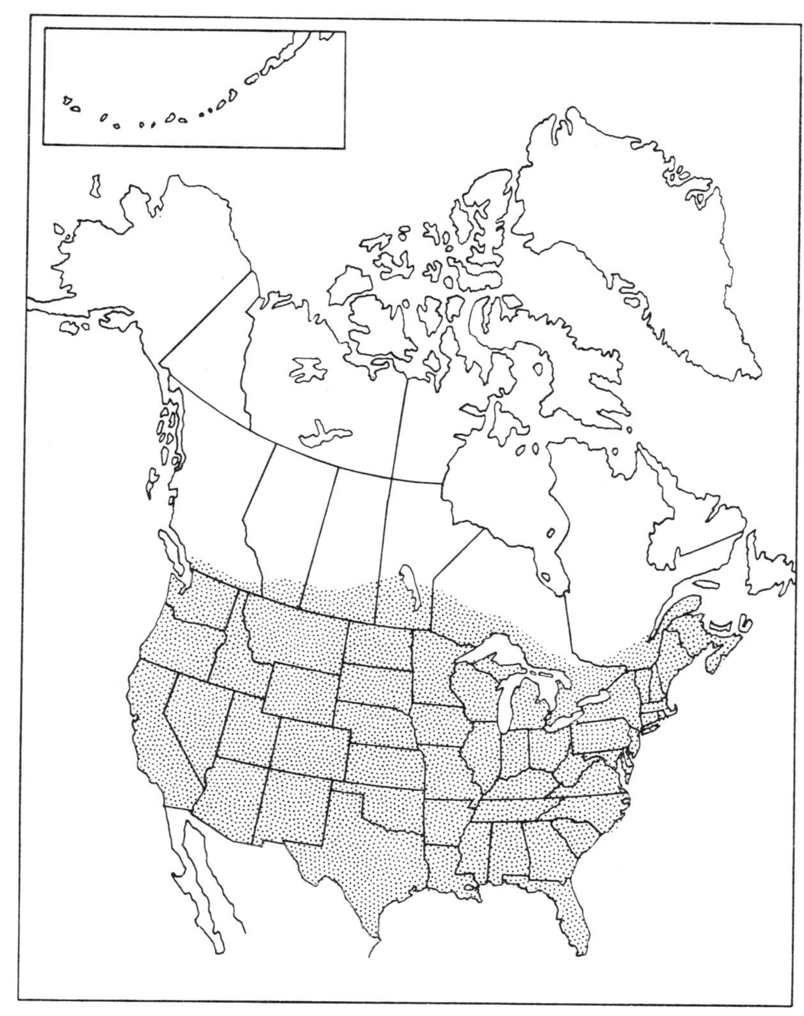

EASTERN LEAST BITTERN

Ixobrychus exilis exilis (Gmelin)

MIGRATION

The Eastern Least Bittern withdraws in winter from a very large portion of its northern summer range and tends to congregate in the Gulf coastal areas as well as the middle halves of the southern states and also into Mexico, Central America, and South America. In winter it has been found as far north as northern Georgia and central South Carolina, as well as central Arizona and southern California.

XXIII LIMPKIN

Aramus guarauna pictus (Meyer). Female. Moore County, Florida. July 10, 1956. A.O.U. Number 207

XXIV KING RAIL

Rallus elegans elegans Audubon. Bensenville, Du Page County, Illinois, August 30, 1963. A.O.U. Number 208

COMMON NAME

Western Least Bittern
(Color Plate XIV)

SCIENTIFIC NAME

Ixobrychus exilis hesperis Dickey & van Rossem. *Hesperis* is Greek for western.

BASIC SUBSPECIFIC DIFFERENCES

The Western Least Bittern differs from the Eastern Least Bittern in that the former is considerably larger.

WESTERN LEAST BITTERN
Ixobrychus exilis hesperis Dickey & van Rossem

WOOD STORK

SUBORDER:	*CICONIAE*
SUPERFAMILY:	*CICONIOIDEA*
FAMILY:	*CICONIIDAE*
SUBFAMILY:	*MYCTERIINAE*
GENUS:	*MYCTERIA* Linnaeus
SPECIES:	*AMERICANA* Linnaeus

COMMON NAME

Wood Stork
(Color Plate XV)

SCIENTIFIC NAME

Mycteria americana Linnaeus. From the Greek *mycteros,* meaning nose.

OTHER COMMON OR COLLOQUIAL NAMES

FLINTHEAD The most commonly used colloquial name, especially favored in Florida and other southern states; after the dark, bare, flintlike head.

GOURDHEAD (Sometimes written as Goardhead.) After the naked gourdlike head of the bird.

IRONHEAD See derivation of Flinthead.

PREACHER For the solemn demeanor the bird often assumes as it stands motionless and contemplative, especially after a heavy meal.

WOOD IBIS Formerly the common name, though changed because the term ibis is inaccurate.

SHAPE AT REST AND IN FLIGHT

The Wood Stork assumes, at rest, a very hunched posture, often perched on just one leg, head drawn in on shoulders, the huge beak resting on the breast feathers and pointing downward, the whole mien one of solemnity or dejection. It is a big white bird, 10 to 12 pounds, with a bare head and a huge beak. These traits, along with its distinctive combination of white and black plumage, unmistakably identify it in the field.

This is also an easily recognizable bird in flight, jet-black flight feathers contrasting with the prevailing whiteness of the bird, a long neck fully extended, long legs which trail far beyond the short black tail, and a very heavy beak. The black flight feathers make a fringe of black on the outer edge and rear of the outspread wing. The wingbeat is regular and strong, sometimes alternately flapping and gliding.

Now and then great flocks of the birds rise together and engage in spectacular aerial displays, seemingly for the sheer enjoyment of flying. The entire flock rises in an ever heightening spiral, the birds crossing and recrossing as they rise until they are mere specks in the sky and all but lost to human vision. For a while all will flap in unison and then, as if on signal, all will set their wings and sail along in great smooth circles. Abruptly the entire flock will dive down toward the earth, their plummeting bodies fairly whistling through the air and seeming sure to crash into the marsh or swamp below. Then, at the last moment, the great wings cup the air and thrust them into a long low glide which once more becomes a great spiraling climb upward to repeat the whole process. This is one of the really thrilling sights of nature.

LENGTH AND WINGSPAN

The average length of the Wood Stork is just short of 44 inches (43.8 inches—

1123mm) and its average wingspan is 63.6 inches (1631mm).

BEAK

The beak is not only long (8.7 inches average), is is unusually thick, normally measuring about 2 inches through at the base. It is a dingy yellow on the sides and the lower mandible, and dusky along the upper ridge. It does not have a nasal groove or membrane and the nostrils directly perforate the beak high up at the base of the upper mandible. It is a long stout beak, gradually tapering and ending in a downward curve at the tip.

LEGS, FEET, AND CLAWS

The toes are well lengthened and the claws are compressed. The tibia, bare for half its length, averages about 160mm in length (6.24 inches), and the middle toe and claw average 123.70mm (4.82 inches). The legs of the Wood Stork range from a deep bluish-gray to bluish-black, with the toes blackish. The anterior toes are webbed at the base and this webbing is tinged with yellow.

EYES

The irides are a deep brown, so dark as to appear almost black under certain conditions of light.

CRESTS, PLUMAGE, ANNUAL MOLT

The Wood Stork has no crests nor even any peculiar plumage. A complete molt of the adults occurs annually beginning in September, and this molt is normally completed by early November.

VOICE

Mycteria americana is capable of producing quite a variety of sounds, although in most circumstances it is an essentially silent species. The most commonly uttered note is a deep, grating croak ordinarily uttered when the bird has been disturbed or has become frightened. The Wood Stork can also voice very sharp and grating squalling noises. The young birds make a sound similar to the squeaking of a newly hatched alligator. They also croak like bullfrogs.

SEXUAL DIFFERENCES: SIZE, COLORATION, VOICE

The male bird has a deeper voice and is larger than the female, often by a considerable margin. There are no differences in coloration or markings.

COLORATION AND MARKINGS: ADULT

Mostly, the plumage is all pure white, the only exceptions being that the primaries, the primary coverts, and the rectrices are all rather blackish—the flight feathers a distinct bronzed greenish-black and the tail a similarly bronzed bluish-black, but sometimes shading to greenish. The head is bare of plumage and crowned with a horny plate. The naked, scaly skin of the head and down the neck is a dark blackish-gray.

COLORATION AND MARKINGS: JUVENILE

In juvenile birds up until the time of the first molt, the head is well covered with a fuzzy brown down. This same down also covers the neck. All this fuzz, however, disappears with the first molt. The plumage is quite different in coloration from that of the adults, a dark grayish as opposed to the adult bird's white, and with the blackish feathering showing much less of the glaucous green.

GENERAL HABITS AND CHARACTERISTICS

This is an uncommonly gregarious bird at almost all times and is rarely if ever seen alone. In eating, roosting, nesting, migration, and all other activities, it prefers the company of its own kind and often the company of other wading birds as well, such as Roseate Spoonbills, Great Egrets, Great Blue Herons, White Ibises, and others. However, gregarious though it is, occasionally small groups of birds, numbering from three or four to a half dozen or more, will break away from the main flock and wander off together. The Wood Stork is the only native stork in North America north of Mexico.

HABITAT AND ROOSTING

Thickly wooded swamps and marshes with dense growths of reeds and bushes are especially favored areas, although now and again the Wood Stork will forsake the favored woodlands of cypress and mangrove for open pasturelands, sloughs, pond edges, and even roadside ditches. Though generally a freshwater bird, it is frequently observed in saltwater marshes as well. The hot, moist bottomlands of the southern states are greatly favored, especially in conjunction with stands of water oaks, large stands of cypress, willows, tupelo, and gums heavy with Spanish moss, and dense underbrush interlaced with tangled vines in areas of dark muddy pools of water. Such areas are favorite roosts of the Wood Stork, where hundreds, perhaps even thousands, of the birds gather.

FOOD AND FEEDING HABITS

Wood Storks eat a wide variety of small life from the swamps and marshes they habitually visit. Fish of any kind, as long as they are small enough to be handled, frogs, baby alligators, water snakes, lizards, minnows, wood rats, fiddler crabs and other crustaceans, nestling grackles and rails, small turtles, tadpoles, water beetles, dragonfly nymphs, a variety of seeds, mosses and pond slime, catfish, carp, and crickets—all these and more make up the diet of the Wood Stork.

WOOD STORK

Mycteria americana Linnaeus

NEST AND NESTING HABITS

Stands of huge cypress trees rising from water are the favorite nesting areas of the Wood Storks, although they will nest in other trees as well. They much prefer a high nest, from 50 to 100 feet up. Every major tree within the rookery is occupied by nests, with some of the larger trees containing as many as five to fifteen nests. At times the nests are so close together they are almost touching. A typical nest is constructed basically of large twigs, many of them torn from living trees and bushes by the birds, and interwoven together on a sturdy branch, especially at a good junction between two branches. On an especially favored branch there may be half a dozen nests in a row, the edges of each touching one another. As many as five thousand nests in one nesting rookery is not uncommon. On rare occasions, if tall trees are not available, they will nest in the very tops of shorter trees, such as red mangroves about 20 feet high.

For such a large bird, the nests are small and surprisingly flimsy. On the base of interwoven twigs, finer twigs are laced, mixed with finer stems and twigs of willows, oaks, maples, cypress, and other woody growth. The nest, when completed, is usually no more than 1.5 feet in diameter and about 5 inches thick, but with very little depression in the top for the eggs. Occasionally it is lined with Spanish moss or green leaves. Although these big birds are inclined to sharing their feeding areas with other wading birds, this is not the case with the nesting areas and they will normally drive away other birds which attempt to nest in their vicinity.

EGGS AND INCUBATION

Two or three chalky white (but occasionally brown-stained) eggs are laid; the shells range from smooth-surfaced to rather rough and flaky. They are large eggs, averaging 2.7 inches x 1.8 inches (68mm x 46mm).

An interval of about forty to fifty hours (sometimes even longer) occurs between the laying of each egg. Both parent birds incubate, though the female somewhat more extensively than the male. Term of incubation is twenty-seven to thirty days and begins with the first egg laid.

YOUNG

When first hatched, the young are partially covered with a dense white down almost like wool, but the front half of the nestling's head and the spaces of skin between the feather tracts remain bare. The young tend to be noisy in the nest and this tendency increases for the first two thirds of their nest life, after which it decreases sharply.

As soon as they are large enough and strong enough, they begin leaving the nest and perching on the nearby branches, not infrequently losing their balance and hanging by necks and toes, flapping their wings desperately in an effort to regain their perch.

PLEGADIS IBISES

SUPERFAMILY: *THRESKIORNITHOIDAE*
FAMILY: *THRESKIORNITHIDAE*
SUBFAMILY: *THRESKIORNITHINAE*
GENUS: *PLEGADIS* Kaup

SPECIES: *FALCINELLUS* (Linnaeus)
SUBSPECIES: *falcinellus* (Linnaeus)
Glossy Ibis

SPECIES: *CHIHI* Vieillot
White-Faced Ibis

COMMON NAME

Glossy Ibis
(Color Plate XVI)

SCIENTIFIC NAME

Plegadis falcinellus falcinellus (Linnaeus). From *plegadis,* Greek, meaning small sickle, after the shape of the bird's beak, and *falcinellus,* Latin, also meaning small sickle.

OTHER COMMON OR COLLOQUIAL NAMES

BLACK CURLEW Because of its general coloration and, erroneously, because of its resemblance, due to the curved beak, to a curlew.

GREEN IBIS After the glaucous or somewhat metallic bronze-greenish cast to the feathers, especially under ideal conditions of sunlight.

SPANISH CURLEW "Spanish" origin uncertain, and "curlew" erroneously after the species it resembles to some degree.

SHAPE AT REST AND IN FLIGHT

A slender, relatively long-necked bird with very distinctively downturned beak, which makes a graceful downward arc from base to tip. The shape of the head and beak is very reminiscent of that of the curlews, but this ibis is darker and larger than any curlew species.

In flight it presents a long, slender silhouette, with neck and head outstretched and held at a downward angle, and legs trailing behind. Flight is characterized by a generally rapid flapping and gliding at low altitudes, rarely over 500 feet.

LENGTH AND WINGSPAN

The Glossy Ibis averages 2 feet in length (615mm) and has an average wingspan of 3 feet (922mm).

LEGS AND FEET

The legs are grayish-black and the feet are equally dark.

EYES

The irides are brown and the lores are a slaty bluish and broadly naked, with the bare space embracing the eye.

CRESTS, PLUMAGE, ANNUAL MOLT

A complete molt occurs among the Glossy Ibises once a year beginning in mid-July and ending by late October. The plumages and molts of the Glossy Ibis are very similar to those of *Plegadis chihi.* (the White-Faced Ibis, see page 141).

VOICE

Both adult sexes utter a very soft crooning sound in the midst of courtship and as they approach the nest throughout the nesting season. This sound is in marked contrast to their ordinary sound, a sort of bleating grunt, not unlike that made by the White Ibis, *Eudocimus albus.*

SEXUAL DIFFERENCES: SIZE, COLORATION, VOICE

In coloration and voice the sexes are identical.

COLORATION AND MARKINGS: ADULT

In general, the plumage is a rich purplish-chestnut with a greenish and purplish metallic iridescence on the crown, back, rump, wings, and tail. These are very distinct colorations, but the glaucous nature can only be seen well at close range. From a distance the bird looks entirely black.

COLORATION AND MARKINGS: JUVENILE

The head and neck of the juvenile ranges from grayish-brown to grayish-black and is streaked with white. The upper parts are generally a dusky green with a metallic bronze-greenish gloss, while the underparts are an ordinary dull brownish-gray.

GENERAL HABITS AND CHARACTERISTICS

The Glossy Ibis is a fairly quiet bird, content to perch, wade about, and fly in relative silence. It is gregarious within certain limitations with its own species, and occasionally with other ibises.

HABITAT AND ROOSTING

The principal habitat is extensive marshland dotted well with low hammocks of tangled brush and low trees and with, here and there, well-hidden little lakes and ponds. Flooded meadows are also appealing, but the Glossy Ibis rarely lands along canals or ditches. Most roosting is done in densely overgrown willow islands or hammocks, such as those found centrally located in the Everglades. Especially favored for a roost are islands of this nature which have, in their centers, well-hidden little lakes. Although the Glossy Ibis will roost here with other species, it generally remains in little pockets of its own kind rather than intermingling.

FOOD AND FEEDING HABITS

The Glossy Ibis is very definite about establishing feeding areas it particularly likes and then frequenting these areas to the exclusion of others, even though there may be no apparent difference in terrain or the sort of food available. It is not at all unusual for the Glossy Ibis, leaving its roosting area in the early morning, to fly fully 20 miles to a favorite feeding area, when just such an area may be within a mile or two of the roosting area. A wide range of food is eaten, though cutworms, grasshoppers, crayfish, and snakes make up the bulk of its intake. Water insects, frogs, and lizards, along with some snails and tadpoles, complete the Glossy Ibis' diet.

GLOSSY IBIS

Plegadis falcinellus falcinellus (Linnaeus)

NEST AND NESTING HABITS

In by far the majority of cases, nest-site selection is made by the female, but construction of the nest is undertaken by both birds. The nest is sloppily made of poorly interwoven twigs and is rarely completed before the female lays her eggs. Initial construction takes the pair two days, but after the young birds hatch, additional material is often added to the nest. If the first nest is destroyed, as often happens, a whole new nest will be constructed and more eggs laid.

Most nests are located about 10 to 20 feet high in dense tangles of brush and low trees, most often over shallow water. The Glossy Ibis is very jealous about its nesting area and will not permit any other species, regardless of size, to build its nest within 10 to 12 feet of its own. Sometimes it will tolerate such a nearby nest for a while, but when its own eggs are ready to hatch it will attack the other bird, even if it is the size of a Great Blue Heron, and eventually run it off. Then it will watch with disinterest as fish crows steal the eggs from the other nest, after which the Glossy Ibis will itself dismantle the other nest and sometimes use the twigs as additional material in its own nest. The nest is usually 1 to 1.5 feet in diameter and has a reasonably well-formed cup in the center.

EGGS AND INCUBATION

Normally four pastel greenish-blue smooth-shelled eggs are laid which have an average size of 2 inches x 1.4 inches (52mm x 37mm). The eggs are laid about twenty-four hours apart. Incubation does not begin until fully twenty-four hours after the last egg of the clutch has been laid. This incubation, which lasts for twenty-one days, is accomplished by both parents. The female incubates about eighteen hours out of each twenty-four.

YOUNG

The beak of the downy young is yellowish and black, and the feet are yellow. During the first five days after hatching, the young are never left alone in the nest. One parent is always on hand. When the adult bird feeds the young, the food is regurgitated into the throat, not into the beak, as is the case with the herons. The young Glossy Ibis then shoves its own head and beak into its parent's mouth and feeds. One young bird is fed until it is entirely filled before another is fed. It takes only about two minutes to feed one of the nestlings and there is rarely a wait of over three minutes before the next nestling is fed. The young Glossy Ibises remain in the nest for six weeks, until they are able to fly. At this point they begin flying with their parents to the feeding ground and return with them at night to roost at the nest.

MIGRATION

There is a casual, disbursement sort of migrational movement northward and westward following the nesting season, and a very strong autumn and spring migration. Winter range in the North American continent is seldom north of southernmost Florida.

XXV NORTHERN CLAPPER RAIL

Rallus longirostris crepitans Gmelin. Yorktown, Virginia. A.O.U. Number 211

XXVI VIRGINIA RAIL

Rallus limicola limicola Vieillot. Franklin Park, Illinois. A.O.U. Number 212

Karl E. Karalus

Karl E. Karalus

Karl E. Karalus

Karl E Karalus

COMMON NAME

White-Faced Ibis
(Color Plate XVI)

SCIENTIFIC NAME

Plegadis chihi Vieillot.

OTHER COMMON OR COLLOQUIAL NAMES

BLACK CURLEW Because of its coloration and its basic similarity in form to the curlew; term mainly used by hunters of this bird in California.

BRONZE IBIS After its general coloration; term used most commonly in Texas.

SHAPE AT REST AND IN FLIGHT

Very similar in silhouette to the smaller curlew, with smooth slender body, erect posture, longish neck, and smoothly arched, downcurved, slender beak. The White-Faced Ibis is difficult to distinguish in flight from the Glossy Ibis.

LENGTH AND WINGSPAN

The White-Faced Ibis has an average length of 23.4 inches (599mm) and an average wingspan of 38.9 inches (996mm).

CRESTS, PLUMAGE, ANNUAL MOLT

The feathers of the head sweep down the forehead, framing the bare skin of the face, and extend back beyond the eye in a posterior point. There are no particular plumes or crests at any season. Adults have a partial pre-nuptial molt beginning in March and a complete post-nuptial molt in July and August.

COLORATION AND MARKINGS: ADULT

In outward appearances the White-Faced Ibis is identical to the Glossy Ibis except for the margin of white feathering that rims the bare flesh of the face and is fairly obvious even from short distances. Legs and feet are dusky reddish. The irides are bright red.

XXVII SORA

Porzana carolina (Linnaeus). Cape Haze, Placida, Charlotte County, Florida, September 14, 1956. A.O.U. Number 214 (Mrs. Joan D. Eckert, collector)

XXVIII YELLOW RAIL

Coturnicops noveboracensis noveboracensis (Gmelin). Cicero and 111 Street, Cook County, Illinois, April 17, 1937. A.O.U. Number 215

COLORATION AND MARKINGS: JUVENILE

With traces of the down still remaining, the first plumage of the young birds is highly lustrous and iridescent. It is almost entirely bronze-greenish, without the violets, reds, and purples of the adults. When adult plumage finally appears, the greenish gives way to grayish-brown and then to the purplish-reds. In its first winter plumage, the young bird is lightly and irregularly streaked with light brownish and dull white on the body, while head and neck are already covered with adult plumage.

HABITAT AND ROOSTING

Plegadis chihi shows a marked preference for tule swamps and marshes, marshy prairies, and lake margins well grown with reeds and rushes. It rarely roosts in trees, as does *Plegadis falcinellus falcinellus,* preferring to roost on low platforms of dead reed stems and rush piles amid heavy cover of marsh or swamp. Sometimes it roosts in plain sight on mud banks or projecting land spits in lakes or streams.

ENEMIES AND DEFENSES

Man had been and to some extent still is the worst enemy of the White-Faced Ibis. Unfortunately for the species, it has a very fine-tasting flesh and was once a game species. Now it is protected, but still taken illegally in considerable numbers annually, as is the case with the White Ibis in Florida, *Eudocimus albus.*

FOOD AND FEEDING HABITS

Plegadis chihi feeds primarily along riverbanks and the shallow shorelines of ponds, lakes, pools, marshes, and swamps, as well as along sluggish streams to a lesser degree. It also frequents marshy meadows, especially those where the ground tends to be torn up by cattle or other stock animals, because these are areas where it finds earthworms and other prey it favors. Almost any small vertebrate or invertebrate animals are eaten, along with a small amount of vegetative matter, but the principal diet items are, in addition to earthworms, crayfish, small mollusks, snails, insects and their larvae, small fish, frogs, leeches, newts, and slugs.

NEST AND NESTING HABITS

Unlike the herons, the White-Faced Ibis makes a rather compact and well-constructed nest with a deep cup that is well and smoothly lined with fine tule reeds and grasses; the outer portion of the nest is 12 to 14 inches in diameter and formed of tightly interwoven dead tule reeds from the preceding year. It does not normally nest in trees or bushes, as does the Glossy Ibis, but instead builds its nest 10 or 12 inches above the water in thick stands of rushes or reeds and attached to these plants. Now and then the nests are actually partially afloat in the water. Almost invariably the water where the nests are built is less than 3 feet deep, but at least 2 feet in depth. The birds nest in very large rookeries numbering, at times, in the thousands of individual birds. They also nest in amiable conjunction with some of the herons.

EGGS AND INCUBATION

Most often three or four eggs are laid which initially are a rather distinct pastel blue or green, but which soon fade to nearly white. Though usually smooth-shelled, sometimes the shells are finely pitted or granulated. The average egg size is 2 inches x 1.4 inches (52mm x 36mm).

The term of incubation is twenty-one days and is done by both parents, the female predominating.

YOUNG

A very dull, unattractive blackish down covers the nestlings and there is a distinctive whitish patch at the back of the crown. The beak is a pale flesh color with a tip of black, a blackish base, and a black band in the middle. (This unusual beak coloration is also a characteristic of the juvenile plumage and does not disappear until the post-nuptial molt in September.) The young birds in the nest are uncommonly timid and, as soon as they are capable of it, they will flee the nest at any disturbance whatever, throwing themselves into the water and flapping across it to the nearest cover where they hide until the danger is past, at which time they return in less haste to the nest.

WHITE-FACED IBIS

Plegadis chihi Vieillot

MIGRATION

The species withdraws from most of its northern range in the autumn and moves into semitropical or tropical climes, remaining in the United States primarily in Florida and to a lesser extent in Louisiana and Texas coastal areas, and in southernmost California. Ordinarily the birds have withdrawn from the northern range by mid-October, and begin returning in late March or early April.

EUDOCIMUS IBISES

GENUS: *EUDOCIMUS* Wagler

SPECIES: *ALBUS* (Linnaeus)
White Ibis
RUBER (Linnaeus)
Scarlet Ibis

COMMON NAME

White Ibis
(Color Plate XVII)

SCIENTIFIC NAME

Eudocimus albus (Linnaeus). *Eudocimus* from the Latin, meaning well known or familiar; *albus* also from the Latin, meaning white.

OTHER COMMON OR COLLOQUIAL NAMES

CURLEW Because of its curved beak, resembling that of the curlews.

SPANISH CURLEW Allegedly because it was extensively hunted by the Spanish in Florida as food.

WHITE CURLEW For coloration and beak resemblance to curlews.

SHAPE AT REST AND IN FLIGHT

This bird often stands dozing or looking about on bare tree branches, sometimes alone, frequently in groups of three to a dozen. If merely looking about, it generally stands erect with head held high. If dozing or resting, it often stands on one leg with the other drawn up and out of sight in the underside plumage, its head hunched down on the shoulders in heron fashion and the distinctly curved beak resting on its breast plumage.

In flight, the bird's head and neck, though outstretched, are angled slightly downward. The wings are fairly broad and the long curved beak is plainly visible in flight.

The flight of *Eudocimus albus* is characterized by rapid wingbeats interspersed by occasional to frequent periods of gliding. Usually such flight is in formation with others in long lines that are either straight abreast or diagonal. The flight is fairly swift and direct, and ordinarily quite low, seldom over 150 feet high. This is particularly true during the morning and evening flights to and from feeding and roosting areas. Sometimes the entire flock will perform spectacular acrobatics, including steep dives and recoveries, with such evolutions generally beginning at a very high altitude. The White Ibis is very partial to soaring high on thermals, as are Wood Storks.

LENGTH AND WINGSPAN

The average length of the White Ibis is 26 inches (666mm) and its average wingspan is 39.3 inches (1008mm).

BEAK

The 6-inch beak is curved downward for its entire length, from base to tip.

Myakka River
Charlotte Co. Florida

Feet and Legs rather stout
compared to other wading birds
wing tip
of white
Ibis
Button wood Rookery
Englewood Florida
White Ibis
Eudocimus albus
immature
Grass shrimp
Leptochela, SP.
* Grass shrimp and Larval
stages of other Shrimps
and some small crabs appear
to be the main food of
the Ibis and Spoon bills
at Buttonwood Rookery
* from stomach
contents.
K.E. Karalus

EYES

The irides of the adults are a distinctive pearly blue, and those of the young birds are brownish.

CRESTS, PLUMAGE, ANNUAL MOLT

There are no crests or unusually developed plumes at any time of the year. The adults undergo a complete postnuptial molt from early July usually into late September. There is also an incomplete prenuptial molt in late December and January. The face of the bird is bare of plumage and dull reddish at all times except after prenuptial molt, when this area becomes brilliant red.

VOICE

The White Ibis is not a particularly vocal bird even during breeding season. If disturbed, it will rise and fly away with a peculiar soft grunting call similar to a muted honking. During the breeding season the females are normally silent, while the males make only a few soft cooing sounds and a gurgling sound sometimes repeated for several minutes and similar to a deep-throated *ulla-ulla-ulla.*

Studies of White Ibis and spoonbills made at Buttonwood Rookery and on the Myakka River, in Charlotte County, Florida.

COLORATION AND MARKINGS: ADULT

The breeding plumage and nonbreeding plumage are about the same, except that the latter has more dusky mottlings on the hind neck and crown rather than pure white. The beak, legs, and feet and the naked area of the face tend to range from flesh-colored to pinkish during the greater part of the year, but become bright red during the breeding season. There is also a throat sac—gular pouch—which becomes visibly extendable during breeding.

COLORATION AND MARKINGS: JUVENILE

A very strong combination of contrasting dark brown and white, though the head is actually grayish. The browns are rich in tone but fade until by late winter they are dingy. The legs of young birds are bluish. The irides are brownish. In the first prenuptial molt the young are still mottled, but generally with more white than before. At the first complete postnuptial molt (when the young bird is about fifteen months old) an almost-adult plumage is assumed, but with a few immature traces remaining. Complete adult plumage is not assumed until the second postnuptial molt, when the bird is over two years of age.

GENERAL HABITS AND CHARACTERISTICS

The White Ibis is generally rather active while on the ground, ordinarily feeding in the shallows and moving about in a sprightly manner, or even continuing the general activity as it groups with others in the low branches of mangroves or high in cypresses. It walks gracefully on the ground, swims well if the need arises, and flies smoothly. It can also climb quite well among the branches, beginning at an early age. Often it will perch for long periods of preening on an open branch. It enjoys the company of its fellows and other waders, such as the Wood Stork and Roseate Spoonbill, but is not garrulous.

HABITAT AND ROOSTING

The White Ibis particularly likes small brushy islands, especially for roosting and nesting, but for feeding, it prefers more open shallow waters of pond margins, shallow swamp, and marsh waters and at times shows a keen fondness for flooded meadowlands. It prefers areas that are muddy to those which are sandy, but will frequent either. The birds especially like exposed tidal flats. Preferred roost tree include myrtle, mangrove, willow, cypress, elders, and bays. When approaching the roosts in the evening, they often travel in long wavering lines, sometimes numerous in the extreme and coming from all directions.

ENEMIES AND DEFENSES

Man remains an enemy, for even though the bird is now fully protected by law, its flesh is so prized as meat that it is still illegally hunted in much of its range.

FOOD AND FEEDING HABITS

Insects, crustaceans, and small snakes are the principal foods. Cutworms are a very big item in the diet, as are crayfish. Grasshoppers, too, are eaten in abundance, and, to a slightly lesser extent, fiddler crabs and soldier crabs. Snails and slugs are eaten, as are the larvae of many insects, especially aquatic varieties.

The White Ibis has developed an enterprising manner of hunting successfully for crayfish. In dry weather, when crayfish must burrow to reach water, they leave behind telltale mounds of mud at the hole entry. The White Ibis, seeing one of these, approaches quietly and, with the long curved beak, nudges some of the mud back into the hole. The bird then steps back a step or two and waits. In a short while the crayfish appears at the entry to dispose of the mud again on the pile already built up. As soon as it emerges from the hole as much as it is going to, the bird darts forward and snatches it.

COURTSHIP AND MATING

Although the breeding coloration changes for both sexes, it is most vividly changed in the male, with the fleshy coloration of beak, face, gular pouch, and legs becoming brilliant red. Occasionally, though, the redness, which is common, gives way to a bright red-orange or true orange. The gular pouch extends about a half inch below the beak and is ordinarily a turkey red in coloration. When this pouch is distended, the male sometimes makes low cooing or clucking sounds to the female, which she may or may not echo.

NEST AND NESTING HABITS

White Ibises nest in considerable colonies of their own species, but also frequently in close conjunction with herons, egrets, anhingas, grackles, and other birds. The nesting area is usually the outer fringe area of a hammock or island of dense brushy growth. If the island or hammock has a pond or lake in its center, then often the nesting will take place adjacent to or even overhanging this water. Often numerous nests will be in the same tree and from as low as 3 or 4 feet to as high as 20, but usually around 15 feet in height.

The nest is a poorly constructed one of coarse sticks, with a small depression in the center, that is occasionally lined with Spanish moss, leaves, or grasses. Sometimes, however, the eggs will be laid on the bare twigs. Surprisingly, for the size of the bird, the nests are quite small, often no more than 6 or 7 inches in diameter and seemingly hardly big enough to hold more than one or two eggs. In most cases, the nesting areas are inland, rather than in the immediate coastal areas.

EGGS AND INCUBATION

Ordinarily four eggs are laid which are creamy-buff in color, often with some blotchings of brown at the larger end. The shell is smooth or very finely granulated and the average egg size is 2.25 inches x 1.5 inches (58mm x 40mm).

The incubation period is twenty-one

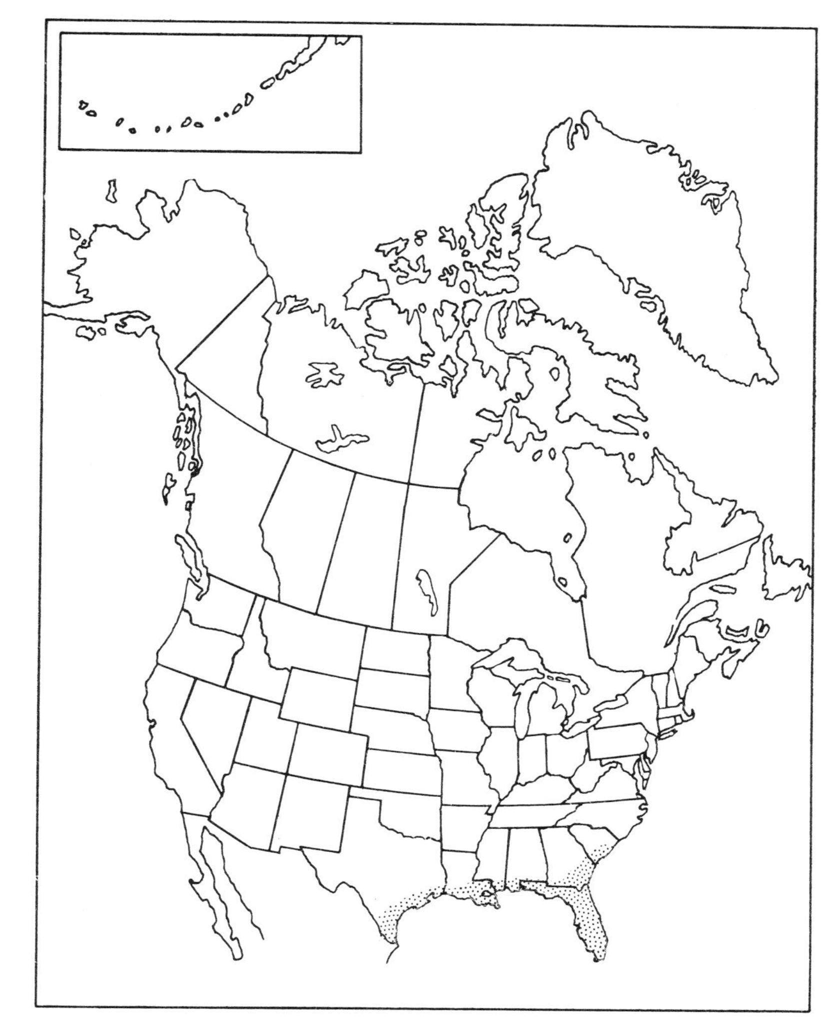

WHITE IBIS

Eudocimus albus (Linnaeus)

days and the incubation duties are shared by both parents on a relatively equal basis.

YOUNG

The downy young, which peep much like chicks fresh from the egg, have glossy black heads, brownish-black throats and necks, and a mouse-gray body down, darker above than below. The beak is a pale flesh color with a dark tip and dark central band. Even when still unable to fly, the young birds are adept at climbing and usually move about in the trees around their nesting area with great agility. Falls are rare and when they do occur, the young bird swims to the first emergent branches and crawls out again quickly. In climbing, it uses not only its feet, but beak and wings as well. Within five weeks the young are able to fly and very quickly after this they are abandoned by the parents.

MIGRATION

There is a general northerly movement of some degree from the breeding range in late summer and early autumn, but this does not last very long. During this period, however, individuals may appear with some regularity in southern California and, in the middle portion of its North American breeding range, as far north as Colorado, Illinois, Minnesota (rarely), Missouri, South Dakota, Ohio, New Jersey, New York, Pennsylvania, Virginia, North Carolina, and occasionally even Vermont.

ECONOMIC INFLUENCE

The White Ibis, because of its propensity for devouring grasshoppers which cause crop damage, and crayfish which feed on the spawn of fish which are good mosquito controllers, is generally considered a very valuable and economically beneficial bird. In past years it was considered valuable for the quality of its flesh as table fare.

COMMON NAME

Scarlet Ibis
(Color Plate XVIII)

SCIENTIFIC NAME

Eudocimus ruber (Linnaeus). *Ruber* is Latin for red.

OTHER COMMON OR COLLOQUIAL NAMES

BLOOD BIRD After its coloration.
RED IBIS After its coloration.

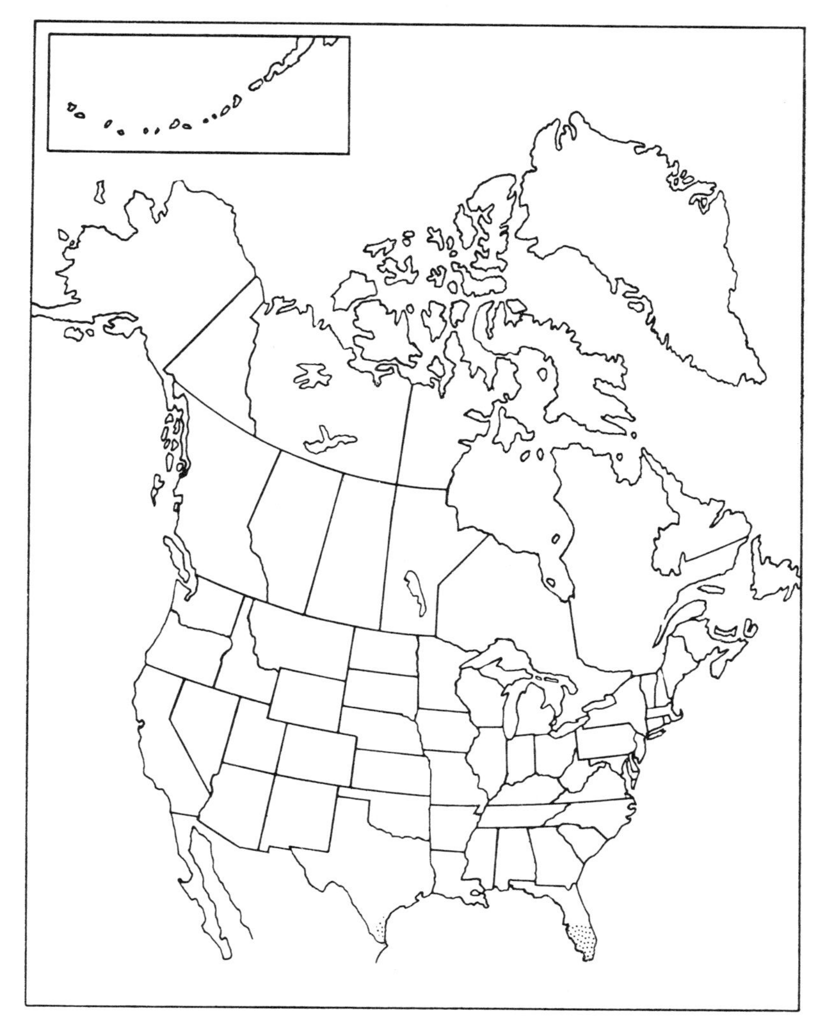

SCARLET IBIS

Eudocimus ruber (Linnaeus)

PRINCIPAL DIFFERENCES FROM *EUDOCIMUS ALBUS*

The most immediate and striking difference between the two closely related birds is, of course, the coloration. The Scarlet Ibis is, as its name indicates, a brilliantly scarlet bird, especially so in its breeding plumage. The beak, bare skin of the face, gular pouch, plumage, and legs are all a deep blood-red, the only exception being the outermost tips of the primaries, which are a deep blue. Unlike the young of the White Ibis, which take two years to assume full adult plumage, that plumage does not occur completely in the Scarlet Ibis until the bird's fourth year. First-year birds are generally brown, but gradually begin assuming increasing areas of reddish coloration, mixed with some grayish and white. Incubation is slightly longer than that for the White Ibis—twenty-four days instead of twenty-one.

Much more wary than the White Ibis, the Scarlet Ibis is rarely seen except at a distance. Although it has been known to interbreed with the White Ibis, this does not occur on a regular basis, and the pink offspring do not breed true color even with its own kind; resultant offspring are usually white.

At one time this bird was very rare anywhere in North America north of Mexico, but in recent years breeding colonies have become artificially established in southern Florida and possibly in south coastal Texas.

(Overleaf) Sketches of ibis and spoonbills made near Peterson Island in Lemon Bay, Englewood, Florida. (Sketches were made with the aid of 10 x 50mm glass.)

Karalus

ROSEATE SPOONBILL

SUBFAMILY: *PLATALEINEA*
GENUS: *AJAIA* Reichenbach
SPECIES: *AJAJA* (Linnaeus)

XXIX BLACK RAIL (left)

Laterallus jamaicensis jamaicensis Gmelin. Ithaca, New York. A.O.U. Number 216

FARALLON RAIL (right)

Laterallus jamaicensis coturniculus (Ridgway). Point Reyes, California, October 29, 1913. A.O.U. Number 216.1

XXX COMMON GALLINULE

Gallinula chloropus cachinnans Bangs. Cape Haze, Charlotte County, Florida. A.O.U. Number 219

Karl E. Karalus

Karl E. Karalus

Karl E. Karalus

Karl E. Karalus

COMMON NAME

Roseate Spoonbill
(Color Plate XIX)

SCIENTIFIC NAME

Ajaia ajaja (Linnaeus). *Ajaia* is the Brazilian name for the bird.

OTHER COMMON OR COLLOQUIAL NAMES

Most common or colloquial names other than Roseate Spoonbill have to do with the shape of the beak and the coloration of the bird. Some of the names used are:

BIGBILL
FLAME BIRD
FLATNOSE
PADDLEBEAK
RED SPOONBILL
SPOONBILL

XXXI PURPLE GALLINULE

Porphyrula martinica (Linnaeus). Lake Wales, Florida. A.O.U. Number 218

XXXII AMERICAN COOT

Fulica americana americana Gmelin. Charlotte Harbor, Charlotte County, Florida. A.O.U. Number 221

SHAPE AT REST AND IN FLIGHT

The Roseate Spoonbill is a tall bird but most distinctive because of the large, spatulate character of the beak. Generally the bird stands quite erect, but with beak angled downward or hanging straight down.

In flight the head and neck are fully outstretched and, again, the spoonlike beak as it points straight forward is the most obvious distinguishing characteristic. Feet extend backward under the tail and beyond it during flight.

The flight pattern of the Roseate Spoonbill underlines its close relationship to the ibises, for the wingbeating and gliding are very nearly identical. In flock flight, which is customary, the Roseate Spoonbills generally assume long diagonal lines, but rarely fly abreast, as do the White and Scarlet Ibises. The Spoonbill, however, unlike those ibis species, frequently group together in wedge formation for flight, as in the manner of geese. The wingbeats are low and slow, interspersed with periods of gliding.

LENGTH AND WINGSPAN

The Roseate Spoonbill has an average length of 33 inches (847mm) and a wingspan of 52.8 inches (1354mm).

BEAK

The beak, as we have said, is extremely distinctive, a sure means of identifying the species at a glance. It is long and flat, narrow most of its length, and very much widened spoonlike at the outermost quadrant, (at that point it is about 2 inches wide). The nostrils are near the base and are long rather than round. The beak itself is a variety of colors, ranging from greenish and bluish to yellowish and black.

EYES

The irides are carmine in coloration.

CRESTS, PLUMAGE, ANNUAL MOLT

The finest plumage occurs with the completion of the prenuptial molt, which begins in November and is usually finished by late December. The postnuptial molt, which is complete in adults, begins about late May and finishes by mid-July. The highest perfection of adult plumage is not acquired until the bird has passed three years of age and sometimes not until four. There are no crests or plumes of a spectacular nature, although the species was once endangered by plume hunters who sought the wing feathers for hats. In some cases the entire opened wings were dried and sold as fans. Only a remnant population of the birds remained when legislation was enacted prohibiting the plume-hunting.

VOICE

The young birds in the nest give voice to a number of different trilling and peeping sounds, which increase in speed and become more tremulous as the parent bird approaches the nest. The adults are largely quiet, even during courtship, although occasionally both sexes will exchange low-pitched grunts not unlike the clucking of a hen and not audible at any great distances. The author once heard a low murmuring, muted honklike sound from a flight of about a dozen Roseate Spoonbills passing overhead in the first light of dawn, but never encountered this sound from the birds again.

COLORATION AND MARKINGS: ADULT

The head of the Roseate Spoonbill is bare, with yellowish-green to yellowish green-blue skin. The neck, breast, and back plumage is pure white, while the rest of the body and wings are a pale rose-pink, with the shoulders and tail coverts boldly splashed with a rich carmine. A tuft of small curly carmine feathers occurs in the center of the breast. In some birds, there is a suffusion of carmine or at least pinkish in the breast plumage. The tail is a rich ochraceous buff. The legs are red.

COLORATION AND MARKINGS: JUVENILE

The juvenile plumage, acquired before the young birds leave the nest, is mainly white suffused with pinkish be-

Field sketches of spoonbills made at Buttonwood Rookery, Lemon Bay, Englewood, Florida, September 1976.

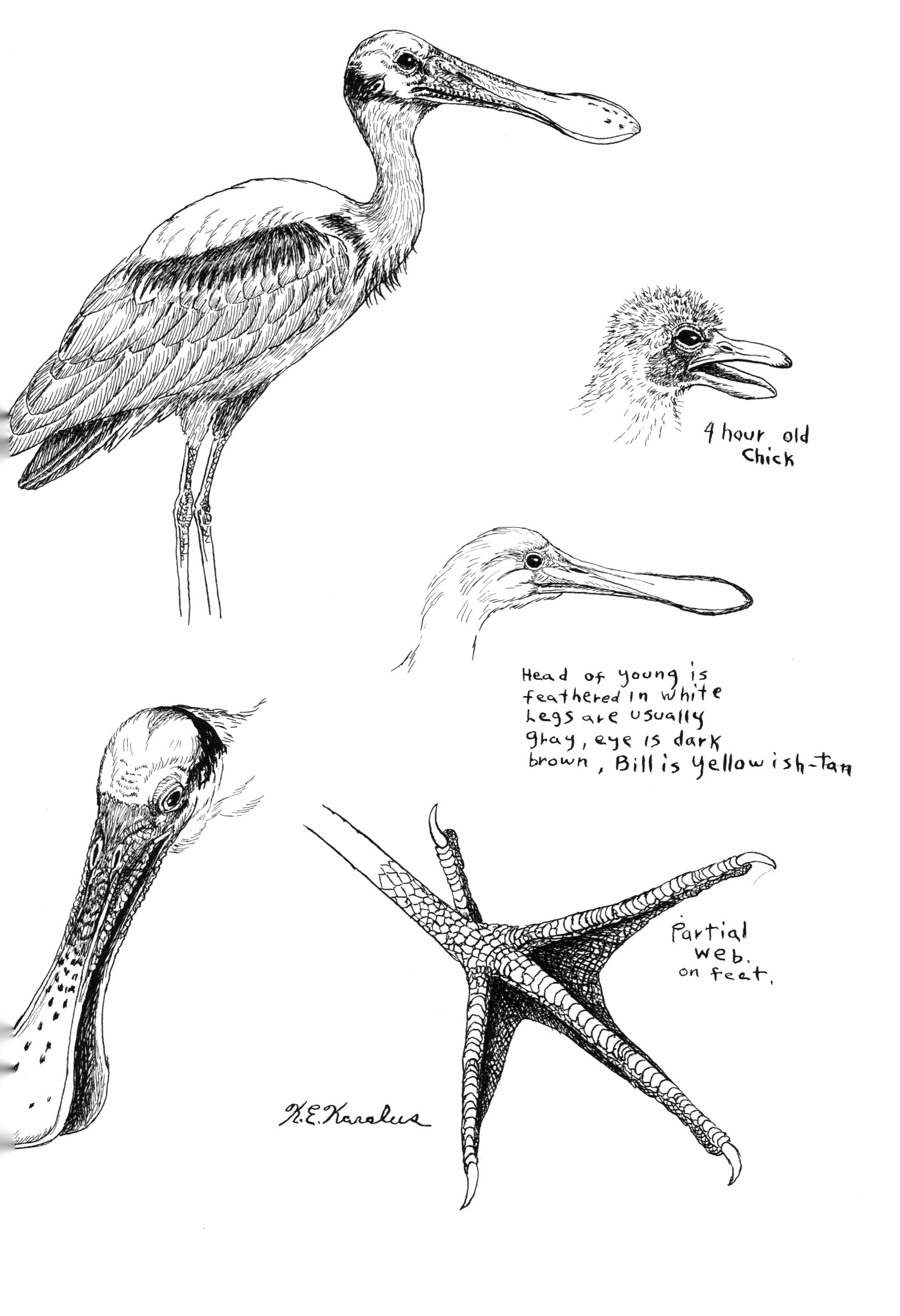
4 hour old
Chick
Head of young is
feathered in white
Legs are usually
gray, eye is dark
brown, Bill is yellowish-tan
Partial
web.
on feet.
K.E. Karalus

neath wings and tail. The crown, cheeks, and throat are covered with white plumage and are not, as in the adults, naked. The outer primaries have dusky tips. First winter plumage is simply a continuation of development toward mature plumage, with a little carmine appearing in the lesser wing coverts and upper tail coverts.

GENERAL HABITS AND CHARACTERISTICS

While not generally considered nocturnal, Roseate Spoonbills are just as apt to be abroad and active at nighttime as during the day. This is particularly true on brightly moonlit nights. However, as with most of the wading birds, the principal feeding times are dawn and dusk, but with more extensive night feeding than day feeding.

Quite frequently the birds will stand together in groups with their wings opened as if drying themselves. In group flight, the Roseate Spoonbills will sometimes lift from the ground simultaneously and then rise to great heights in ascending spirals, crossing back and forth the way vultures and ibises are prone to do. Descent is usually swift, in a series of zigzagging drops. Although they tend to be essentially gregarious at all seasons, their groups are smaller at non-breeding times.

HABITAT AND ROOSTING

The Gulf coastal estuaries are particularly favored areas of habitat, especially if isolated. The rookeries are almost always on dense mangrove islands, which at times literally become covered with the birds. Probably the most favored habitat is a tidal flat area in association with tiny islets of buttonwood and both red and black mangrove. The muddy, marshy borders of estuaries and river-mouth systems are highly favored, too. Roseate Spoonbills often visit salt or brackish ponds. Sometimes the birds will wander far inland, but most often they are seen within a mile of the coastline.

ENEMIES AND DEFENSES

As with so many of the more colorful and beautifully plumed wading birds, man has been the worst enemy. In the case of *Ajaia ajaja,* the species was very nearly wiped out and has never recovered its former numbers, although it is no longer so severely endangered.

FOOD AND FEEDING HABITS

The food is primarily crustaceans—especially prawns and shrimp—as well as fish and grasshoppers. In feeding, the birds alight in shallow water which they proceed to muddy up by swishing their beaks back and forth in the water, all the while collecting in the beaks water life, such as small crustaceans. Sometimes the entire head and part of the neck will be submerged while feeding. Practically all feeding is done in saltwater areas; sometimes in brackish areas, but almost never in fresh water. If, during the movements of the beak through the water, a small fish is caught, the bird will beat it to death against the surface of the water before swallowing it.

COURTSHIP AND MATING

The courtship dance is engaged in by both sexes, though more strenuously by the male. Generally he approaches the female on the ground and as he walks toward her he opens his wings and vibrates them. He seems to make a point of approaching the female with the sun behind him so that the rays shining through the open plumage of his wings will bathe him in a rosy glow. Now and then he will execute little hops as he nears her and then she, too, will engage in small jumps. This may or may not be accompanied by more extensive wing opening (and some flapping) on the part of both. Head raising and lowering sometimes occurs with almost metronomic regularity. Actual copulation more often takes place on the ground than in a tree or bush.

NEST AND NESTING HABITS

Prior to 1879, when plume-hunting began decimating the species, the Roseate Spoonbill nested all along the Gulf Coast of the United States. Huge nesting rookeries containing many thousands of birds could be found from southern Texas to southern Florida. Now most of the breeding is in the area south of a line across Florida which bisects Lake Okeechobee on an east-west direction. The Roseate Spoonbill's present breeding colonies are much smaller and are frequently found in conjunction with Louisiana Herons, Little Blue Herons, Great Egrets, anhingas, White Ibises, and Florida cormorants. Most often the nests are located in the outer fringe of small mangrove islands in saltwater areas or brackish estuarial systems, but always well hidden in the densest areas of the mangrove fringe.

The nests are almost always located in red mangroves at a height of about a dozen feet off the water or mud and are more often constructed on a horizontal branch than in the fork of branches. Though they nest in conjunction with White Ibises and medium-sized herons, nests of Roseate Spoonbills are easily recognizable because they are built of larger sticks and have a diameter of about 1.5 feet. The egg depression is shallow—only about 1 to 2 inches deep maximum—and about 6 inches in diameter. Occasionally the nest will be lined with smaller twigs, but not as a rule. Even more rarely, there will be a lining of moss or grasses or sometimes some leaves of the mangrove. On the whole, the nest is better constructed than are those of neighboring species.

EGGS AND INCUBATION

There are usually four eggs to a clutch, of varied coloration. At times they are pinkish-creamy and speckled with dots and blotches of lavender, purple, brown, and gray-drab. Most often, though, the ground coloration is a dingy white, more or less regularly blotched and spotted with browns ranging from umber to russet. The eggs are thick-shelled, without gloss, and rather roughly granulated. The average egg size is 2.6 inches x 1.7 inches (65mm x 44mm). Incubation is shared by both parents.

ROSEATE SPOONBILL

Ajaia ajaja (Linnaeus)

YOUNG

When first hatched, the young Roseate Spoonbills are very feeble and almost entirely helpless. For some hours they have difficulty even raising their heads. They are very strange-looking creatures, unable to stand, having enormous stomachs and a generally salmon-colored skin which is, at first, only very scantily covered by a soft down. The wing quills are well started at this time, but are still in sheaths and take a long time developing. The soft beak is turned downward slightly and rather ducklike at first. The down increases in quantity and length until, within a few days, the bird is entirely covered.

The young are fed through regurgitation, with a parent bird feeding one and then resting, then feeding another, until all the young are fed. Within a couple of weeks, the young birds begin to venture out onto nearby branches and quickly become skilled in climbing about, although they still fall quite frequently. When the parent birds are away from the nest, the young, after the first few days, rarely make any sounds.

MIGRATION

There is not a general species-wide migration as such among the Roseate Spoonbills, although, as is the case with some others of the wading birds, there is a general northerly movement after the nesting seasons. The birds from southern Florida will sometimes go as far north as South Carolina and there have even been sightings recorded in Wisconsin, Illinois, Ohio, Pennsylvania, New York, and Indiana, as well as in Colorado, Utah, New Mexico, Arizona, and California, but these are isolated cases. The Roseate Spoonbill very rarely travels any great distances inland, and not too far northward from its normal range.

AMERICAN FLAMINGO

SUBORDER: *PHOENICOPTERI*
FAMILY: *PHOENICOPTERIDAE*
GENUS: *PHOENICOPTERUS* Linnaeus
SPECIES: *RUBER* Linnaeus

COMMON NAME

American Flamingo
(Color Plate XX)

SCIENTIFIC NAME

Phoenicopterus ruber Linnaeus. From the Greek *phoenikopteros,* meaning a red wing.

SHAPE AT REST AND IN FLIGHT

A very distinctive bird, immediately recognizable due to its long legs, relatively short, horizontal body, and very long neck. Also, the bent beak is unique among North American birds. Standing, the bird is about 5 feet tall.

In flight, as well as at rest, flamingos are very recognizable. The very long legs stretch far out behind, as with the herons. However, unlike the herons, the neck is well outstretched as in the manner of cranes and ibises. The tail is relatively short and the surprisingly narrow, pointed wings are just about exactly midway between beak and feet.

The strong, level, purposeful flight with medium-speed wingbeat is faster than the Great Blue Heron's, but slower than that of the White Ibis.

HEIGHT AND WEIGHT

The American Flamingo has an average height of just over 5 feet (61.1 inches—1567mm) and an average weight of 7.33 pounds (3.3 kg).

LENGTH AND WINGSPAN

The average length is 47.75 inches (1225mm) and wingspan averages 61.3 inches (1571mm).

BEAK

The beak of the flamingo is unique in shape; abruptly bent at midpoint, the beak's front upper surface faces straight forward and when the bird's head is upside down for feeding, the upper beak is on the bottom. The length of the beak actually exceeds the length of the head. Very large and thick, the beak is black at the tip, orange in the middle portion, and yellowish at the base.

CRESTS, PLUMAGE, ANNUAL MOLT

The flamingo has no crests and no particularly elongated plumes at any season. The annual complete molt is postnuptial, but it begins while the adults are still nesting. The first feathers to be affected are those of the scapulars and crown. By the time this molt occurs, the breeding plumage is very worn and faded almost white. The least amount of fading has occurred on upper and under wing coverts. By mid-June the molt is full upon the bird, at which time it may be incapable of flight or at least greatly handicapped; if danger threatens at such time, the bird depends upon its running ability to escape. The molt is completed, at the latest, by early August. A partial prenuptial molt, which brings the spectacularly beautiful red breeding plumage, begins in about November and is completed by January.

VOICE

The American Flamingo has a fairly extensive range of notes, most of which are guttural and croaky in character. Perhaps the most common is a sort of in-flight honking sound of three notes repeated regularly, the second note loudest. Another call, also usually uttered in flight, is more gooselike in character—a deep but not terribly melodious four-note or five-note honking. This is a call that may come from many of the birds simultaneously when they are in flight, and which becomes harsher and more strident if danger threatens. There is also a murmuring groanlike cry which is uttered upon approaching the nest, and a similar but slightly more grating cry uttered as a flight is terminated.

COLORATION AND MARKINGS: ADULT

The perfect breeding plumage is practically all scarlet except for the primaries and most of the secondaries which are black on the terminal ends. In the words of the late Dr. Frank Chapman, "No other large bird is so brightly colored, and no other brightly colored bird is so large."

COLORATION AND MARKINGS: JUVENILE

The first winter plumage of the immature flamingo begins to appear at five weeks of age, first on the scapulars and sides of the breast. The general coloration is a grayish-brown barely tinged with pinkish on the underside and wings. The back feathers have well-marked shaft streaks and the tail is pinkish in coloration with the feathers black-edged. The secondaries are black in the center and have white margins. The following July to August, when the bird is about eighteen months old, a postnuptial molt occurs in which the young bird assumes full adult plumage with the possible exception of some dusky discoloration on the wing coverts. Immature birds are always lighter in coloration than adults and they fly together, apart from the adults.

HABITAT

The extremely rare American Flamingo favors the marl and mud flats of the coastal shallows. The author, who lived in southern Florida for many years and observed birds closely during all that time, saw American Flamingos only once—thirteen of them in flight just at dawn at the lower end of Lemon Bay in 1969.

FOOD AND FEEDING HABITS

The flamingo's food consists almost entirely of shells of genus Ceritheum,

---

American Flamingo, *Phoenicopterus ruber* Linnaeus (no scale intended).

Feet Webbed
chick
nest
of mud
a few inches to
2 feet high
Karalus

AMERICAN FLAMINGO

Phoenicopterus ruber Linnaeus

which are picked out by the beak as it probes and swishes and sifts through the muddy bottom, swallowed whole and then ground up in the stomach.

EGGS AND INCUBATION

Most often only one egg is laid. Occasionally there will be two and very rarely three. They are dingy white, with an uncommonly thick shell that is often lumpy with flaky white calcium deposits on the surface. These are large eggs, averaging 3.6 inches x 2.2 inches (91mm x 56mm).

The incubation is about equally divided between both parents, with the parent not on the eggs ordinarily feeding during this period or standing guard near the incubating parent bird (guard duty usually falls to the male). The change of shift on the nest usually occurs in early morning and late afternoon. The incubation period is about thirty-one days.

YOUNG

At the time it is first hatched, the American Flamingo chick is clad in a coat of thick white down which is a dingy blue on crown and back. The lores and areas surrounding the eyes are bare of down. At the age of one month, this coat of down is shed and another, ash-gray in color, replaces it. This second downy coat lasts for only seven to nine days. Before the hatchling begins feeding on its own, it is fed through regurgitation by the parent birds. The first material that the chick eats on its own is the trampled egg fragments still on the nesting platform. This is believed to be crucial to the bone-formation process. The young chick issues a series of sounds, including a puppylike yapping, a whistling sound, and then a slightly melodious crowing call.

NORTH AMERICAN DISTRIBUTION

Phoenicopterus ruber, beyond any doubt one of the most spectacular birds of the Western Hemisphere, was once abundant in the southern portion of North America, but is largely extinct there now. Only rarely is it seen in southernmost Florida.

THE CRANES

ORDER: *GRUIFORMES*
SUBORDER: *GRUES*
SUPERFAMILY: *GRUOIDEA*
FAMILY: *GRUIDAE*
SUBFAMILY: *GRUINEA*
GENUS: *GRUS* Pallas

SPECIES: *CANADENSIS* (Linnaeus)
SUBSPECIES: *canadensis* (Linnaeus)
Sandhill Crane

tabida (Peters)
Little Brown Crane

pratensis Meyer
Florida Crane

SPECIES: *AMERICANA* (Linnaeus)
Whooping Crane

COMMON NAME

Sandhill Crane
(Color Plate XXI)

SCIENTIFIC NAME

Grus canadensis canadensis (Linnaeus). From the Latin *grus*, a crane.

OTHER COMMON OR COLLOQUIAL NAMES

COMMON BROWN CRANE After basic coloration.

COMMON CRANE

RATTLING CRANE After peculiar vocal sounds.

SHAPE AT REST AND IN FLIGHT

A very tall, upright, stately bird with a sharply pointed heron-like beak, long neck, no showy plumes, a heavy body, long legs, and long sturdy toes. Not as tall as the Whooping Crane, *Grus americana.*

During flight the birds gives the immediate impression of great wing force and direction with little real effort and without rapid wingbeating at any time. Occasionally long glides are enacted, especially in descent from high altitudes. This bird often soars and circles in a dizzying manner at great altitudes, evidently for the sheer enjoyment of flying.

LENGTH AND WINGSPAN

The Sandhill Crane has an average length of 43.75 inches (1122mm) and an average wingspan of 80 inches (2053mm).

LEGS AND FEET

The legs and feet are sturdily built, with considerably less of the long narrow delicacy characteristic of the legs of the egrets. Both legs and feet are black and heavily scaled and the toe span is very wide.

EYES

The irides are brown, though sometimes with a faint touch of ruddy coloration, or paling down to yellowish.

ANNUAL MOLT

A complete molt begins each year in August with the flight feathers, and lasts until replacement of the body plumage and wing coverts in December. There is said to be very little, if any, prenuptial molt.

VOICE

The voice of the crane is very distinctive and has a powerful, far-carrying resonant quality caused by a peculiar series of tracheal convolutions which allow the windpipe to act as a sort of echo chamber. This capability seems to reach its peak of effectiveness in the Whooping Crane, which has upward of 30 inches of such convolutions. The Sandhill Crane has about 8 inches of convoluted windpipe, but enough to produce a rather thrilling and very far-carrying trumpeting, rattling cry, which, once heard and correctly identified, is never mistaken for the call of any other bird. In addition to the long, rattling, trumpeting cries, there are also numerous shorter, guttural rattles and croakings. Young birds are capable of uttering only a slight peeping sound and a rather plaintive whistling.

COLORATION AND MARKINGS: ADULT

The primaries and coverts, as well as general body plumage, are slate-gray to brownish-gray. The coloration becomes somewhat lighter on head and neck, with the throat and chin sometimes almost whitish. Cheeks, too, are light. A bare space of bright red skin stretches from the base of the beak to mid-crown, the bottom line of this bareness passing through the median line of the eye on both sides. This is a very distinctive marking for the species. The rear portion of the crown, as well as the nape, is darker slaty gray. The underwings are lightish gray, almost white. Legs and beak are black.

COLORATION AND MARKINGS: JUVENILE

For the most part like that of the adult except that the head is fully feathered and thus lacks the bright red bare skin of the face, and the plumage is much more variegated with browns, chestnut, and rusty colorations. These are replaced by full adult plumage colorations with the second complete annual molt, when the bird is just over two years old.

HABITAT AND ROOSTING

The Sandhill Crane particularly enjoys expansive prairie locations with relatively short grass, but is often found in sparse stands of cypress and pine. It prefers dry ground to wading, although is not disinclined to entering water which may be deep enough to reach almost to the abdomen. Wet meadows and slough edges are often frequented. Most often the roosting is done on low sturdy branches or the ground, usually in the company of a dozen or more of its own kind, but sometimes with only one or two others. It rarely roosts alone.

FOOD AND FEEDING HABITS

Sandhill Cranes are probably most often observed as they walk slowly and sedately through the prairie grasses, here and there plucking things up with graceful movements of the head and neck and murmuring softly among themselves, in groups of from two or three to six or seven birds. The food matter they pick up at such times is considerably varied. A great deal of vegetation is eaten, espe-

---

Sandhill Crane, *Grus canadensis canadensis* (Linnaeus).

chick
Display
Albion Nebraska
1964
Feet stout and more chicken like
than other wading birds
Sleeping
6 miles south of Englewood
Florida
♀ shot by Poacher and left to rot
stomach contained June beetles, grubs
and many small roots
Karl E. Karalus

cially seeds of many kinds, along with hard gravel to aid in grinding it up in their gizzards. Berries and small fruits of numerous kinds are also eaten and a surprisingly varied diet of animal matter—insects of almost any kind, lizards, snakes, moles, mice, rats, small turtles, frogs, fish, tadpoles, small birds, young rabbits, etc. The birds are often held in disfavor by farmers for the amount of crop materials they consume, from voluminous quantities of wheat, oats, barley, and other grains, through fruits and vegetables of many types, even including potatoes that have been unearthed for harvest.

COURTSHIP AND MATING

Grus canadensis canadensis generally has a preselected courtship ground in its own territory, used by itself and others of its species and to which, when the time is right, numerous Sandhill Cranes will come. This usually occurs at sunrise or shortly thereafter, with individual flocks of from five to ten birds arriving from different directions until perhaps fifteen to thirty birds have gathered together. The dancing ground is usually located on the prominence of a rolling prairie, where there is good visibility in all directions. As soon as the birds arrive, the dance begins. A number of the birds raise their beaks skyward and begin a slow and rather stately circular walk, sometimes with wingtips hanging downward. Abruptly the heads are lowered right to the ground, the wings drawn in tightly, and the body looks like a ball supported by three legs. In this pose the birds begin a more bouncing walk until they are actually jumping and finally leaping high into the air, sometimes with the wings dropping again, and at other times with the wings raised to full extent. In this manner they cut back and forth in front of one another, croaking and trilling and trumpeting in their highly distinctive voices, as the speed and wild abandon of their dancing increases. The whole thing reaches a violent climax of sound and motion, abruptly dies away, and then begins again, usually with some birds who danced before dropping out and others that have not yet danced taking their places. The entire dancing group may reach upward of three hundred birds at times, although fifty to eighty seems the more usual number. Now and then the entire flock breaks into a weird sort of group skipping and light leaping with upraised wings. The dance lasts for about two or three hours and then the individual groups begin to head for their morning feeding grounds.

NEST AND NESTING HABITS

The Sandhill Crane sometimes nests among fairly low grasses in prairie country, where the eggs are laid in a simple scooped-out area of earth lightly lined with broad-leaved grasses. An advantage of such a locality is that the bird can see well in all directions. Far more commonly, though, the nest is in the fringe of a marsh or slough in water from a few inches to a foot deep, the nesting platform constructed of dense rushes and reeds to form a bulky platform. Such a nest is usually about 2 feet high and 4 feet in diameter.

EGGS AND INCUBATION

Almost always two eggs are laid which range from a pasty pale green to a pale brownish-green of pastel nature, overlaid by a series of brown, dark buffy-gray or purplish-gray spots and blotches. In general, the eggs are slightly lighter-colored than those of the other North American cranes. The shell is thick and usually smooth, though it is sometimes lightly pitted or granulated. The eggs are quite large, averaging about 3 inches x 2.4 inches (97mm x 63mm). Incubation is by both parent birds, but predominantly by the female.

SANDHILL CRANE

Grus canadensis canadensis (Linnaeus)

YOUNG

Sandhill Crane chicks emerge from the egg in about two to four hours, remain helpless for another hour or so beyond that, and within another hour are standing and demanding food from the parent birds. Although they tend to remain near the nest for the first couple of days, they can, if need be, leave the nest within three or four hours of hatching. In all cases the nest is abandoned fairly early and the chicks wander about under the protective care of the parent birds, being fed by them and learning to feed themselves. They remain with the parent birds until and even after they can fly very well themselves, with some families staying close-knit up until the time of the next nesting.

The downy young bird is clad in thick soft down which ranges from chestnut to a deep rich brown on crown, nape, back, and wings, to a rather lighter tawny-buff on the sides and throat, to a grayish-white on the underparts. These colors fade as the chick grows older and by the time the first juvenile plumage is appearing, the down has become dingy. Young cranes do not acquire their complete adult plumage until they are about thirty months of age.

MIGRATION

Highly migrational, Sandhill Cranes, beginning usually in August and continuing into late September, gather in great migratory flocks which gradually grow larger and larger and which regularly take to wing and soar about at great altitudes and in thrilling performances prior to the actual directional movement of the migration. An almost constant din of their rattling, trumpeting cries fills the air as they whirl and circle and dip; this vocal demonstration tends to diminish somewhat during the actual migrational flights. The flights north and south are swift and strong and direct, occurring both day and night, with the birds stopping for brief hours here and there to feed and rest. A major migrational staging area is at Nebraska's Platte River. The Sandhill Crane is absent in winter from about the northern four fifths of its range north of Mexico. The northward migration sometimes extends across Alaska's Aleutian Islands and into Siberia.

ECONOMIC INFLUENCE

Sandhill Cranes have gained the enmity of many farmers because of their depredations in grain fields, and in areas where fruit and vegetable crops are maturing. To some extent this adverse influence is offset by the considerable insect-eating and rodent-eating habits of the birds during practically any season.

COMMON NAME

Little Brown Crane
(Color Plate XXI)

SCIENTIFIC NAME

Grus canadensis tabida (Peters). *Tabida* from the Latin *tabidus,* meaning lesser.

BASIC SUBSPECIFIC DIFFERENCES

The Little Brown Crane, also known as the Canadian Crane, Northern Brown Crane, and Big Brown Crane, is, despite its most common name, somewhat larger than the Sandhill Crane. Coloration is essentially the same, although with less grayish and more brownish-buff than in the Sandhill Crane.

The Little Brown Crane breeds in the far northern regions of the North American continent, across the northern portion of Alaska and Canada eastward to about the region of Hudson Bay. It is absent from all of that territory during winter, occurring in great abundance during the fall migration in the western states west of the Rockies. Lemmings make up a large portion of their summer diet.

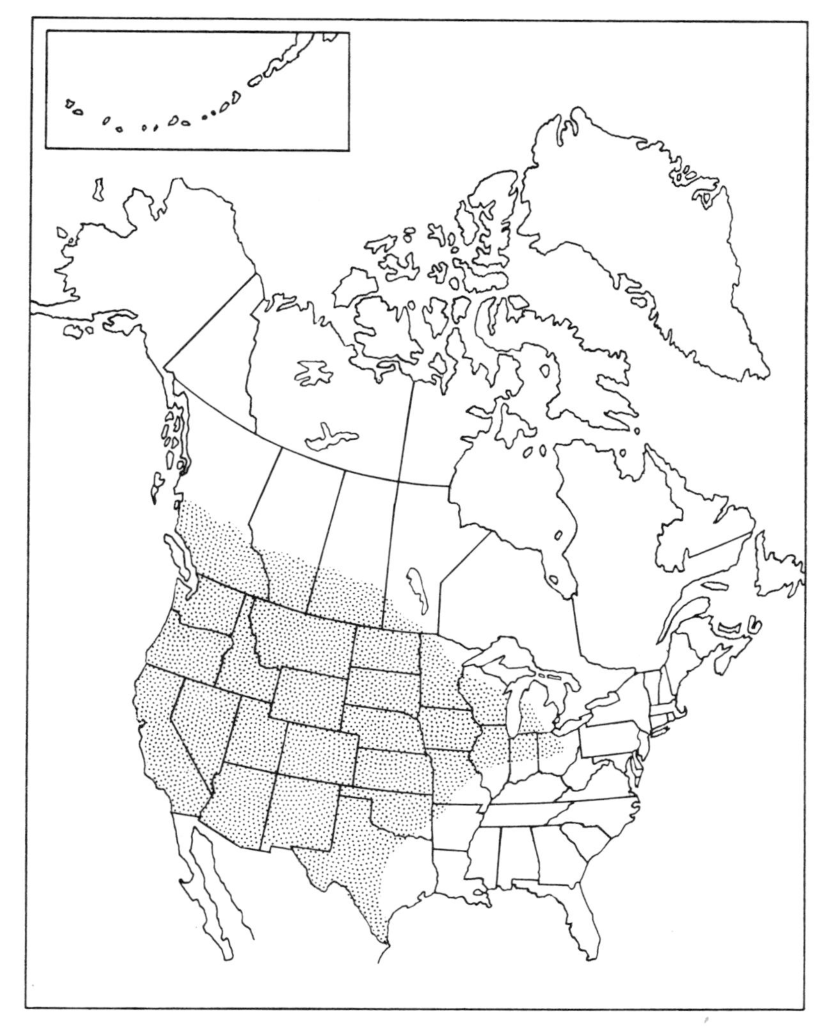

LITTLE BROWN CRANE
Grus canadensis tabida (Peters)

More often than the Sandhill or Florida Crane, the Little Brown Crane prefers a relatively dry nesting area on the ground. The nest is often no more than a cavity hollowed out of sandy soil, most often rather thickly lined with fine (rather than coarse, as with the other cranes) grasses and perhaps a few feathers. The eggs—usually two—are pale green with dark chocolate-colored blotches and spots. Average egg size is 3.5 inches x 2.2 inches (90mm x 55mm).

COMMON NAME

Florida Crane
(Color Plate XXI)

SCIENTIFIC NAME

Grus canadensis pratensis Meyer. From the Latin *pratensis,* meaning of the meadow.

OTHER COMMON OR COLLOQUIAL NAMES

SANDHILL CRANE

FLORIDA CRANE

Grus canadensis pratensis Meyer

BASIC SUBSPECIFIC DIFFERENCES

The Florida Crane is on the average considerably smaller than the Little Brown Crane and slightly smaller than the Sandhill Crane.

There is a greater difference of coloration between the Florida Crane and the Sandhill than there is between the Sandhill and the Little Brown Crane. In the Florida Crane, the forehead and crown, as in the other subspecies, are bare and red, but the chin and throat are white, with the rest of the body mainly a rather darkish smoke-gray, with back and scapulars overlaid heavily with wood brown or fuscous. The primaries are a fuscous-black.

The Florida Crane depends to a greater extent on a diet of vegetation than the other subspecies, with animal matter (including insects, mammals, reptiles, amphibians, etc.) comprising only 2.5 per cent of the bird's diet. *Grus canadensis pratensis* most often frequents marshy meadows and wet prairies, but is also found in the pine flats and open pine forests in the vicinity of small ponds. It is in the area of such ponds that the Florida Crane ordinarily builds its nest, which is bulkier for the most part than that of the Little Brown Crane and usually more so than that of the Sandhill Crane.

The Florida Crane nest is 4 or 5 feet in diameter and constructed of sticks, grasses, reeds, and palmetto fronds, often to a height of more than a foot. There is no finer lining in the nest and usually not even very much of an egg depression.

COMMON NAME

Whooping Crane
(Color Plate XXII)

SCIENTIFIC NAME

Grus americana (Linnaeus).

OTHER COMMON OR COLLOQUIAL NAMES

GREAT WHITE CRANE After general coloration and size.
WHITE CRANE For general coloration.
WHOOPER For vocal attributes.

SHAPE AT REST AND IN FLIGHT

A very tall (over 5 feet), stately bird which, at a distance, looks pure white, with a distinctive red fleshy marking on the forecrown, extending from beak base to slightly below occipital area.

The Whooping Crane in flight is clearly recognizable by its well-extended neck and head, snow-white plumage with black primaries and secondaries, and black legs and feet extending far behind the tail. The beak is clearly yellow. This is one of America's most distinctive birds.

LENGTH AND WINGSPAN

The average length of the Whooping Crane is 54.2 inches (1390mm) and the average wingspan is 7.5 feet (2308mm).

CRESTS, PLUMAGE, ANNUAL MOLT

The Whooping Crane has no particularly elongated plumes at any season and no crest. However, the dull red fleshy area of the face and head becomes a much brighter carmine during the breeding season. There is a complete molt of the plumage once annually, beginning about early July and extending through November.

VOICE

One of its most distinctive characteristics, the voice of the Whooping Crane is a far-carrying trumpeting call which is thrilling to hear and unforgettable. Its tremendous carrying power and clarion quality are the result of an extraordinarily long and amazingly convoluted windpipe that amplifies and trumpets the sounds made by the bird. This windpipe is often longer than the total length of the bird itself, averaging about 1428mm (55.69 inches). The cry is loud, clear and piercing and said to be audible for 2 or 3 miles under proper conditions. It has a greater clarity and less of a rattling quality than the calls of the Sandhill, Little Brown, or Florida Cranes.

COLORATION AND MARKINGS: ADULT

The adult *Grus americana* is pure white throughout its plumage except for the primaries and secondaries, which are deep black and, in some lights, faintly iridescent with a bronze-green tone. Legs and feet are black and the beak is a dull greenish except during breeding season when it becomes more yellowish. The eye is a brilliant lemon-yellow and the fleshy area of the face and head, extending from the base of the beak to mid-crown and slightly beneath the eyes, is dull red except during breeding season, when it becomes more of a bright blood-red. There are scattered black hairlike feathers in this red fleshy area at all seasons.

COLORATION AND MARKINGS: JUVENILE

The head of the juvenile bird is completely feathered and does not become bare until full adult plumage is acquired at the second annual molt. The plumage of the young bird is basically white, but with a rusty-brownish overcast at times.

HABITAT AND ROOSTING

During its breeding season, the Whooping Crane (which now breeds almost solely in the area of Great Slave Lake) prefers slough country that is marshy and swampy, especially areas with extensive growths of aspen. During its migration, when it passes from the prairie wetlands of northwestern Canada southward through the Dakotas, Nebraska, Kansas, Oklahoma, and Texas, it lands to feed in grainfields and it is at this time that it becomes most vulnerable to waterfowl gunners.

ENEMIES AND DEFENSES

Man is, of course, by far the worst enemy of the species. To his shame, man very nearly exterminated this bird, bringing its total wild population down to thirteen birds at one time. But, to his credit, man has, through extensive endeavors and great care, brought the total number into the hundreds again. The Whooping Crane is still an extremely endangered bird and conditions still remain all too precarious for it. One great natural blow in the form of a hurricane or other disaster striking the wintering birds at the National Wildlife Refuge at Port Aransas, Texas, near Corpus Christi, could well cause the ultimate extinction of the bird.

FOOD AND FEEDING HABITS

Though generally omnivorous, the Whooping Crane eats somewhat more vegetative matter than animal matter. Nevertheless, it is known to eat large quantities of grasshoppers, beetles, dragonflies and other large insects and their larvae, as well as small rodents, shrews, lizards, snakes, frogs, and birds. Plant bulbs, tubers, succulent leaves and stems, small fruits, berries, grains, and other vegetable crops and foliage make up the bulk of the diet.

NEST AND NESTING HABITS

Most often the nest is built in relatively shallow water, from a few inches to perhaps a foot or a little more in depth. The nest itself, made up of matted rushes, reeds, and grasses, extends anywhere from 6 to 14 inches above the water and is about 2 feet in diameter. Invariably it is extremely well hidden from casual view, yet almost always within mere feet of fairly open areas. The adult birds are very cautious about approaching the nest and if any sort of danger threatens, will walk casually past it as if it didn't exist and then try to make the intruder think the nest is elsewhere, some distance away. The nest itself is not just a floating platform of woven grasses and reeds, but a very dense structure built up from the bottom surface so that it can support considerable weight without sinking or even lowering appreciably.

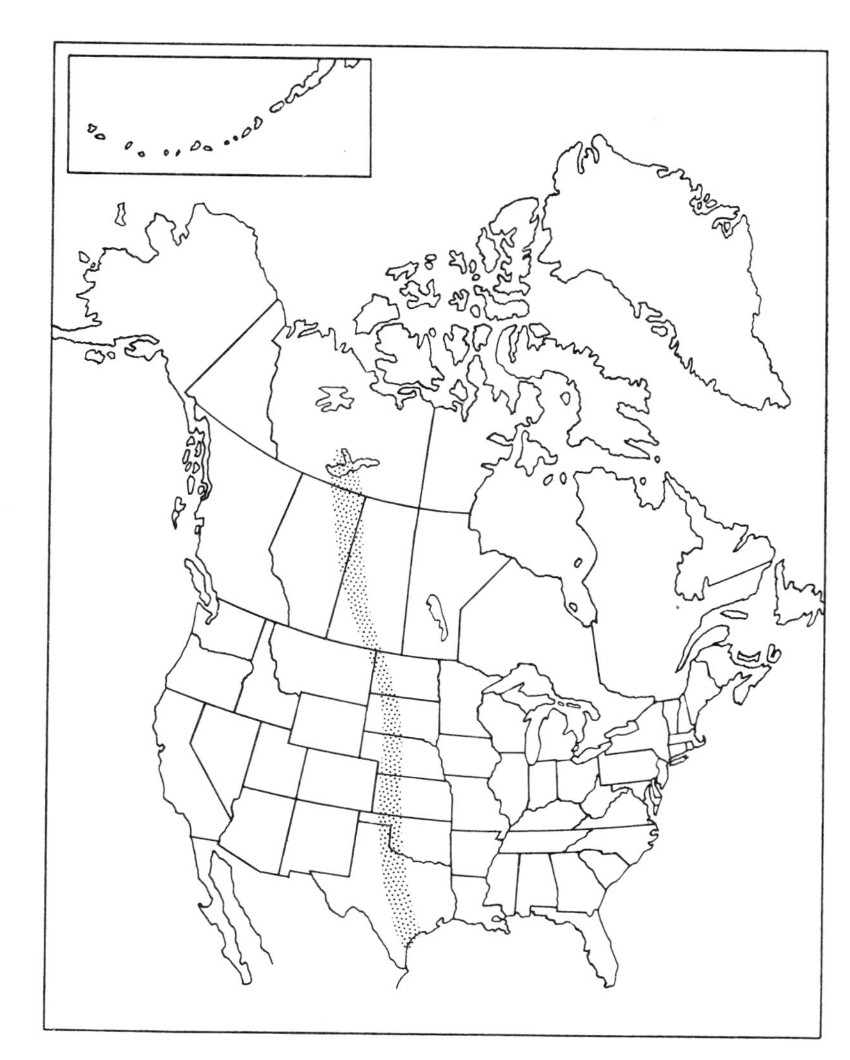

WHOOPING CRANE

Grus americana (Linnaeus)

EGGS AND INCUBATION

Most often two eggs are laid, although occasionally there will be only one, and on very rare occasions, three. The base color of the egg is a heavy buff to dull greenish-buff. In addition, the larger end of the egg is rather heavily blotched and spotted with brown. There is a slight granulation and glossiness to the shell, but it is nevertheless rather smooth and faintly glossy.

Arthur Cleveland Bent in *Life Histories of North American Marsh Birds* gives the average size of thirty-eight measured eggs as being 3.8 inches x 2.4 inches (98mm x 62mm).

Incubation is shared by both parent birds.

YOUNG

The downy hatchling is generally pale beige in coloration, but darker on the back than elsewhere. The chicks are said to peep vigorously and plaintively while emerging from the egg, and are able to move about freely and well within a few hours of hatching. Within twenty-four hours of emerging from the egg, the chick will move off the nest platform and swim into hiding in the surrounding grasses and rushes if danger threatens.

Young birds are fed by regurgitation and this sort of feeding continues for several weeks, even after the chicks have begun eating food on their own.

In the first winter plumage the entire head, including even the lores, is feathered and there is no real indication of the reddish flesh of face and crown which the bird will have as an adult. The young are believed to remain with the parent birds up to and possibly through the fall migration, and it is even possible that the family groups again fly north together the following spring.

NORTH AMERICAN DISTRIBUTION

While the Whooping Crane was once abundant all throughout America east of the Rocky Mountains, it is now extremely scarce and its distribution very limited—ranging from the breeding area in Canada down a narrow migrational corridor to the Texas coast. A few wild pairs are known to breed in Wood Buffalo Park, Mackenzie.

MIGRATION

The Whooping Cranes leave the Great Slave Lake area of Mackenzie on their southward migration around October 1 and arrive at the Texas coast two or three weeks later. In spring, the northward migration generally begins about mid-April and ends by mid-May.

ECONOMIC INFLUENCE

While no longer of any real economic influence, the Whooping Crane has a very great aesthetic value and its decline and gradual partial recovery provide an important lesson in conservation practices.

LIMPKIN

FAMILY: *ARAMIDAE*
GENUS: *ARAMUS* Vieillot
SPECIES: *GUARAUNA* (Linnaeus)
SUBSPECIES: *pictus* (Meyer)

COMMON NAME

Limpkin
(Color Plate XXIII)

SCIENTIFIC NAME

Aramus guarauna pictus (Meyer). *Aramus,* derivation unknown; *guarauna,* a Brazilian name; *pictus,* painted.

OTHER COMMON OR COLLOQUIAL NAMES

The Limpkin (a name derived from the bird's peculiar halting gait) has a wide range of common or colloquial names, including:

CARAU
CLUCKING HEN
COURLAN
COURLIRI
CRYING BIRD
FLORIDA COURLAN
GREATER COURLAN
HAMMOCK TURKEY
INDIAN PULLET
NIGGERBIRD
SCOLOPACEOUS COURLAN
SWAMP GROUSE
UP-N-DOWN

SHAPE AT REST AND IN FLIGHT

The Limpkin is a large-bodied bird with relatively long legs and medium-long neck.

In flight, the down-angled neck and head, with distinctive oversized beak, are clearly evident. The long legs dangle at first but are drawn up to trail behind the tail, which is very short. Its flight, which seldom lasts long, always seems very heavy, effortful and quite slow. The Limpkin rarely flies more than a few feet above the reeds or grasses.

LENGTH AND WINGSPAN

The average length of the Limpkin is 26.7 inches (684mm) and its wingspan is 3.5 feet (1077mm).

BEAK

The beak is a dingy brownish shading to dark gray.

CRESTS, PLUMAGE, ANNUAL MOLT

The Limpkin has no crests and grows no special plumes for the breeding season. Adults have a complete prenuptial molt which begins in February and concludes in April, and another complete molt, postnuptially, beginning in August and ending in November. The plumage is generally very dense, even though relatively short.

VOICE

The voice of the Limpkin is a lonely, disconsolate, and yet altogether delightful sound of the marsh. Oddly, it is one of the few birds whose vocal qualities inspire almost completely different reactions in different people. For some it is chilling. For others it is a beautiful, gentle, and wholly pleasant auditory experience. Why this should be could make an interesting study. Whatever the case, the voice of the Limpkin is so completely distinctive that, like the voice of the Sandhill Crane, once heard it is never mistaken for that of any other bird. The call is a high-pitched rattling sound, followed by two equally high-pitched plaintive notes.

COLORATION AND MARKINGS: ADULT

The basic coloration of *Aramus guarauna pictus* is a milk-chocolate brown, with sharp streakings and spottings of white throughout the plumage. The legs are a dingy green, the beak dark brownish-gray, and the eyes brown, sometimes with a faint orangish cast.

COLORATION AND MARKINGS: JUVENILE

Young Limpkins are essentially the same color and pattern as the adults, except that the browns are paler and the whites duller.

HABITAT AND ROOSTING

Although the Limpkin will frequently alight on low scrub-growth trees (especially those devoid of leaves) growing in marsh or swamp, and perch there for long sleepy minutes, most often it does not roost in trees at all but rather in the saw grass and reeds and rushes of the marsh habitat it favors. It is slow to take flight and quick to end its flight once airborne, dropping into the tall water grasses much in the manner of the rails. And, like the rails, it is an expert at slipping through the dense vegetation with the utmost facility. In addition to ordinary marsh-grass areas, the Limpkin favors areas of tree growth containing scattered cypresses, magnolias, maples, oaks, sabal palms, and pines, and also areas where the undergrowth of vines and brush are very thick. It also favors areas where there is little water current and extensive growths of water hyacinth and swamp lettuce, upon which it often walks as it searches for food.

FOOD AND FEEDING HABITS

Aramus guarauna pictus eats very little vegetable matter, feeding almost exclusively on small animal life of the marshlands, especially snails, mollusks, crustaceans, insects, frogs, worms, and lizards, as well as occasional small snakes. Undoubtedly its favorite food is the apple snail so common to the Everglades and other Florida marsh areas. The Limpkin has a habit of bringing the snails and crustaceans it catches to a particular log or stump or clump of matted swamp grass and devouring them there, leaving behind the shells, which eventually grow into a telltale mound. The Limpkin is quite skilled at shaking the large snails free of their shells without breaking the shells themselves.

Limpkin, *Aramus guarauna pictus* (Meyer).

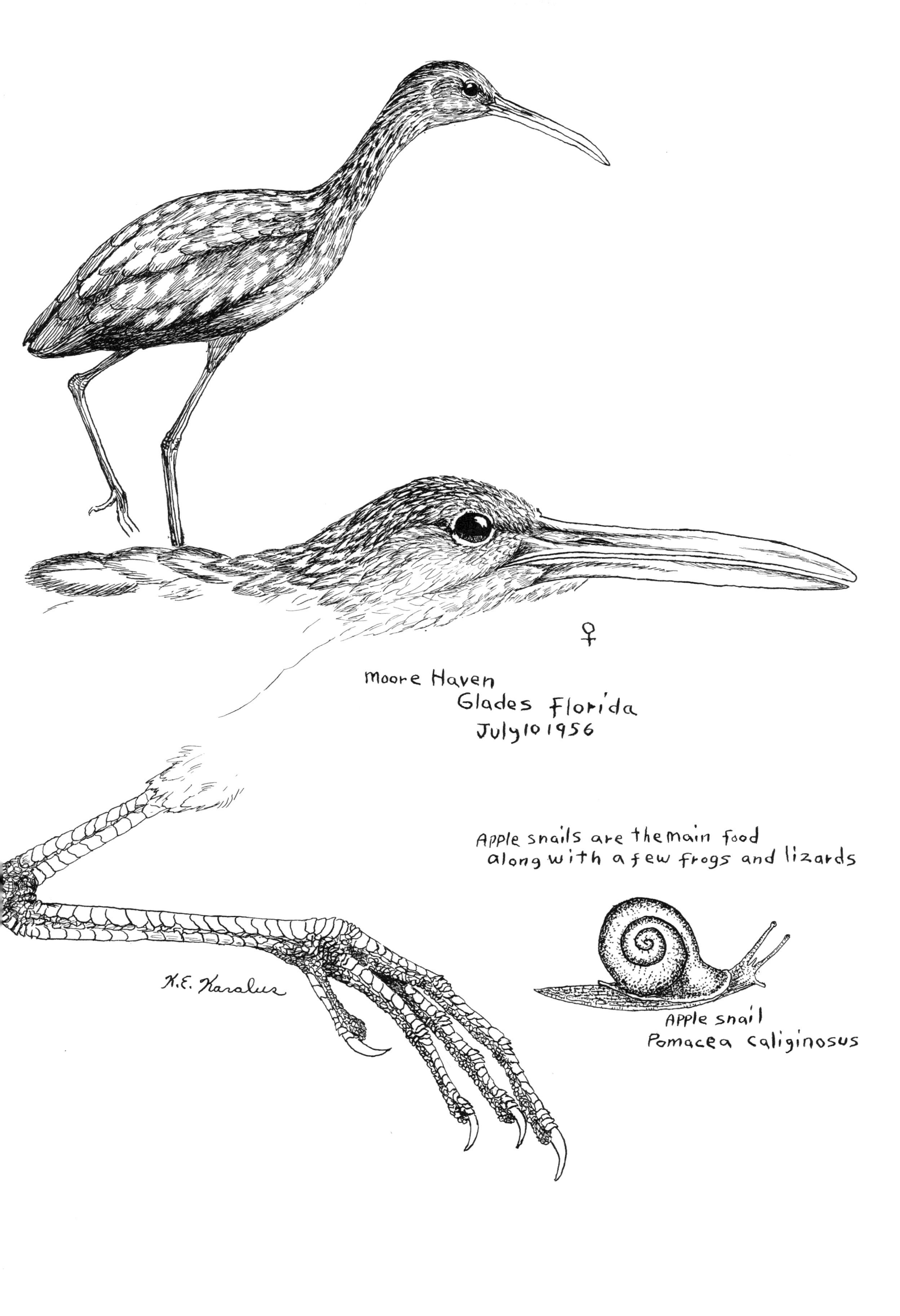
♀
moore Haven
Glades Florida
July 10 1956
Apple snails are the main food
along with a few frogs and lizards
K.E. Karalus
Apple snail
Pomacea caliginosus

LIMPKIN

Aramus guarauna pictus (Meyer)

NEST AND NESTING HABITS

Most often the nest of *Aramus guarauna pictus* is built in thick sawgrass. The bird constructs its bulky platform by bending over stalks of saw grass, upon which it places much vegetative matter in various states of decomposition, and then interweaves this with the living saw grass surrounding the nest. The platform upon which the eggs are laid has only the slightest of depressions, hardly as much as that of a dinner plate, but it seems to suffice quite well for the species and its particular nesting conditions. Almost invariably the Limpkin nest is well hidden, yet only a step or two from open water, most often from 18 inches to 2 feet in depth.

EGGS AND INCUBATION

The Limpkin usually lays five to eight buff-colored eggs which are often streaked or blotched with brown at the large end. They are smooth and have a faint gloss. In size they average 2.3 inches x 1.8 inches (60mm x 46mm). Both parent birds incubate.

YOUNG

Like young rails, the hatchling Limpkin is well covered with a thick and rather long, soft down ranging from a reddish cinnamon-brown to very dark snuff-brown on the back and head, but much lighter buffy-brown on the throat and underparts. The actual plumage appears first on the body, and only very gradually develops on the wings. (When the bird reaches full growth, its wings still bear only half-developed primaries and secondaries.) Full adult plumage is acquired when the young bird is a year old. The fledgling birds, like their parents, can swim well if the need arises. They are also exceptionally skilled at moving through the dense marsh grasses with a minimum of effort or disturbance.

RALLUS RAILS

SUPERFAMILY: *RALLOIDEA*
FAMILY: *RALLIDAE*
SUBFAMILY: *RALLINAE*
GENUS: *RALLUS* Linnaeus

SPECIES: *ELEGANS* Audubon
SUBSPECIES: *elegans* Audubon
King Rail

SPECIES: *LONGIROSTRIS* Boddaert
SUBSPECIES: *crepitans* Gmelin
Northern Clapper Rail

saturatus Ridgway
Louisiana Clapper Rail

scotti Sennett
Florida Clapper Rail

waynei Brewster
Wayne's Clapper Rail

insularum Brooks
Mangrove Clapper Rail

obsoletus Ridgway
California Clapper Rail

yumanensis Dickey
Yuma Clapper Rail

levipes Bangs
Light-Footed Rail

SPECIES: *LIMICOLA* Vieillot
SUBSPECIES: *limicola* Vieillot
Virginia Rail

COMMON NAME

King Rail
(Color Plate XXIV)

SCIENTIFIC NAME

Rallus elegans elegans Audubon. From the Latin, *rallus* signifying a rail, and *elegans* meaning choice.

OTHER COMMON OR COLLOQUIAL NAMES

FRESHWATER MARSH HEN This same name is applied to most of the rails without regard to species or subspecies.

MARSH HEN Probably the most common term, but too indefinite to be of value.

MUD HEN Also very common, though this name is also used in reference to the American Coot.

SHAPE AT REST AND IN FLIGHT

The King Rail is not at all large in comparison to other Gruiformes, such as the cranes. It is well adapted to its life among close-growing reed stems, the body highly compressed and almost pointed in the front, then tapering back in a sort of wedge shape to a blunt, thick posterior with short up-tipped tail.

The wings are extremely short and rounded. When it first springs into the air, its legs dangle awkwardly beneath. They are not drawn up unless the flight is to be long, which is rare, since the bird ordinarily drops out of sight into the marsh grass after a very short flight just over the tops of the reeds. If, however, flight is to be protracted, the legs and the neck are fully extended.

Flight is slow and laborious in practically all circumstances. This is so pronounced that one wonders how the long migrational flights can be made. Even when in full flight with neck extended and legs fully back, the King Rail's movements appear difficult, slow, and weak. Yet, extensive migrations do take place. In most circumstances the flight is very short and vacillating, with rapid wingbeats which seem essentially ineffective. When pursued, they usually run for escape rather than take flight.

LENGTH AND WINGSPAN

The King Rail has an average length of 1.5 feet (464mm) and an average wingspan of 2 feet (615mm).

CRESTS, PLUMAGE, ANNUAL MOLT

There are no distinctive plumage changes throughout the seasons or from one molt to another. The flank feathers are barred, black and white. Adult birds undergo a complete molt which takes about two months, beginning in early August. There is also a partial molt of the contour plumage in spring prior to nesting.

VOICE

The King Rail utters a three-note call, which sounds most like *kark-kark-kark,* and can be heard both day and night.

COLORATION AND MARKINGS: ADULT

The King Rail has a general resemblance to the Northern Clapper Rail, *Rallus longirostris crepitans,* but is larger and slightly more brightly colored. The coloration and markings, in fact, are almost identical to those of the much smaller Virginia Rail, *Rallus limicola limicola.* On the upper portions, the adult King Rail is generally brownish and distinctly streaked. These markings enable the bird to camouflage itself very well among the reeds and rushes of the marsh. On the underside, the plumage is a cinnamon color, brightest on the breast. There is a light line from the base of the beak to over the eye, and a dark line through the eye. The irides are a rich chestnut. The lower eyelid is white. The flanks, as well as the lining of the wings, are quite blackish and very distinctly barred with white. Legs and feet are pale dusky green.

HABITAT AND ROOSTING

Reedy marshes are the preferred habitat of the King Rail and the location where roosting occurs. It does not like tidal marshes and is rarely found along saltwater fringes, preferring a freshwater habitat for roosting, breeding, nesting, and feeding.

FOOD AND FEEDING HABITS

The food of the King Rail consists of both animal and vegetable matter. Snails, slugs, leeches, insects, crayfish, tadpoles, small frogs, and lizards seem to make up the bulk of the animal matter, while seeds of various water and marsh plants, such as water cane, marsh oats, etc., make up the vegetable matter. Food matter is never probed for in the mud, as is the custom with woodcocks and shorebirds, but instead is plucked from the surface of the water or mud by the nimble bird.

NEST AND NESTING HABITS

The nest is ordinarily a slightly raised platform—1 inch to 3 inches above the water surface—of matted reeds and other vegetation, often with surrounding vegetation bent over the top in a concealing manner.

EGGS AND INCUBATION

Most often six to ten creamy beige (sometimes faintly olive) eggs are laid. Irregular spots and blotches appear toward either end of the eggs, which are smooth and faintly glossy. The eggs average about 1.6 inches by 1.2 inches (42mm x 30mm).

Incubation is divided equally between the parent birds and lasts for about 21 to 24 days.

Field sketches of various rails made at Cape Haze, Placida, Florida, March 22, 1964.

Virginia Rail
Rallus limicola
King Rail
Rallus elegans
Clapper Rail
Rallus longirostris
Florida clapper Rail
Rallus longirostris scottii
♀
Cape Haze Florida
March 22, 1964
virginia
Rail
K. E. Karalus

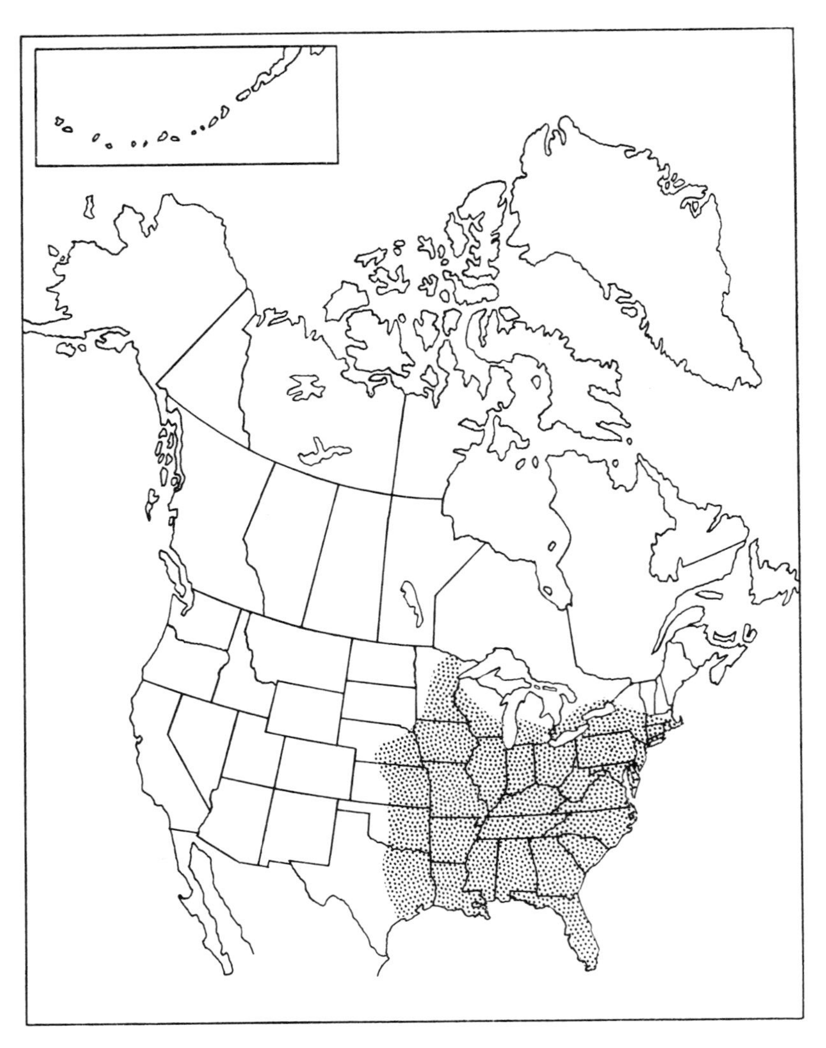

KING RAIL

Rallus elegans elegans Audubon

YOUNG

A heavy coat of thick, short, black fluffy down covers the hatchling. By the November following its hatching, the fledgling bird has acquired virtually adult plumage, though the full richness of adult coloration is not acquired until the next August's molt. When all the young have hatched, they follow their parent birds dutifully about the marsh, quickly learning to snatch up and devour small insects and water life, along with the tender shoots of plants and some seeds. They become very quick in their movements quite soon and, if unexpectedly encountered, scatter in such a manner that one might well mistake them for a group of mice disappearing into the cover.

MIGRATION

In the fall, the King Rail withdraws from most of its breeding range in North America north of Mexico except for southern Texas, southern Mississippi and Alabama, southernmost Georgia, and all of Florida, though with concentrations heavier in the south than in the north. The migrational flights, usually nocturnal, leave the north in about mid-September and return in April.

COMMON NAME

Northern Clapper Rail
(Color Plate XXV)

SCIENTIFIC NAME

Rallus longirostris crepitans Gmelin. The Latin *crepitans* signifies clattering, and *longirostris,* long-billed.

OTHER COMMON OR COLLOQUIAL NAMES

SALT-MARSH HEN For habitat and appearance.
SEDGE HEN Same.

NORTHERN CLAPPER RAIL
Rallus longirostris crepitans Gmelin

BASIC SUBSPECIFIC DIFFERENCES

This essentially grayish subspecies is more muted in coloration than the King Rail and lacks the reddishness which marks that species. As an adult the Northern Clapper Rail is variegated in color, with dark brownish to greenish-brown streaks. The same colors, but paler, appear underneath, becoming more grayish-white on throat and sides of breast, without chestnut shadings. The flanks, undertail, and underwings are deep gray with a brownish cast, sharply and narrowly barred with white. The primaries, secondaries, and tail are dull brown shading to gray and without ruddiness. The eyelids and the short line over the eye are grayish-white. Hatchlings are sooty black and juveniles are much like the adults but dusky white below.

The Northern Clapper Rail is particularly fond of salt marshes and is usually found in coastal areas.

LENGTH AND WINGSPAN

The average length of the Northern Clapper Rail is about 15 inches (386mm) and average wingspan is 20 inches (513mm).

EGGS

Six to fifteen buffy-white eggs are laid. These are randomly speckled and blotched with brown and faint lavender. In size they average 1.75 inches x 1.1 inches (45mm x 29mm).

COMMON NAME

Louisiana Clapper Rail
(Subspecies Sketch 9)

SCIENTIFIC NAME

Rallus longirostris saturatus Ridgway. The Latin *saturatus* signifies dark-colored.

BASIC SUBSPECIFIC DIFFERENCES

Generally, the Louisiana Clapper Rail is similar to the Northern Clapper Rail in shape and size, but with considerably darker coloration. On the back and upper areas it is a dark olive-gray and quite broadly striped in dark brown to black. The underside lacks the lightness of the Northern Clapper Rail and is a dull cinnamon-red.

LOUISIANA CLAPPER RAIL

Rallus longirostris saturatus Ridgway

9. LOUISIANA CLAPPER RAIL

Rallus longirostris saturatus Ridgway. Gulfport, Louisiana. A.O.U. Number 211a

K. E. Karalus

COMMON NAME

Florida Clapper Rail
(Subspecies Sketch 10)

SCIENTIFIC NAME

Rallus longirostris scottii Sennett. Named after W. E. D. Scott, who discovered the bird.

OTHER COMMON OR COLLOQUIAL NAMES

BLACK CLAPPER
SCOTT'S CLAPPER

FLORIDA CLAPPER RAIL
Rallus longirostris scottii Sennett

BASIC SUBSPECIFIC DIFFERENCES

This common Florida subspecies is just a bit smaller than either the Northern Clapper Rail or the King Rail, but the principal difference is in the coloration. On its upper portions, this bird is a deep sooty gray, shading into blackish and only a slight edging of olivaceous on the feather rims. On the underside the bird is very dark gray with just a faint touch of cinnamon. As in similar rails, the flanks, axillars, and undertail are well barred with white. The wing coverts are olive-brown to buffy-brown.

---

10. FLORIDA CLAPPER RAIL

Rallus longirostris scottii Sennett. Englewood, Florida. A.O.U. Number 211b

from life
Button wood Rookery
Lemon Bay Conservancy Land
Englewood Florida
May 1-1975

COMMON NAME

Wayne's Clapper Rail
(Subspecies Sketch 11)

SCIENTIFIC NAME

Rallus longirostris waynei Brewster.

BASIC SUBSPECIFIC DIFFERENCES

This subspecies is about the size of the Florida Clapper Rail and its range overlaps that of *Rallus longirostris scottii,* with some intergrading no doubt occurring. However, in general, Wayne's Clapper Rail does not have the overall conspicuous darkness of the Florida Clapper Rail. Its upper parts are generally much more grayish and the underparts, especially the breast, much lighter.

WAYNE'S CLAPPER RAIL

Rallus longirostris waynei Brewster

11. WAYNE'S CLAPPER RAIL

Rallus longirostris waynei Brewster. Cedar Key, Florida. A.O.U. Number 211c

K. E. Karalus
Cedar Key florida
Nov 16-1976

COMMON NAME

Mangrove Clapper Rail
(Subspecies Sketch 12)

SCIENTIFIC NAME

Rallus longirostris insularum Brooks. *Insularum* is Latin for of islands.

BASIC SUBSPECIFIC DIFFERENCES

The Mangrove Clapper Rail is very similar in size and markings to Wayne's Clapper Rail, except that the feathers of the upper parts of the Mangrove Clapper Rail are considerably more broadly edged with gray. The area beneath and behind the eyes on the sides of the head is a light neutral gray and the sides of the neck and the breast have a wash of the same coloration.

MANGROVE CLAPPER RAIL

Rallus longirostris insularum Brooks

12. MANGROVE CLAPPER RAIL

Rallus longirostris insularum Brooks. Big Pine Key, Florida. A.O.U. Number 211d

K. E. Karalus
Big Pine Key
Florida
10 June 1973

COMMON NAME

California Clapper Rail
(Subspecies Sketch 13)

SCIENTIFIC NAME

Rallus longirostris obsoletus Ridgway. The Latin *obsoletus,* meaning obsolete, refers to the lack of those markings on the upper parts that characterize the King Rail, *Rallus elegans elegans.*

BASIC SUBSPECIFIC DIFFERENCES

One of the better-marked subspecies, the California Clapper Rail is unique in that it has the characteristics of the Northern Clapper Rail, *Rallus longirostris crepitans,* on the upper parts, and the characteristics of the King Rail on the underparts.

CALIFORNIA CLAPPER RAIL

Rallus longirostris obsoletus Ridgway

13. CALIFORNIA CLAPPER RAIL

Rallus longirostris obsoletus Ridgway. Los Angeles, California. A.O.U. Number 210

K.E. Karalus

COMMON NAME

Yuma Clapper Rail
(Subspecies Sketch 14)

SCIENTIFIC NAME

Rallus longirostris yumanensis Dickey.

BASIC SUBSPECIFIC DIFFERENCES

This rail, which is confined strictly to freshwater areas (as opposed to other California rails, which inhabit tidal estuarial salt-marsh systems), is similar in appearance to the Light-Footed Rail, *Rallus longirostris levipes,* but its general color is duller and with more of an olive tone on the upper wing and tail coverts; it also has paler underparts and more slender legs and beak.

NORTH AMERICAN DISTRIBUTION

The Yuma Clapper Rail is non-migratory and has a very limited distribution. It occurs only in the fresh or (rarely) brackish marshes of the Colorado River in both California and Arizona, from Laguna Dam to Yuma and at the southeastern end of Salton Sea.

YUMA CLAPPER RAIL

Rallus longirostris yumanensis Dickey

14. YUMA CLAPPER RAIL

Rallus longirostris yumanensis Dickey. Grand Junction, Colorado. A.O.U. Number 210a

COMMON NAME

Light-Footed Rail
(Subspecies Sketch 15)

SCIENTIFIC NAME

Rallus longirostris levipes Bangs.

BASIC SUBSPECIFIC DIFFERENCES

Despite its name, the Light-Footed Rail is not really any more light-footed than any other of the rails. It most resembles the California Clapper Rail—*Rallus longirostris obsoletus*—but its beak is more slender, and it is generally darker than *obsoletus.* The breast and the sides of the neck are rusty in coloration rather than grayish, with a tinge of rufous. The ground color of the flanks is darker and the superciliary streak is white instead of rusty.

NORTH AMERICAN DISTRIBUTION

This is another of the non-migratory rails. It resides in the salt marshes and, occasionally, brackish or freshwater marshes of southern California from Hueneme in the north (formerly Santa Barbara) to San Diego and southward.

LIGHT-FOOTED RAIL
Rallus longirostris levipes Bangs

15. LIGHT-FOOTED RAIL
Rallus longirostris levipes Bangs. Rosario, Baja California. A.O.U. Number 210.1

K.E. Karalus

COMMON NAME

Virginia Rail
(Color Plate XXVI)

SCIENTIFIC NAME

Rallus limicola limicola Vieillot. *Limicola* is Latin for mud-dweller.

LENGTH AND WINGSPAN

Average length of the Virginia Rail is about 9.5 inches (245mm) and its average wingspan is 13.5 inches (348mm).

VOICE

The very distinctive voice of the Virginia Rail is often heard, even though the bird itself is very infrequently seen. The sound has a strong metallic timbre and might well be compared to that of an anvil being struck by a light hammer. The Virginia Rail's call is best rendered as *ku-tic ku-tic ku-tic ku-tic.* This is sometimes repeated incessantly day and night.

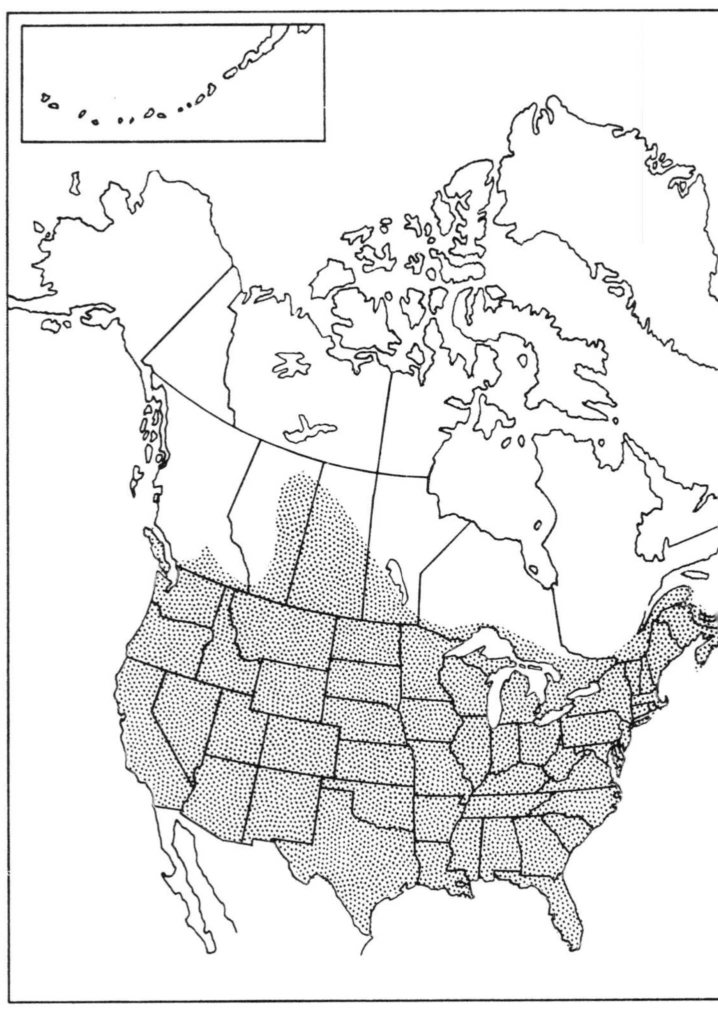

VIRGINIA RAIL

Rallus limicola limicola Vieillot

EGGS

Normally there are six to ten eggs in a clutch, though sometimes as many as a dozen or as few as five. They are generally a pale buff, sometimes with a pinkish cast and liberally to sparingly sprinkled with blotches, spots, and streaks of dark brown to reddish-brown.

SORA

GENUS: *PORZANA* Vieillot
SPECIES: *CAROLINA* (Linnaeus)

COMMON NAME

Sora (or Sora Rail)
(Color Plate XXVII)

SCIENTIFIC NAME

Porzana carolina (Linnaeus).

OTHER COMMON OR COLLOQUIAL NAMES

CAROLINA CRAKE From its most common distributional area and from the sound of its voice.

CAROLINA RAIL Distributional nomenclature.

CHICKEN-BILLED RAIL For the character of its beak.

COMMON RAIL Because it is the most common and most widely distributed rail in North America.

LITTLE AMERICAN WATER HEN Descriptive.

MEADOW CHICKEN After its habitat and, to some extent, after its general appearance.

ORTOLAN After the Italian and French (and derived from the Latin *hortulanus*), relating to a garden; the true ortolan is *Emberiza hortulana,* a European bunting deemed a delicacy by gourmets, which is also true of the Sora.

LENGTH AND WINGSPAN

The Sora's average length is about 8.5 inches (219mm) and its wingspan averages about 12.5 inches (322mm).

CRESTS, PLUMAGE, ANNUAL MOLT

There are no particularly elongated or exceptional plumes and no crest. The adult birds undergo an incomplete molt, prenuptially, between January and March, but this molt involves only the contour plumage. Another molt, this one complete, occurs postnuptially beginning in July and ending in September.

VOICE

The call of the Sora is a piglike *oink-oink,* and a loud, descending warbling whistle.

COLORATION AND MARKINGS: ADULT

The upper parts are a light sepia well marked with black patches and narrow white streakings. The underparts are essentially a neutral gray; while the flanks are very distinctly marked with narrow, back-curved barrings of white. The undertail and underwing are dingy white. The crown is very dark, as are the face, chin, and lores. A dark, broad stripe (usually gray in the female and black in the male) runs down the throat. A light line originates at the base of the beak, runs over the eyes, and trails down the back sides of the head, fading out gradually. The beak is yellow and rather chickenlike in form.

COLORATION AND MARKINGS: JUVENILE

Much like the adults except that the underparts are mainly white and there is no black on the throat.

FOOD AND FEEDING HABITS

The primary foods seem to be small mollusks or gastropods of the marsh, along with aquatic insects and their larvae and, to a lesser extent, seeds and the tender shoots of some young vegetation. Occasionally the bird will eat small tadpoles or earthworms and evidently at some times of the year caterpillars are important in the diet. In autumn, as seeds ripen, this sort of vegetation becomes important in the overall diet, too.

NEST AND NESTING HABITS

The nest is very much like that of other rails. It is ordinarily constructed a few inches to a foot above the water level in densely reeded or rushed areas of the marsh. The fibers of the nest are interwoven with the surrounding grasses and the whole is rather haphazardly concealed by a canopy of grasses bent over the nest. The actual nest is about 6 inches in diameter, with an inner cavity about 3 inches across and a couple of inches deep. Quite frequently a small runway of grasses leading the last yard or two to the nest will be constructed.

EGGS AND INCUBATION

Ordinarily there are between eight and fourteen eggs to each nesting. These eggs range from a reddish to a yellowish beige, with this ground color overlaid with irregular streakings and spottings of brown, chestnut, and dark olive. They are smooth and quite glossy —much glossier, in fact, than those of the Virginia Rail. The average egg size is about 1.25 inches x .9 inch (32mm x 22mm).

Because there are so many eggs in the nest, the Sora, as a rule, puts the eggs in two layers, but even then the bird is hard put to cover and incubate well all that are in the clutch. Both parents incubate, evidently about equally, and incubation begins with the first, second, or third egg laid. Hatching is therefore staggered. The incubation period is fourteen days. As the first eggs hatch, one parent takes the young off, leaving the other parent to continue incubation.

YOUNG

As with most other rail species, the downy chicks of the Sora are black and

---

Sora, *Porzana carolina* (Linnaeus). Field sketches made at Cape Haze, Placida, Florida, September 14, 1956. In the nest in which the female on the lower right was found were two normal eggs, plus a third that was one third larger than the others (the latter was in fact two eggs bound into one).

♂
K. E. Karalus

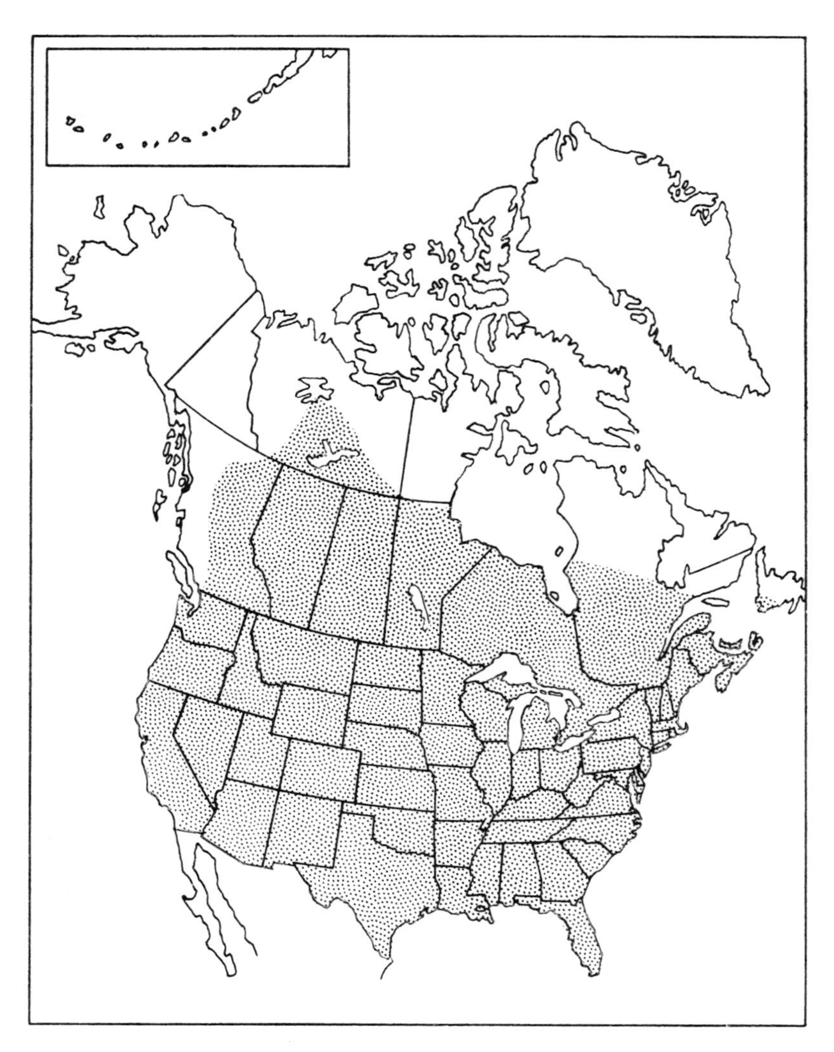

SORA

Porzana carolina (Linnaeus)

fluffy and very soon after hatching are able to move about and follow the parent birds. The only real difference between the down covering of the Sora and that of other rails is its glossiness and the fact that there are some stiff and usually curly bright yellow hairs on the chin. Full adult plumage is assumed by the first postnuptial complete molt, when the bird is about sixteen months old.

NORTH AMERICAN DISTRIBUTION

The Sora is one of the most common and widely distributed rails in all of North America.

YELLOW RAIL

GENUS: *COTURNICOPS* Gray
SPECIES: *NOVEBORACENSIS* (Gemlin)
SUBSPECIES: *noveboracensis* (Gemlin)

♀
white wing patch
visible only when flushed
which is rare
K. E. Karalus

COMMON NAME

Yellow Rail
(Color Plate XXVIII)

SCIENTIFIC NAME

Coturnicops noveboracensis noveboracensis (Gmelin). From *coturnicops,* meaning quail-like, and *noveboracensis,* meaning New York.

BASIC SPECIES DIFFERENCES

Slightly smaller than the Sora, the Yellow Rail, as its name suggests, is basically yellowish, especially on the underside and flank plumage, where the Sora is gray; it also lacks the blackness of face and lores that the Sora shows. Instead of red eyes, as the Sora has, its irides are yellowish.

There is a very basic quail-like appearance to the Yellow Rail when it is afoot, although this similarity vanishes as the bird takes wing, since its weak, fluttery flight pattern, like that of the other rails, has no quail-like quality. Basically in coloration it is streaked with blackish and brownish yellow on the upper parts, and thickly marked with narrow white semicircles and transverse barrings. The underparts are a pale brownish-yellow, deepest on the breast and fading on the belly. Many of the breast feathers are tipped in black. The flanks are generally black with numerous barrings of white. The lining of the wings and the secondaries is white. A dark brownish stripe is under each eye. The average length of the Yellow Rail is 6.4 inches (164mm) and its average wingspan is 10 inches (254mm).

Although its distribution is quite wide on the continent, it is nowhere nearly as abundant as the Sora.

YELLOW RAIL

Coturnicops noveboracensis noveboracensis (Gmelin)

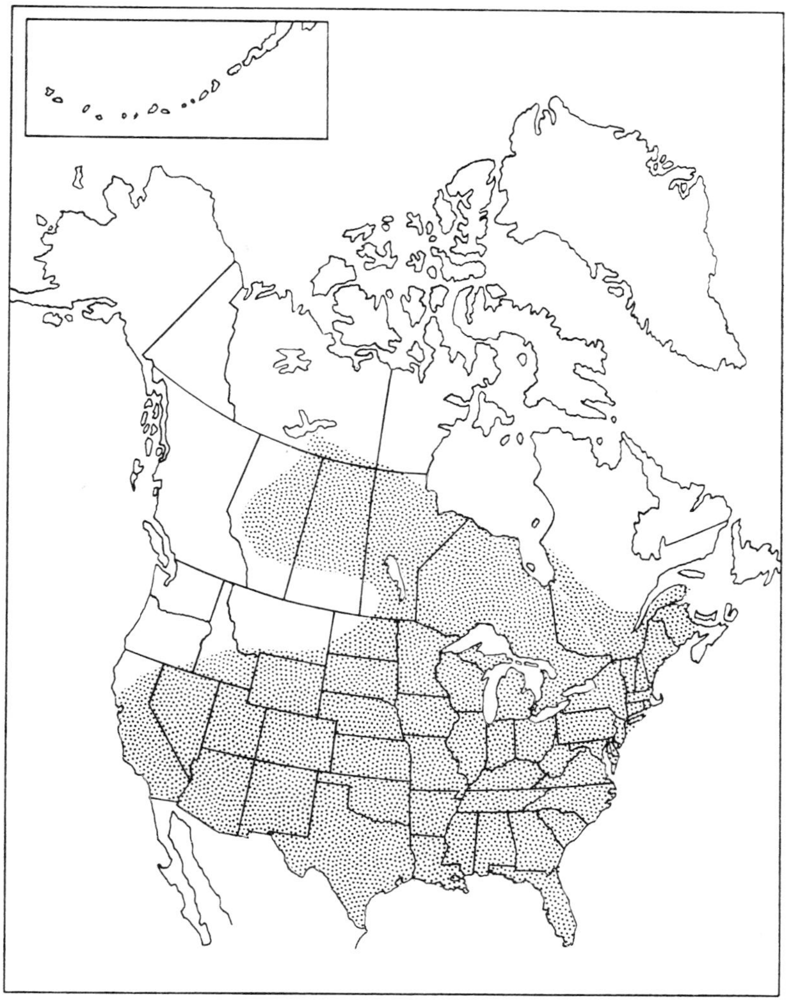

EGGS

The usual clutch contains seven to ten eggs. These are a buffy warm brown with reddish-brown to dark brown spots and blotches, mostly at the larger end.

Yellow Rail, *Coturnicops noveboracensis noveboracensis* (Gmelin).

LATERALLUS RAILS

GENUS:	*LATERALLUS* Gray
SPECIES:	*JAMAICENSIS* (Gmelin)
SUBSPECIES:	*jamaicensis* (Gmelin)
	Black Rail
	coturniculus (Ridgway)
	Farallon Rail

Laterallus ♂
jamaicensis
coturniculus
Point Reyes
California oct 29
1913
one specimen observe
near Dayton museum
of Natural History
Dayton Ohio
oct 1974
Englewood florida
March 1973
Chick
Karl E. Karalus

COMMON NAME

Black Rail
(Color Plate XXIX)

SCIENTIFIC NAME

Laterallus jamaicensis jamaicensis (Gmelin). From *laterallus,* a rail.

OTHER COMMON OR COLLOQUIAL NAMES

LITTLE BLACK CRAKE
LITTLE BLACK RAIL
JAMAICAN CRAKE
JAMAICAN RAIL

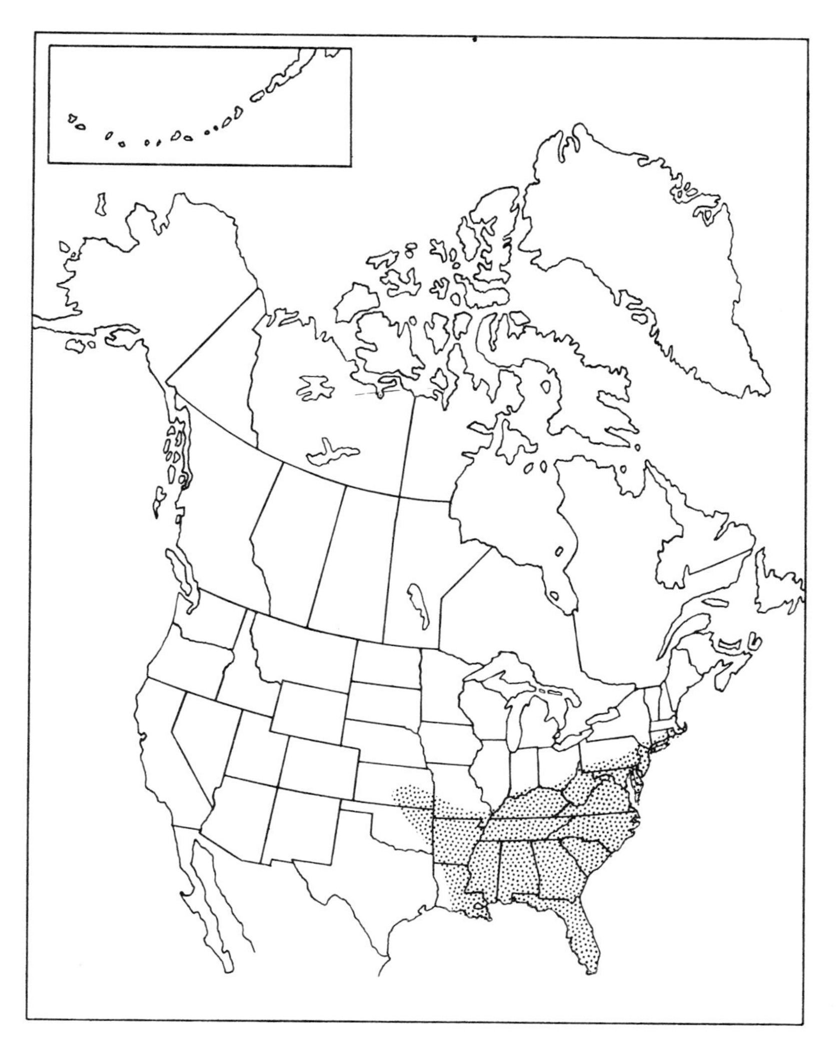

BLACK RAIL
Laterallus jamaicensis jamaicensis (Gmelin)

BASIC SPECIES DIFFERENCES

A very small rail, no longer than a large sparrow. The crown is black, the nape and upper back are a deep red-brown, and the lower back a dark brown, flecked with white. The beak is black. Young birds are similar to the adults except that they are paler on the underside and white on the throat. The crown is brownish rather than black. Not terribly abundant, yet not as rare as it was once thought to be, an impression due to the extreme secretiveness of the bird in most circumstances.

Black and Farallon Rails (*Laterallus jamaicensis jamaicensis* [Gmelin] and *Laterallus jamaicensis coturniculus* [Ridgway]).

EGGS

Quite different from those of either the Sora or the Yellow Rail. The usual clutch is from six to nine eggs which are 1.1 inches x .8 inch (27mm x 21mm) on the average. The basic coloration is cream-white with fine cinnamon to drab brown speckles on the large end of the egg.

COMMON NAME

Farallon Rail
(Color Plate XXIX)

SCIENTIFIC NAME

Laterallus jamaicensis coturniculus (Ridgway).

OTHER COMMON OR COLLOQUIAL NAMES

CALIFORNIA BLACK RAIL (infrequent)
FARALLON BLACK CRAKE
FARALLON BLACK RAIL

FARALLON RAIL
Laterallus jamaicensis coturniculus (Ridgway)

BASIC SUBSPECIFIC DIFFERENCES

Even smaller than the Black Rail, *Laterallus jamaicensis jamaicensis,* the Farallon Rail has an average wing length of only 2.5 inches (64mm). In almost all respects it is very similar to the Black Rail, except that it is much more uniform in its coloration and does not have the white specks which are so significant on the Black Rail. The bird is very rarely seen and very limited in its population north of Mexico.

NORTH AMERICAN DISTRIBUTION

The subspecies is known to breed in a very limited scope in the southwesternmost point of California, specifically in the immediate area of San Diego. There was one record of a nesting near Chino, California. During the winter, it has been known to migrate coastally as far north as San Francisco. It is also found inland casually as far as Stockton, Riverside, and the Salton Sea in southern California.

COMMON GALLINULE

GENUS: *GALLINULA* Brisson
SPECIES: *CHLOROPUS* (Linnaeus)
SUBSPECIES: *cachinnans* Bangs

COMMON NAME

Common Gallinule
(Color Plate XXX)

SCIENTIFIC NAME

Gallinula chloropus cachinnans Bangs. From the Latin, *gallinula,* meaning little hen; *chloropus,* meaning green-footed; and *cachinnans,* meaning laughing.

OTHER COMMON OR COLLOQUIAL NAMES

MUD HEN A term descriptive of its habitat but one more commonly applied to the American Coot and certain of the rails, such as the King Rail and Northern Clapper Rail.

SHAPE AT REST AND IN FLIGHT

This is a long-legged, short-bodied, and relatively short-necked marsh bird with a chickenlike beak and a rather sloping forehead marked by a scarlet unfeathered frontal plate. The toes are very long and with a considerable span. Generally, the tail is held upright.

In flight, the wings are rather short and rounded. The tail is short.

The flight of *Gallinula chloropus cachinnans* is not really very strong and has an excessively flapping, fluttery quality. If the flight is short, which is ordinarily the case, the legs will dangle very awkwardly below. On longer flights the legs will extend back and be tight against the abdomen, extending far beyond the short tail. On long flights the head becomes more outstretched in front and the wingbeat somewhat smoother and stronger, with less visible effort.

LENGTH AND WINGSPAN

The Common Gallinule has an average length of 13.1 inches (336mm) and a wingspan which averages 20.8 inches (533mm).

LEGS, FEET, AND CLAWS

The feet, of a beautiful lime hue, are narrow-boned with long, slender toes. The legs are the same shade as the feet up to the first joint, above which they turn a shade of orange. The toes are marked by an evident (although only very slight) marginal membrane.

EYES

The Common Gallinule's irides are generally red, sometimes shading into a chestnut-brownish.

CRESTS, PLUMAGE, ANNUAL MOLT

There are no particular plumes of note, nor any crest. The adults have a complete molt, usually beginning in early August and lasting through most of September or into early October. There is also a partial prenuptial molt occurring in the spring, but neither molt brings much of a difference in coloration.

COLORATION AND MARKINGS: ADULT

Most often the very tip of the beak will have a faint yellowish or even greenish-yellow cast, but the remainder is bright red, and this scarlet coloration is clearly offset by the slate-black coloration of the entire head and throat. This slate-black shades to a deep coot-like neutral gray on the foreback and belly. The mid and rear back is very dark brown and the wings fuscous. The middle undertail coverts are black and the outer ones are white (the latter appear as the bird moves as a couple of white patches). A ring of scarlet encircles the leg just above the heel and the rest of the tarsus (or shank) and foot is greenish.

COLORATION AND MARKINGS: JUVENILE

Very similar to the adult, though less intense generally. The throat is white and the underparts are more or less mixed with white. The crown is a medium brown. Otherwise gray.

HABITAT AND ROOSTING

The Common Gallinule is strictly confined to swampy areas, preferably where muddy conditions provide a good growth of lily pads and other surface vegetation upon which the bird can walk and search for food. It is less often seen in marsh areas that are strictly of a saw grass, rush, or reed character. The edges of slow rivers and bayous, especially where they are broadly muddy or overgrown with water hyacinth, are especially favored. Roosting is sometimes done in heavy marsh vegetation and at other times in dense brush which is contiguous to the water.

FOOD AND FEEDING HABITS

Practically all the food eaten by the Common Gallinule is found amid floating or surface vegetation in water where there is little or no current. Popular belief had it that *Gallinula chloropus cachinnans* was essentially insectivorous, but recent studies have shown this is not the case; the bird is, in fact, about 85 to 90 per cent herbivorous, with the remainder comprised of aquatic insects and occasionally mollusks or gastropods. The vegetation eaten is primarily tender new shoots, rootlets, leaves, and seeds of various water plants.

COURTSHIP AND MATING

When the male approaches the female he wishes to win, they are ordinarily in the water, either standing on floating vegetation or swimming. Usually it is the latter, at least for the male. As he nears her, he begins uttering his *tikka-tikka-tikka-tikka* mating call, at the same time holding his head so near the water surface that occasionally the beak touches the water and his neck is curved in a manner curiously like a swan's. His wings open partially and he raises and spreads his short tail to its utmost, exposing as much as possible the white undertail coverts, which seem to be the most important breeding feathers. He swims with his head bobbing back and forth, much in the manner of the American Coot. He paddles back and forth before her, drawing ever closer, occasionally raising his head high. At last, though no apparent visible or audible sign is given to signify her acceptance, he abruptly swims to her and they move off together into heavier cover to copulate. The copulation, and occasionally the male's display, are repeated daily for at least three or four days, at the end of which time the pair gets ready to build their nest.

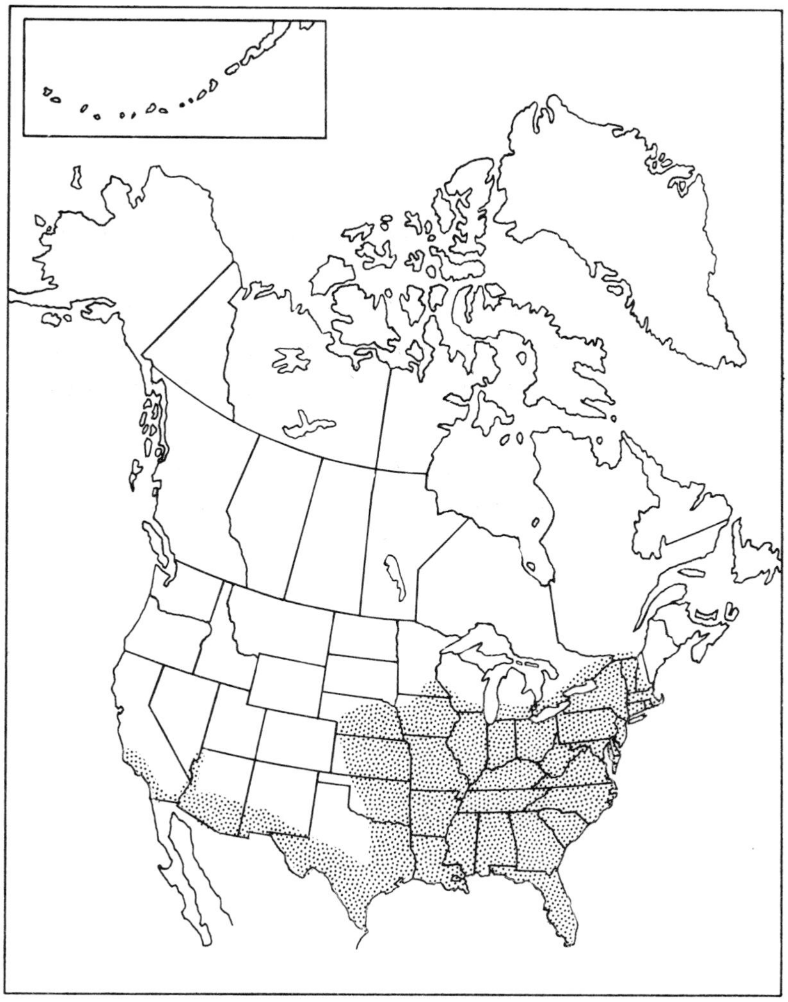

COMMON GALLINULE

Gallinula chloropus cachinnans Bangs

NEST AND NESTING HABITS

Ordinarily the nest is built amid dense stands of reeds or rushes, but with close access to reasonably open water. The nest is a dense interweaving of reeds to a height of about 8 inches above the water surface. The diameter of the nest is about 20 inches, but with an inner cavity diameter of only about 7 inches and a depth of less than 3 inches. Such a nest is usually anchored and often has an interwoven reedwork pathway leading to the nest from the water.

EGGS AND INCUBATION

Most often there are from eight to twelve eggs, which vary from a pale buffy-olive to a distinct cinnamon-buff in their ground color. On this ground color are numerous irregular spots, dots, blotches and irregular streakings of dark brown, cinnamon-red, and olive-drab. The eggs are smooth, but with little or no gloss. In size they average about 1.5 inches x 1.2 inches (40mm x 31mm).

The incubation, by both parents, commences with the first egg, and lasts for twenty-one days.

YOUNG

The downy young bird has only a few hairlike feathers on its head, but the remainder of the bird is covered with a thick and soft down of glossy greenish-black on the upper parts and dull black on the underparts. At this time the skin at the base of the beak is bright scarlet and there is a sharp spur protruding at the bend of the wing, which the young bird uses in climbing through dense cover. It is capable of leaving the nest and swimming shortly after being hatched. Curly white hairs occur frequently on the throats of the hatchlings. Full adult plumage is not acquired until the first postnupital molt the next year, when the bird is about fourteen or fifteen months old.

PURPLE GALLINULE

GENUS: *PORPHYRULA* Blyth
SPECIES: *MARTINICA* (Linnaeus)

COMMON NAME

Purple Gallinule
(Color Plate XXXI)

SCIENTIFIC NAME

Porphyrula martinica (Linnaeus). From the Latin *porphyra,* meaning purple.

BASIC SPECIES DIFFERENCES

In size, shape, and bearing, the Purple Gallinule is virtually identical to the Common Gallinule, but the immense difference is in the coloration. The Purple Gallinule is one of North America's most gorgeously colored birds. Sometimes called "Blue Pete," the Purple Gallinule has a beak much like a chicken's in shape, but bright yellow at the tip and bright red for the remaining two thirds of its length. The frontal shield, instead of continuing red, as in the case of the Common Gallinule, is a light pastel blue. The head and underparts are a very distinct, eye-catching purple with a certain amount of gloss if not true iridescence. The hind part of the bird from mid-back and the wings are a dark to very deep green, often shading into bluish-green. The legs and feet are greenish-yellow, but with more yellowish apparent than in the greenish-yellow legs of the Common Gallinule. The undertail coverts are white and, importantly, show as a very prominent white patch when the tail is raised.

PURPLE GALLINULE
Porphyrula martinica (Linnaeus)

The immature birds are less vividly colored, with the top of the head a warm sepia color, the throat white, and the breast a pale buff to tawny. The entire back is solidly greenish-brown except at the rump, which is a clove brown. Downy young are an unbroken greenish-black in coloration.

AMERICAN COOT

SUBFAMILY: *FULICINAE*
GENUS: *FULICA* Linnaeus
SPECIES: *AMERICANA* Gmelin
SUBSPECIES: *americana* Gmelin

COMMON NAME

American Coot
(Color Plate XXXII)

SCIENTIFIC NAME

Fulica americana americana Gmelin. From the Latin *fuligo,* meaning soot, or a sooty color, referring to the general coloration of the bird.

OTHER COMMON OR COLLOQUIAL NAMES

Because it is so common and so frequently seen, the American Coot is a very familiar American bird and, as a result, is known by a great number of common or colloquial names. Most are of obvious origin and some of the most frequently used names are

BLUE PETER
COOT
CROW-BILL
CROW-DUCK
FLUSTERER
HEN-BILL
IVORY-BILLED COOT
LA FOULQUE AMÉRICAINE
MARSH HEN
MEADOW HEN
MOOR HEN
MUD COOT
MUD HEN
PELICK
POND CROW
POND HEN
PULL-DOO (POULE D'EAU)
SEA CROW
SHUFFLER
SPLATTERER
WATER CHICKEN
WATER HEN
WHITE-BILL
WHITE-BILL COOT
WHITE-BELLIED MUD HEN

SHAPE AT REST AND IN FLIGHT

The American Coot is rather ducklike when resting on the water surface as it ordinarily does, but easily distinguished from a duck by its white beak, very much like that of a chicken. When standing on the ground, its legs are slightly longer than those of a duck and the toes are lobed rather than webbed.

It is even more ducklike when in full strong flight, but differs from a duck when first taking off, at which time it begins flapping and running along the water surface until it is actually stepping on the water surface faster and faster until the rapidly beating wings can lift a body which seems too heavy. Often the American Coot will seem to give up before takeoff speed is reached and simply settle back onto the water surface, or dive if there is danger. The wings are are set well back in flight, like those of a duck. The neck is well extended, also in ducklike fashion, but the beak, instead of being pointed straight forward, is pointed slightly downward. The feet extend behind the tail a short way, with

(Overleaf) American Coot, *Fulica americana americana* Gmelin.

Near Dayton
Museum of
Natural History

April 1975
Still Water River
Dayton Ohio
Montgomery Co.

the toes pointing upward and helping to serve as a rudder to aid the tiny and ineffective tail. In local flight, the altitude is quite low, often just above the water surface. On longer flights, especially migrations, the flight is high and quite frequently in company with flocks of ducks.

LENGTH AND WINGSPAN

The American Coot has an average length of just over 15 inches (386mm) and its wingspan averages about 25.5 inches (653mm).

BEAK

The beak ranges from pure milk white to a sort of fleshy color, often with a clayish cast. It is marked with reddish-black near the tip and at the base of the frontal plate.

LEGS, FEET, AND CLAWS

The legs and feet range from dull grayish-green to a rather bright yellowish-green, with black claws. All of the toes are lobed, facilitating better swimming than is possible for the gallinules, yet also permitting pad-walking, an ability shared with the gallinules. The hind-toe lobe is rudimentary.

EYES

The irides are a bright carmine at all seasons.

CRESTS, PLUMAGE, ANNUAL MOLT

Beginning in August, adults have a complete molt, which is usually finished before the end of September. A rather limited partial molt occurs prenuptially early each spring.

VOICE

The American Coot is capable of a wide range of vocal utterances, most of them far from melodious. Some are simply guttural squawks and croakings. A few of the calls, however, have a somewhat pleasant sound. Foremost among these is a rather common early morning cooing sort of chatter that passes back and forth among them as they feed in the marsh fringe of open waters. There is also a less melodious clucking sound which is quite common and, less often, a heavy quack similar to that of a mallard duck.

COLORATION AND MARKINGS: ADULT

The plumage is generally a dark slate-gray in color, slightly paler on the underside and noticeably darker, almost to black, on the head and neck. The dark gray gets a sort of olivaceous cast on the back. The crissum, the edge of the wing, and the tips of the secondaries are white, but these markings are generally hidden except when the bird is in flight. The primaries are dusky gray except for the outer edge of the first, which is white. The tail is gray-black.

COLORATION AND MARKINGS: JUVENILE

The young are colored very much like the adults except that the grays and blacks are not as crisp; there is a more general dullness of tone and the overall coloration is slightly paler than in the adult. There is considerably more white or dingy white on the underparts than in the adult. The frontal shield at the base of the beak is not developed and the beak is dingy in its coloration and lacks the distinctive reddish spots seen in adult birds. Full adult plumage is acquired after the first postnuptial molt when the young bird is over a year old.

HABITAT AND ROOSTING

The marsh fringe is the American Coot's favored habitat, because of the plentiful food and security the marsh provides. Roosting is normally in small open pockets in the reed or rush banks and usually occurs in groups of from six to twenty birds, though the flocks grow much larger as migrational periods near. In migration and on wintering grounds, the bird often associates in large numbers with diving ducks.

FOOD AND FEEDING HABITS

The great majority of the American Coot's food is vegetative—primarily seeds, tender grass sprouts, and some different sorts of greenery. Wild celery, milfoil, corn, millet, various cereal grains—all these are food for the American Coot, along with occasional animal matter such as grasshoppers and other insects. Another item of the diet is green algae, which the American Coot seems to have a special fondness for at certain times. Occasionally it will eat tadpoles, snails, and small fish.

COURTSHIP AND MATING

Rivalry is very keen among the American Coots and reasonably serious fights between males during the courtship period are frequent. These fights are sometimes over territory and at other times to gain the acceptance of a female. In addition to fighting, the males will display before the females. Most often this amounts to the male swimming toward the female, his head and neck on the water surface, his wingtips raised high above the tail, and the ridiculous little tail itself spread and elevated so that the white markings on either side become very obvious. As he gets very near to her, the female, deciding in his favor, assumes the same position. When he gets to within a couple of feet of her, the male turns, shows his tail and starts slowly swimming away, encouraging her to follow. If she does not, he returns and repeats the act. When they are finally paired, the two birds will frequently swim directly toward one another, scatter droplets of water on each other, and then begin nuzzling and preening one another's neck and upper breast and back feathers.

NEST AND NESTING HABITS

Although the male stays close at hand, most of the nest construction is under-

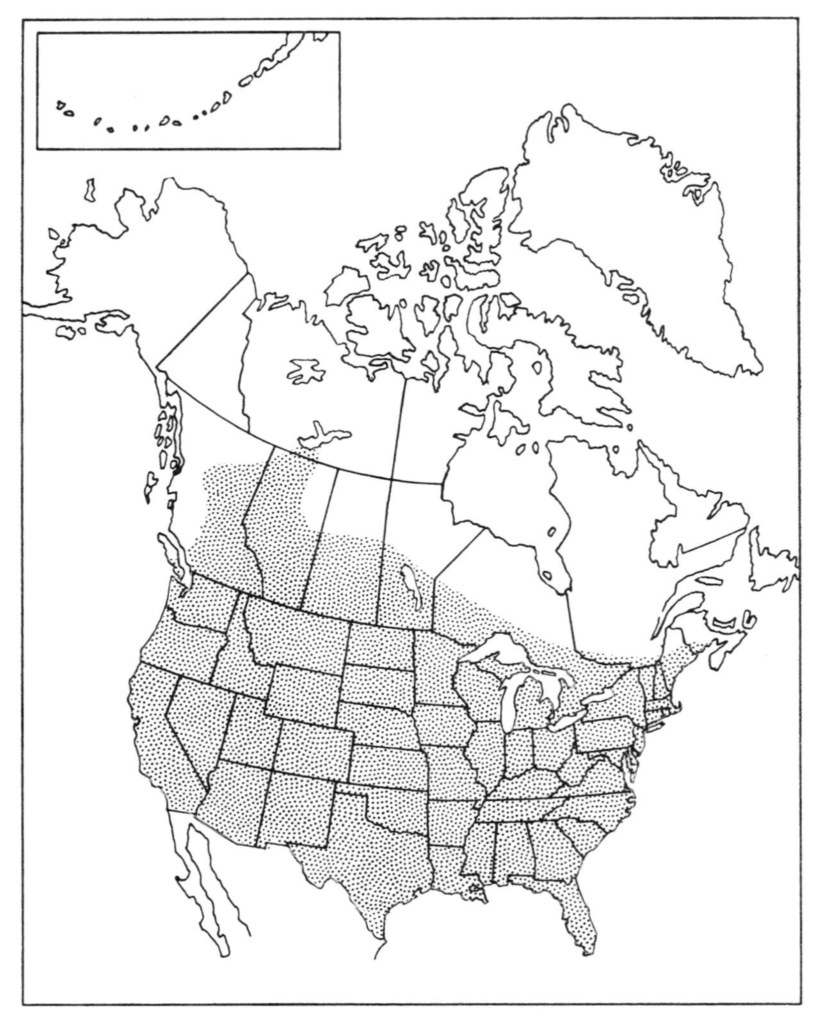

AMERICAN COOT

Fulica americana americana Gmelin

taken by the female. She starts the nest by gradually building up a platform of living reed stems, which she bends over and fastens down by interlacing them together. In this manner a nesting platform is eventually built up. It is quite firmly fastened to the growing reeds of the area and well woven into a substantial basket. The outside diameter of the completed nest is about 15 inches. The inner diameter, well lined with soft plant materials, is about 7 inches, with the egg basin of the nest fully 8 inches above the water.

EGGS AND INCUBATION

The usual number of eggs laid is from eight to sixteen, most commonly nine to eleven. They are a warm buffy color well covered with a multitude of tiny dots and blotches of dark brown and black over the entire surface. They are smooth with a slight gloss and in size they average about 1.9 inches x 1.3 inches (49mm x 34mm).

The incubation, shared by both parent birds, extends over a period of twenty-two days. Frequently the male will guard the female while she incubates, but rarely is the opposite true.

YOUNG

The downy young are strikingly colored but not really very pretty. They appear shaggy, with a body down coloration of black and scattered orange hairs here and there. There are also scattered hairlike feathers, some curly and some short and stiff and straight of pure yellow or pure white. The bald crown is very reddish. The hatchlings are quite precocious; they leave the nesting platform and begin swimming within an hour or so of emergence. By the end of just a few hours they can dive with remarkable skill and stay under water for a surprising length of time—upward of three minutes. The feet grow much too fast for the body, resulting in chicks with enormously oversized legs and feet. Not until it is over a year old, at the first postnuptial molt, does the young bird assume full adult plumage. Swimming or walking, it bobs its head—as does the adult—with each movement of the feet.

MIGRATION

American Coots are very hardy and, though they migrate long distances, they are among the last of the summer birds to leave the northernmost portions of their range in fall, and among the first to return in spring. Quite often they will not leave the northern lakes until forced to do so by the freezing of lake surfaces and the increasing scarcity of food. The birds come together into flocks numbering in the thousands and they literally darken the sky when they fly. In the dead of winter, they are rarely found north of the United States and, depending upon the severity of the winter, are often scarce in the northernmost tier of states.

ECONOMIC INFLUENCE

While American Coots cannot be considered a top-notch game bird, they are nevertheless on the migratory waterfowl game lists and are hunted extensively each year. They travel with duck flocks quite often but, since they are not as maneuverable as ducks, nor as wary, nor as fast in flight, they are often killed when the ducks are not.

BIBLIOGRAPHY

It is not possible to list here every source consulted in the preparation of *The Wading Birds of North America.* Oftentimes certain books, papers, theses, leaflets, and similar materials provided only a single minor datum which was incorporated into this volume; to list these, except in the most unusual of cases, would be virtually pointless. The following works, therefore, are those which we relied upon most heavily in the research of this book.

* * *

Allen, Robert P. "Additional Data on the Food of the Whooping Crane," *The Auk,* No. 71, Vol. II, page 198, April 1954

——— "The Whooping Crane," *National Audubon Society Research Report,* No. 3, xxvi, July 1952

American Ornithologists' *Union Check-list of North American Birds,* Fifth Edition, Lord Baltimore Press, Baltimore, Maryland, 1957

Applegarth, John H. "The Ecology of the California Clapper Rail on the South Arm of San Francisco Bay," AM thesis, Stanford University, 1938

Bancroft, Griffing "Northern Breeding Record for Reddish Egret," *The Auk,* Vol. 88, No. 2, page 429, April 1971

Bent, Arthur Cleveland "Life Histories of North American Marsh Birds," *U.S. National Museum Bulletin,* No. 35, Washington, 1926

Billard, Ruth S. "An Ecological Study of the Virginia Rail *(Rallus limicola limicola)* and the Sora *(Porzana carolina)* in Some Connecticut Swamps," MS thesis, Iowa State College, 1947

Blaker, D. "Behaviour of the Cattle Egret *Ardeola ibis,*" *The Ostrich,* Vol. 40, No. 3, September 1969

Campbell, R. Wayne "The Green Heron in British Columbia," *Syesis,* Vol. 5, 1972, and *Biological Abstracts,* Vol. 55, No. 9, 1973

Caslick, James W. "Sandhill Cranes in Yellowstone Park," *The Auk,* Vol. 72, No. 1, January 1955

Chapman, Frank L. *Handbook of Birds of Eastern North America,* D. Appleton Co., New York, 1929

Cottam, Clarence "Food of the Limpkin," *Wilson Bulletin,* Vol. 48, No. 1, March 1936

——— "Supplementary Notes on the Food of the Limpkin," *The Nautilus,* Vol. 55, No. 4, April 1942

Coues, Elliott *Key to North American Birds,* Fifth Edition, Vol. II, The Page Co., Boston, Mass., 1927

Crosby, Gilbert T. "Spread of the Cattle Egret in the Western Hemisphere," *Bird Banding,* Vol. 43, No. 3, July 1972

Dennis, Clifford J. "Observations on the Feeding Behaviour of the Great Blue Heron," *The Passenger Pigeon,* Vol. 33, No. 4, Winter 1971

DeVore, Jon E. "The Sandhill Crane in Tennessee," *The Migrant,* Vol. 43, No. 2, June 1972

Dinsmore, James J. "Foraging Success of Cattle Egrets, *Bubulcus ibis,*" *The American Midland Naturalist,* Vol. 89, No. 1, January 1973

Drewien, Roderick C., and Elwood C. Bizeau "Status and Distribution of Greater Sandhill Cranes in the Rocky Mountains," *Journal of Wildlife Management,* Vol. 38, No: 4, October 1974

Dunmire, William W. *Birds of the National Parks in Hawaii,* Hawaii Natural History Association, Honolulu, Hawaii, 1961

Engeling, Gus A. "King and Clapper Rail," *Texas Game and Fish,* Vol. 8, No. 11, October 1950

Ferrigno, Frederick "Some Aspects of the Nesting Biology, Population Dynamics, and Habitat Associations of the Clapper Rail," MS thesis, Rutgers University, 1966

Friedmann, Herbert, Ludlow Griscom, and Robert T. Moore *Distributional Check-list of the Birds of Mexico,* Cooper Ornithological Club, Pacific Coast Avifauna, No. 29, Part I and Part II, Berkeley, California, 1950

Friley, Charles E., Jr., Logan J. Bennett, and George O. Hendrickson "The American Coot in Iowa," *The Wilson Bulletin,* Vol. 50, No. 2, June 1938

Glahn, James F. "Study of Breeding Rails with Recorded Calls in North-Central Colorado," *The Wilson Bulletin,* Vol. 86, No. 3, September 1974

Godfrey, W. Earl *The Birds of Canada,* Queen's Printer, Ottawa, 1968

Gullion, Gordon W. "The Displays and Calls of the American Coot," *The Wilson Bulletin,* Vol. 64, No. 2, June 1952

——— "Observations on Molting of the American Coot," *The Condor,* Vol. 55, No. 2, March–April 1953

——— "The Reproductive Cycle of American Coots in California," *The Auk,* Vol. 71, No. 4, October 1954

——— "Sex and Age Determination in the American Coot," *Journal of Wildlife Management,* Vol. 16, No. 2, April 1952

——— "Territorial Behaviour of the American Coot," *The Condor,* Vol. 55, No. 4, July–August 1953

Hall, Henry M. "Wakulla Limpkins," *Audubon Magazine,* Vol. 52, No. 5, September–October 1950

Hamerstrom, F. N., Jr. "Central Wisconsin Crane Study," *The Wilson Bulletin,* Vol. 50, No. 3, September 1958

Hamilton, Anne P. "Roseate Spoonbills in Georgia and Tennessee in 1972," *The Oriole,* Vol. 40, Nos. 1 & 2, March–June 1975

Harmon, William Z. "Notes on Cranes," *The Florida Naturalist,* Vol. 27, No. 1, January 1954

Henika, Franklin S. "Sandhill Cranes in Wisconsin and Other Lake States," *Proceedings of the North American Wildlife Conference,* 1936

Henny, Charles J., and Michael R. Bethers "Population Ecology of the Great Blue Heron with Special Reference to Western Oregon," *The Canadian Field Naturalist,* Vol. 85, No. 3, July–September 1971

Hopkins, Milton N., Jr. "Does the Little Blue Heron Breed in the White Plumage?" *The Oriole,* Vol. 36, No. 4, December 1971

Hopkins, Milton N., Jr., and Philip G. Murton "Rookery Data from South Georgia," *The Oriole,* Vol. 34, No. 1, March 1969

Houston, C. Stuart "Longevity Record for Black-Crowned Night Heron: 16½ Years," *The Blue Jay,* Vol. 32, No. 3, September 1974

Howell, Arthur H. *Florida Bird Life,* Coward-McCann, Inc., New York, 1932

Jaeger, Edmund C. *A Source Book of Biological Names and Terms,* Charles C. Thomas, Publisher, Springfield, Illinois, 1955

Jenni, Donald A. "A Study of the Ecology of Four Species of Herons During the Breeding Season at Lake Alice, Alachua County, Florida," *Ecology Monographs,* Vol. 39, No. 3, Summer 1969

Johnson, Douglas H., and Robert E. Stewart "Racial Composition of Migrant Populations of Sandhill Cranes in the Northern Plains States," *The Wilson Bulletin,* Vol. 85, No. 2, June 1973

Jones, John C. "Food Habits of the American Coot, with Notes on Distribution," USDI, *Biological Survey Research Bulletin* 2, 1940

Kiel, William H., Jr. "Nesting Studies of the Coot in Southwestern Manitoba," *Journal of Wildlife Management,* Vol. 19, No. 2, April 1955

Kiel, William H., Jr., and Arthur S. Hawkins "Status of the Coot in the Mississippi Flyway," *Transactions of the 18th North American Wildlife Conference,* 1953

Kozicky, Edward L., and Francis V. Schmidt "Nesting Habits of the Clapper Rail in New Jersey," *The Auk,* Vol. 66, No. 4, October 1949

Kushlan, James A. "Aerial Feeding in the Snowy Egret," *The Wilson Bulletin,* Vol. 84, No. 2, June 1972

——— "Least Bittern Nesting Colonially," *The Auk,* Vol. 90, No. 3, July 1973

——— "Promiscuous Mating Behaviour in the White Ibis," *The Wilson Bulletin,* Vol. 85, No. 3, September 1973

——— "White Ibis Nesting in the Florida Everglades," *The Wilson Bulletin,* Vol. 85, No. 2, June 1973

Lemmon, Robert S. *Our Amazing Birds,* Doubleday & Company, Inc., Garden City, New York, 1952

Lewis, James Chester "Ecology of the Sandhill Crane in the Southeastern Central Flyway," Ph.D. thesis, Oklahoma State University, December 1974

Littlefield, Carroll D. "Flightlessness in Sandhill Cranes," *The Auk,* Vol. 87, No. 1, January 1970

Lowery, George H., Jr. *Louisiana Birds,* Louisiana State University Press, Baton Rouge, Louisiana, 1955

Lumsden, Harry G. "The Status of the Sandhill Crane in Northern Ontario," *The Canadian Field Naturalist,* Vol. 85, No. 4, October–December 1971

Mangold, Robert E. "Noisy Phantom of the Salt Marsh: The Clapper Rail," *New Jersey Outdoors,* Vol. 23, No. 12, June 1973

McLeod, Edith R. "Sandhill Cranes at Meiss Lake, Northern California," *The Condor,* Vol. 56, No. 4, July–August 1954

Meanley, Brooke "Natural History of the King Rail," *North American Fauna,* No. 67, May 1969

——— "Nesting of the King Rail in the Arkansas Rice Fields," *The Auk,* Vol. 70, No. 3, July 1953

Miller, Richard S. "The Brood Size of Cranes," *The Wilson Bulletin,* Vol. 85, No. 4, December 1973

——— "The Florida Gallinule: Breeding Birds of the Philadelphia Region (Part III)," *Cassinia,* Vol. 36, 1946

Miller, Richard S., Daniel S. Botkin, and Roy Mendelssohn "The Whooping Crane *(Grus americana)* Population of North America," *Biology and Conservation,* Volume 6, No. 2, April 1974

Mock, Douglas W. "Aerial Hunting by Little Blue Herons," *The Wilson Bulletin,* Vol. 86, No. 3, September 1974

Munro, David A. "A Study of the Economic Status of Sandhill Cranes in Saskatchewan," *Journal of Wildlife Management,* Vol. 14, No. 3, July 1950

Naylor, A. E., A. W. Miller, and M. E. Foster "Observations on the Sandhill Crane in Northeastern California," *The Condor,* Vol. 56, No. 4, July–August 1954

Nesbitt, Stephen A. "Wood Stork Nesting in North Florida," *The Florida Field Naturalist,* Vol. 1, No. 2, Fall 1973

Oberholser, Harry C. "A Revision of the Clapper Rails *(Rallus longirostris* Boddaert)," Smithsonian Institution, *Proceedings of the United States National Museum,* Vol. 84 (3018), 1937

Oney, John "Fall Food Habits of the Clapper Rail in Georgia," *Journal of Wildlife Management,* Vol. 15, No. 1, January 1951

——— "Final Report: Clapper Rail Survey and Investigation Study," *Georgia Game and Fish Commission Final Report Federal Aid Program for Georgia,* W-9-R, 1954

Partch, Max "The 1972 Great Blue Heron Migration in Minnesota," *The Loon,* Vol. 44, No. 3, Fall 1972

Pearson, T. Gilbert *Birds of America,* Garden City Publishing Co., Garden City, New York, 1936

Peterson, Roger Tory *A Field Guide to the Birds,* Second Edition, Houghton Mifflin Co., Boston, Massachusetts, 1947

Phillips, Allan, Joe Marshall, and Gale Monson *The Birds of Arizona,* University of Arizona Press, Tucson, 1964

Pospichal, Leo B., and William H. Marshall "A Field Study of Sora Rail and Virginia Rail in Central Minnesota," *The Flicker,* Vol. 26, No. 1, March 1954

Pratt, Helen M. "Breeding Biology of Great Blue Herons and Common Egrets in Central California," *The Condor,* Vol. 72, No. 4, October 1970

——— "Nesting Success of Common Egrets and Great Blue Herons in the San Francisco Bay Region," *The Condor,* Vol. 74, No. 4, Winter 1972

Ramsey, J. J. "The Status of the Cattle Egret in Texas," *Bulletin of the Texas Ornithological Society,* Vol. 4, 1971 (from *The Auk,* Vol. 89, No. 4, 1972)

Rapp, William F., Jr. "The Status of Cranes in Nebraska," *The Wilson Bulletin,* Vol. 66, No. 3, September 1954

Reese, Jan G. "Unusual Feeding Behavior of Great Blue Herons and Common Egrets," *The Condor,* Vol. 75, No. 3, Autumn 1973

Reynard, George B. "Some Vocalizations of the Black, Yellow, and Virginia Rails," *The Auk,* Vol. 91, No. 4, October 1974

Ridgway, Robert, and Herbert Friedmann "The Birds of North and Middle America, Part IX," *U.S. National Museum Bulletin,* No. 50, 1941

Roberts, Thomas S. *Bird Portraits in Color,* University of Minnesota Press, Minneapolis, 1934

Rudegeair, Thomas "The Gular Pouch of the Female White Ibis," *The Auk,* Vol. 92, No. 1, January 1975

Schmidt, F. V., and Paul McLain "The Clapper Rail in New Jersey," *New Jersey Division of Fish and Game,* 9-page mimeo, 1951

Shields, Robert H., and Earl L. Benham "Farm Crops as Food Supplements for Whooping Cranes," *Journal of Wildlife Management,* Vol. 33, No. 4, October 1969

Siegfried, W. R. "Communal Roosting of the Cattle Egret," *Transactions of the Royal Society of South Africa,* Vol. 39, No. 4, 1971

——— "The Nest of the Cattle Egret," *The Ostrich,* Vol. 42, No. 3, 1971

Sooter, Clarence A. "Ecology and Management of the American Coot *(Fulica americana americana* Gmelin)," *Iowa State College Journal of Science,* 1941

Stephenson, James Dale "Plumage Development and Growth of Young Whooping Cranes," MS thesis, Oregon State University, June 1971

Stevenson, James O., and Richard E. Griffith "Winter Life of the Whooping Crane," *The Condor,* Vol. 48, No. 4, July–August 1946

Stewart, Robert E. "Clapper Rail Populations of the Middle Atlantic States," *Transactions of the North American Wildlife Conference,* No. 16, 1951

——— "Migratory Movements of the Northern Clapper Rail," *Bird Banding,* Vol. 25, No. 1, January 1954

Sturgis, Bertha B. *Field Book of Birds of the Panama Canal Zone,* Putnam, Washington, D.C., 1928

Sutton, George Miksch *An Introduction to the Birds of Pennsylvania,* J. Horace McFarland Co., Harrisburg, Pennsylvania, 1928

——— *Mexican Birds: First Impressions,* University of Oklahoma Press, Norman, 1951

Tanner, Dean "Autumn Food Habits of the Sandhill Crane," *The Flicker,* Vol. 13, No. 2, May 1941

Thompson, Richard L. "Florida Sandhill Crane Nesting on the Loxahatchee National Wildlife Refuge," *The Auk,* Vol. 87, No. 3, July 1970

Turcotte, W. H. "The Sandhill Crane in Mississippi," *Mississippi Game and Fish,* Vol. 10, No. 12, June 1947

Vermeer, Kees, and Gary G. Anweiler "Great Blue Heron Colonies in Saskatchewan in 1970," *The Blue Jay,* Vol. 28, No. 4, December 1970

Vermeer, Kees, and David R. M. Hatch "Additional Information on Great Blue Heron Colonies in Manitoba," *The Blue Jay,* Vol. 30, No. 2, June 1972

Walkinshaw, Lawrence H. "The Sandhill Cranes," *Cranbrook Institute of Science Bulletin,* No. 29, 1949

Wilbur, Sanford R. "The Status of the Light-Footed Clapper Rail," *American Birds,* Vol. 28, No. 5, October 1974

Wilke, Ford, and Brooke Meanley "Fluctuation in the Fall Food of the Sora Rail," *Maryland Conservation,* Vol. 19, No. 4, Fall 1942

Williams, Lovett E., Jr., and Robert W. Phillips "North Florida Sandhill Crane Populations," *The Auk,* Vol. 89, No. 3, July 1972

Williams, Lovett E., Jr. "Spring Departure of Sandhill Cranes from Northern Florida," *The Auk,* Vol. 87, No. 1, January 1970

Wolford, James W., and David A. Boag "Distribution and Biology of Black-Crowned Night Herons in Alberta," *Canadian Field Naturalist,* Vol. 85, No. 1, January–March 1971

——— "Food Habits of the Black-Crowned Night Herons in Southern Alberta," *The Auk,* Vol. 88, No. 2, April 1971

Youngworth, William "Migration of the Sandhill Crane in Nebraska," *Iowa Bird Life,* Vol. 17, No. 4, December 1947

INDEX

Karl E Karalus
1975